The Mid-Youth Market

The Mid-Youth Market

Baby Boomers in Their Peak Earning and Spending Years

by Cheryl Russell

New Strategist Publications, Inc.
Ithaca, New York

New Strategist Publications, Inc.
P.O. Box 242, Ithaca, NY 14851
607 / 273-0913

ISBN 1-885070-06-3

Printed in the United States of America

For my husband, Rick

Table of Contents

List of Tables

Chapter 4. Wealth and Spending

Chapter 5. Labor Force

Chapter 6. Health and Fitness

Chapter 7. Education

Chapter 8. Attitudes and Behavior

Why Boomers Matter

American business has an insatiable appetite for the baby-boom generation. When you think you've heard everything there is to hear about the big generation, there's more. When you think you've explored every opportunity, another baby-boom market emerges.

Baby boomers, born between 1946 and 1964, are now between the ages of 32 and 50. They account for 40 percent of Americans aged 18 or older. They are more than half of all workers. They are the parents of 75 percent of the nation's children under age 18. Few consumer markets are not dominated by this generation. Yet the importance of boomers to business is still growing.

For years, the nation's 78 million boomers have determined what's hot and what's not simply because of their numbers. Now there is an even more compelling reason to target boomers—they are in their peak earning, spending, and saving years. The generation that brought us minivans is behind the boom in mutual funds. The generation that put Orlando on the map with its quasi-religious zeal for anything Disney has yet to reach the peak years of travel spending. In industry after industry—automotive, home furnishings, entertainment, apparel—the baby-boom generation has only just begun to boost the bottom line.

Businesses stubbornly waiting for the next youth market have been surprised to discover their best customers are still boomers, and that boomers are still the youth market. Baby boomers in their teens and twenties created the youth market over three decades ago. Now, as they enter their 40s and 50s, millions of self-indulgent, demanding, and fun-loving boomers are creating the mid-youth market. They have shown the youth market to be a state of mind.

When all 78 million boomers were under the age of 35, it looked like young adults were the nation's big spenders. Their numbers inflated the market share controlled by young adults in most product categories, obscuring the fact that the biggest spenders are people in their 40s and 50s. Fast-forward twenty years, and the demographic landscape could not be more different. Today, both the numbers and the spending power are in the 35-to-54 age group.

The mid-youth market of the next twenty years will be every bit as exciting and surprising as the youth market of the last three decades. And it will be far more profitable. The middle-age of the baby-boom generation will be unlike that of any previous generation. Boomers have not adopted the attitudes and lifestyles of their parents. They have different wants and needs. As boomers bring the mid-youth market to life, their fierce independence and self-indulgence will reshape products and services. Businesses savvy enough to determine what boomers want will catch a wave of consumer spending that will be the ride of a lifetime.

How to Use This Book

This book is designed to be easy to use. It is divided into eight chapters to guide you in your search for information: Population, Households and Living Arrangements, Labor Force, Income and Assets, Spending, Health, Education, and Attitudes and Behavior.

Each chapter includes tables of demographic statistics for 35-to-54-year-olds, as well as explanatory text. If you want more information than the statistics in the tables provide, you can locate the original source of the data which is listed at the bottom of each table.

The book contains a lengthy table of contents to help you locate the information you need. Or for a more detailed search, use the index in the back of the book. Also in the back of the book is the glossary, which defines many of the terms commonly used in the tables and text.

Most of the tables in this book are based on data collected by the federal government, in particular the Census Bureau, the Bureau of Labor Statistics, the National Center for Education Statistics, and the National Center for Health Statistics. The federal government continues to be the best source of up-to-date, reliable information on the changing characteristics of Americans.

To explore the opinions of boomers in mid-youth, many of the tables in the Attitudes and Behavior chapter use data from the 1994 General Social Survey (GSS) of the University of Chicago's National Opinion Research Center (NORC). To show how attitudes differ by generation, GSS respondents are separated into four generations based on year of birth: Generation X (born from 1965 through 1976), baby boomers (1946 through 1964), the Swing generation (1933 through 1945) and the World War II generation (before 1933). The results for all generations are shown for comparative purposes. For more information about the General Social Survey, contact the National Opinion Research Center, University of Chicago, 1155 East 60th Street, Chicago, IL, 60637; telephone (312) 753-7500.

—Cheryl Russell

1

Population

♦ The oldest boomers turned 50 in 1996, to much fanfare. While these pioneers get the most media attention, the mass of the boomer market is younger.

♦ The mid-youth market is largely a couples market. Most men and women aged 35 to 54 are married.

♦ Although people aged 35 to 54 are less diverse than those who are younger, nearly one in four is an ethnic or racial minority—a share too large to ignore.

♦ While people aged 35 to 54 dominate most markets, they account for just 22 percent of all movers.

♦ In every state, the number of 40-to-44-year-olds grew faster than any other middle-aged group between 1990 and 1995.

♦ During the next five years, the most rapid growth in the 35-to-54 age group will be among 50-to-54-year-olds.

Mid-Youth Power

The mood of Americans—our problems and concerns, hopes and fears—are influenced by the age structure of our population. Today, the middle-aged share of the population is at an all-time high. Never before have so many Americans—both numerically and proportionately—been in the 35-to-54 age group. For the next decade and beyond, the wants and needs of the middle-aged will shape consumer markets.

In 1980, the dominant demographic segment in the United States was young adults. Less than two decades later, it is the middle-aged. This shift is not only unprecedented, but a youth-dominant culture is all most of us have ever known. Few Americans now alive can even remember a time when young adults did not wield more influence than any other consumer segment. Most business strategies, marketing campaigns, products, and services have been designed to serve the wants and needs of youth.

In 1980, the youth market was in its heyday. The share of the population in the 35-to-54 age group was at a low of 21 percent. At that time, baby boomers were aged 16 to 34. Now the tide has turned: the 35-to-54 share of the population rose to 25 percent in 1990 and is on its way to 30 percent by 2000. This shift has not gone unnoticed, but its importance has been ignored. Many businesses still pursue the young adult market as though it was the only market that mattered, obsessively targeting youth even as sales fall. In the apparel industry, revenues have dropped sharply as manufacturers and retailers offer styles for teens and young adults rather than the middle-aged. The network television audience is shrinking because producers create shows for the young rather than the burgeoning middle-aged—all because misinformed advertisers demand a youthful audience. One stock market analyst has even suggested that the ups and downs in consumer spending (and stock values) are tied to the actions of 25-year-olds, the age when many young adults establish households. But that was the way things used to be, when boomers were inflating the number of people in their twenties and making it look like young adults were big spenders. Now it's the actions of 45-year-olds that shape the consumer economy.

Many businesses are asleep at the wheel while the consumer landscape changes around them. Between 1990 and 2010, the number of people in the 35-to-54 age group will expand by over 19 million people, a 30 percent gain. Marketers who are on top of this trend have a once-in-a-lifetime opportunity to capture the mid-youth market from their competitors.

Not only is the 35-to-54 age group large, but its influence extends well beyond those age brackets as it guides the younger generation—its children—and aides the older generation—its parents. The mid-youth market will be the most powerful consumer force this nation has ever known.

The middle-aged share of the population will peak in 2000.

(percent of population aged 35 to 54, 1920-2020)

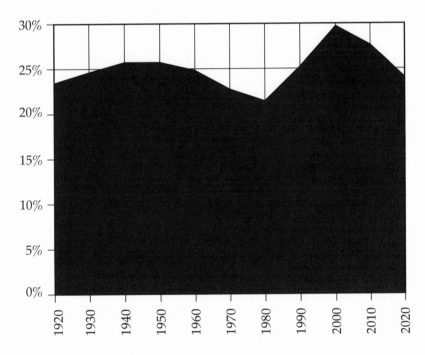

Mid-Youth Market
to Peak at 82 Million

The baby-boom's wants and needs and those of the 35-to-54 age group are one and the same.

The baby-boom generation, aged 32 to 50 in 1996, almost entirely fills the 35-to-54 age group. Today, there are 27 million more people in the 35-to-54 age group than there were in 1980, when the middle-aged share of the population hit its 20th century low. Never before has the number of middle-aged Americans grown by so much— and it's not over yet. In the next four years, the number of 35-to-54-year-olds will grow by another 6 million, peaking in 2000 at 82 million.

Within the 35-to-54 age group, growth rates will vary. Between 1996 and 2000, the number of people aged 35 to 39 will fall by 2 percent as boomers begin to age out of this segment. In contrast, the number of people aged 50 to 54 will surge by 24 percent as the oldest boomers fill this segment.

♦ The oldest boomers turned 50 in 1996, to much fanfare. While these pioneers get the most media attention, the mass of the boomer market is younger.

♦ The median age of the baby boom, which reached 40 in 1996, is the best predictor of boomer wants and needs. This is the age marketers should target if they want to appeal to the broadest number of boomers.

Population Aged 35 to 54, 1996 to 2000

(total number of persons and number aged 35 to 54 in 1996 and 2000; numerical and percent change, 1996-2000; numbers in thousands)

			change, 1996-2000	
	2000	*1996*	*number*	*percent*
Total	274,634	265,253	9,381	3.5%
Total, aged 35 to 54	81,689	75,652	6,037	8.0
Total, aged 35 to 44	44,659	43,311	1,348	3.1
Total, aged 45 to 54	37,030	32,341	4,689	14.5
Total, aged 35 to 39	22,180	22,536	-356	-1.6
Total, aged 40 to 44	22,479	20,775	1,704	8.2
Total, aged 45 to 49	19,806	18,420	1,386	7.5
Total, aged 50 to 54	17,224	13,921	3,303	23.7
Aged 35	4,288	4,579	-291	-6.4
Aged 36	4,350	4,511	-161	-3.6
Aged 37	4,469	4,493	-24	-0.5
Aged 38	4,290	4,247	43	1.0
Aged 39	4,783	4,706	77	1.6
Aged 40	4,667	4,390	277	6.3
Aged 41	4,494	4,253	241	5.7
Aged 42	4,488	4,128	360	8.7
Aged 43	4,424	3,970	454	11.4
Aged 44	4,407	4,034	373	9.2
Aged 45	4,268	3,774	494	13.1
Aged 46	4,034	3,637	397	10.9
Aged 47	3,958	3,595	363	10.1
Aged 48	3,681	3,409	272	8.0
Aged 49	3,864	4,005	-141	-3.5
Aged 50	3,721	2,827	894	31.6
Aged 51	3,504	2,784	720	25.9
Aged 52	3,476	2,767	709	25.6
Aged 53	3,754	2,936	818	27.9
Aged 54	2,769	2,607	162	6.2

Source: Bureau of the Census, Population Projections of the United States, by Age, Sex, Race, and Hispanic Origin: 1993 to 2050, *Current Population Reports, P25-1130, 1996*

Women Begin to
Outnumber Men

The fiftysomething age group has more women than men.

The number of men and women in mid-youth is almost equal—37 million men and 38 million women were aged 35 to 54 in 1996. But within the 35-to-54 age group, women begin to outnumber men by a significant margin among those in their 50s. Behind the growing numerical superiority of women is their sturdier biology. Women may get sick more often than men, but men are more likely to die of their illnesses than women.

In the 35-to-39 age group, women outnumber men by only 94,000. But in the 50-to-54 age group, there are 400,000 more women than men. The gap continues to grow as people age into their 60s and beyond because men's mortality rates are higher than women's.

◆ The mid-youth market is largely a couples market. Most men and women aged 35 to 54 are married.

◆ In the 50-to-54 age group, the lifestyles of women and men begin to differ as more women live alone.

Population Aged 35 to 54 by Sex, 1996

(total number of persons and number aged 35 to 54 by sex, and sex ratio by age, 1996; numbers in thousands)

	total	men	women	males per 100 females
Total	265,253	129,522	135,731	95
Total, aged 35 to 54	75,652	37,288	38,364	97
Total, aged 35 to 44	43,311	21,490	21,821	98
Total, aged 45 to 54	32,341	15,798	16,543	95
Total, aged 35 to 39	22,536	11,221	11,315	99
Total, aged 40 to 44	20,775	10,269	10,506	98
Total, aged 45 to 49	18,420	9,038	9,382	96
Total, aged 50 to 54	13,921	6,760	7,161	94
Aged 35	4,579	2,283	2,296	99
Aged 36	4,511	2,247	2,264	99
Aged 37	4,493	2,234	2,260	99
Aged 38	4,247	2,109	2,138	99
Aged 39	4,706	2,349	2,357	100
Aged 40	4,390	2,175	2,215	98
Aged 41	4,253	2,104	2,149	98
Aged 42	4,128	2,038	2,090	98
Aged 43	3,970	1,951	2,019	97
Aged 44	4,034	2,001	2,033	98
Aged 45	3,774	1,858	1,915	97
Aged 46	3,637	1,787	1,850	97
Aged 47	3,595	1,757	1,838	96
Aged 48	3,409	1,665	1,745	95
Aged 49	4,005	1,971	2,034	97
Aged 50	2,827	1,377	1,450	95
Aged 51	2,784	1,354	1,430	95
Aged 52	2,767	1,343	1,424	94
Aged 53	2,936	1,425	1,511	94
Aged 54	2,607	1,261	1,346	94

Source: Bureau of the Census, Population Projections of the United States, by Age, Sex, Race, and Hispanic Origin: 1993 to 2050, *Current Population Reports, P25-1130, 1996*

Mid-Youth Market Less Diverse Than Young Adults

Three out of four 35-to-54-year-olds are non-Hispanic whites.

America's children and young adults are much more racially and ethnically diverse than are the middle or older age groups. Even within the mid-youth market, diversity drops with increasing age.

Overall, 76 percent of 35-to-54-year-olds are non-Hispanic whites, but this proportion is lowest (74 percent) among 35-to-39-year-olds and highest (79 percent) among 50-to-54-year-olds. The Hispanic share is highest among 35-to-39-year-olds (10 percent) and lowest among 50-to-54-year-olds (7 percent).

Blacks are the largest minority within the mid-youth market. Eleven percent of 35-to-54-year-olds are non-Hispanic blacks. The black share of the middle-aged ranges from a high of 12 percent among 35-to-39-year-olds to a low of 10 percent among 50-to-54-year-olds. Non-Hispanic Asians account for 3.5 percent of 35-to-54-year-olds, while Native Americans are just 0.7 percent.

◆ Although people aged 35 to 54 are less diverse than those who are younger, nearly one in four is an ethnic or racial minority—a share too large to ignore.

◆ In some metropolitan areas, the minority share of 35-to-54-year-olds will be much higher. Local and regional marketers need to know the ethnic and racial composition of the middle-aged on a market-by-market basis.

Non-Hispanics Aged 35 to 54 by Race, 1996

(number and percent distribution of total persons and persons aged 35 to 54 who are non-Hispanics, by race, 1996; numbers in thousands)

	total	total non-Hispanic	non-Hispanic			
			white	black	Asian or Pacific Islander	Native American
Total, number	265,253	237,449	194,353	31,999	9,141	1,956
Aged 35 to 54	75,652	69,144	57,678	8,325	2,646	495
Aged 35 to 44	43,311	39,224	32,297	5,058	1,576	293
Aged 45 to 54	32,341	29,920	25,381	3,267	1,070	202
Aged 35 to 39	22,536	20,273	16,598	2,693	828	154
Aged 40 to 44	20,775	18,951	15,699	2,365	748	139
Aged 45 to 49	18,420	17,013	14,356	1,914	628	115
Aged 50 to 54	13,921	12,907	11,025	1,353	442	87
Total, percent	100.0%	89.5%	73.3%	12.1%	3.4%	0.7%
Aged 35 to 54	100.0	91.4	76.2	11.0	3.5	0.7
Aged 35 to 44	100.0	90.6	74.6	11.7	3.6	0.7
Aged 45 to 54	100.0	92.5	78.5	10.1	3.3	0.6
Aged 35 to 39	100.0	90.0	73.7	11.9	3.7	0.7
Aged 40 to 44	100.0	91.2	75.6	11.4	3.6	0.7
Aged 45 to 49	100.0	92.4	77.9	10.4	3.4	0.6
Aged 50 to 54	100.0	92.7	79.2	9.7	3.2	0.6

Source: Bureau of the Census, Population Projections of the United States, by Age, Sex, Race, and Hispanic Origin: 1995 to 2050, *Current Population Reports, P25-1130, 1996*

Hispanics Aged 35 to 54 by Race, 1996

(number and percent distribution of Hispanics aged 35 to 54 by race, 1996; numbers in thousands)

	total	total Hispanic	Hispanic white	Hispanic black	Asian or Pacific Islander	Native American
Total, number	265,253	27,804	25,288	1,612	587	317
Aged 35 to 54	75,652	6,506	5,903	393	139	71
Aged 35 to 44	43,311	4,086	3,703	250	87	46
Aged 45 to 54	32,341	2,420	2,200	143	52	25
Aged 35 to 39	22,536	2,262	2,052	138	47	25
Aged 40 to 44	20,775	1,824	1,651	112	40	21
Aged 45 to 49	18,420	1,406	1,277	84	30	15
Aged 50 to 54	13,921	1,014	923	59	22	10
Total, percent	100.0%	10.5%	9.5%	0.6%	0.2%	0.1%
Aged 35 to 54	100.0	8.6	7.8	0.5	0.2	0.1
Aged 35 to 44	100.0	9.4	8.5	0.6	0.2	0.1
Aged 45 to 54	100.0	7.5	6.8	0.4	0.2	0.1
Aged 35 to 39	100.0	10.0	9.1	0.6	0.2	0.1
Aged 40 to 44	100.0	8.8	7.9	0.5	0.2	0.1
Aged 45 to 49	100.0	7.6	6.9	0.5	0.2	0.1
Aged 50 to 54	100.0	7.3	6.6	0.4	0.2	0.1

Source: Bureau of the Census, Population Projections of the United States, by Age, Sex, Race, and Hispanic Origin: 1995 to 2050, *Current Population Reports, P25-1130, 1996*

Few People in
Their Fifties Move

Mobility rates drop sharply as people enter late 40s and early 50s.

By the age of 50, few people move much anymore. Only 9 percent of people aged 50 to 54 moved from one house to another between March 1993 and March 1994. Mobility rates fall as people enter middle-age because most are committed to a job that keeps them in one location, most own homes they like, and many have children in school.

Overall, 16 percent of Americans moved between 1993 and 1994. The mobility rate of people aged 35 to 39 matches the national rate, but falls steadily with age from there.

Most movers do not go far. Over sixty percent of the moves of 35-to-54-year-olds are within the same county. This suggests that most moves are for housing-related reasons—people are buying their first homes or trading up to better homes. Fewer than 3 percent of moves are to a different state. Among the middle-aged, most interstate mobility is job-related—corporate relocations and career moves.

♦ While people aged 35 to 54 dominate most markets, they account for just 22 percent of all movers.

♦ In the years ahead, the mobility rates of the middle-aged may decline because of the difficulties in relocating for two-income couples.

Geographical Mobility, 1993 to 1994

(total number and percent of persons aged 1 and older, and aged 35 to 54, who moved between March 1993 and March 1994, by type of move; numbers in thousands)

	total	same house (non-movers)	total	same county	different house in the U.S. different county total	same state	different state total	same region	different region	movers from abroad
Total, 1 or older	255,774	212,939	41,590	26,638	14,952	8,226	6,726	3,591	3,135	1,245
Aged 35 to 39	21,967	18,311	3,579	2,287	1,292	653	639	310	330	77
Aged 40 to 44	19,557	16,957	2,523	1,541	981	587	394	220	174	78
Aged 45 to 49	16,562	14,679	1,808	1,137	671	315	356	179	177	75
Aged 50 to 54	12,960	11,747	1,173	705	467	258	210	128	81	40
Median age	33.8	36.0	26.8	26.4	27.5	27.3	27.9	28.0	27.8	26.5
Total, 1 or older	100.0%	83.3%	16.3%	10.4%	5.8%	3.2%	2.6%	1.4%	1.2%	0.5%
Aged 35 to 39	100.0	83.4	16.3	10.4	5.9	3.0	2.9	1.4	1.5	0.4
Aged 40 to 44	100.0	86.7	12.9	7.9	5.0	3.0	2.0	1.1	0.9	0.4
Aged 45 to 49	100.0	88.6	10.9	6.9	4.1	1.9	2.1	1.1	1.1	0.5
Aged 50 to 54	100.0	90.6	9.1	5.4	3.6	2.0	1.6	1.0	0.6	0.3

Source: Bureau of the Census, Geographical Mobility: March 1993 to March 1994, *Current Population Reports, P20-485, 1995*

Middle-Aged Population Will Grow Rapidly in Every Region

The number of 35-to-54-year-olds is growing three times faster than the population as a whole.

While the total U.S. population grew by 5 percent between 1990 and 1995, the number of 35-to-54-year-olds grew by 17 percent.

The number of 35-to-54-year-olds grew rapidly in every region in the first half of the 1990s. The slowest growth for this age group occurred in the Middle Atlantic states of New York, New Jersey, and Pennsylvania (12 percent). The most rapid growth occurred in the Mountain states (27 percent).

In every region, the fastest growth within the 35-to-54 age group was among 45-to-49-year-olds. This age group grew by 26 percent nationally between 1990 and 1995, but by as much as 41 percent in the Mountain states.

♦ During the next five years, the most rapid growth in the 35-to-54 age group will be among 50-to-54-year-olds as boomers enter their 50s. At the same time, the number of 35-to-39-year-olds will shrink in many parts of the country.

Regional Populations, 1990 and 1995

(number of people aged 35 to 54 by region and division in 1990 and 1995, and percent change 1990-95; numbers in thousands)

	1990	1995	percent change
Total, United States	249,403	262,755	5.4%
Total aged 35 to 54	62,953	73,546	16.8
Aged 35 to 39	19,975	22,249	11.4
Aged 40 to 44	17,790	20,219	13.7
Aged 45 to 49	13,820	17,449	26.3
Aged 50 to 54	11,368	13,630	19.9
Total, Northeast	50,858	51,466	1.2
Total aged 35 to 54	13,060	14,633	12.0
Aged 35 to 39	4,057	4,402	8.5
Aged 40 to 44	3,692	3,971	7.6
Aged 45 to 49	2,914	3,493	19.9
Aged 50 to 54	2,397	2,767	15.4
Total, New England	13,220	13,312	0.7
Total aged 35 to 54	3,409	3,844	12.8
Aged 35 to 39	1,080	1,174	8.7
Aged 40 to 44	980	1,047	6.8
Aged 45 to 49	756	916	21.2
Aged 50 to 54	593	707	19.2
Total, Middle Atlantic	37,638	38,153	1.4
Total aged 35 to 54	9,651	10,790	11.8
Aged 35 to 39	2,978	3,228	8.4
Aged 40 to 44	2,712	2,924	7.8
Aged 45 to 49	2,158	2,578	19.4
Aged 50 to 54	1,804	2,060	14.2
Total, Midwest	59,768	61,804	3.4
Total aged 35 to 54	14,944	17,285	15.7
Aged 35 to 39	4,737	5,223	10.3
Aged 40 to 44	4,186	4,777	14.1
Aged 45 to 49	3,270	4,083	24.9
Aged 50 to 54	2,751	3,201	16.4

(continued)

(continued from previous page)

	1990	1995	percent change
Total, East North Central	42,079	43,456	3.3%
Total aged 35 to 54	10,618	12,226	15.1
Aged 35 to 39	3,348	3,688	10.2
Aged 40 to 44	2,980	3,367	13.0
Aged 45 to 49	2,332	2,897	24.3
Aged 50 to 54	1,958	2,272	16.1
Total, West North Central	17,688	18,348	3.7
Total aged 35 to 54	4,326	5,060	17.0
Aged 35 to 39	1,389	1,535	10.5
Aged 40 to 44	1,206	1,410	16.9
Aged 45 to 49	938	1,186	26.4
Aged 50 to 54	793	929	17.1
Total, South	85,731	91,890	7.2
Total aged 35 to 54	21,500	25,511	18.7
Aged 35 to 39	6,744	7,651	13.4
Aged 40 to 44	6,065	6,970	14.9
Aged 45 to 49	4,755	6,085	28.0
Aged 50 to 54	3,935	4,805	22.1
Total, South Atlantic	43,758	46,995	7.4
Total aged 35 to 54	11,125	13,199	18.6
Aged 35 to 39	3,462	3,963	14.5
Aged 40 to 44	3,154	3,588	13.8
Aged 45 to 49	2,475	3,158	27.6
Aged 50 to 54	2,034	2,490	22.4
Total, East South Central	15,209	16,066	5.6
Total aged 35 to 54	3,832	4,463	16.5
Aged 35 to 39	1,175	1,301	10.8
Aged 40 to 44	1,074	1,219	13.5
Aged 45 to 49	852	1,081	26.9
Aged 50 to 54	731	862	17.9
Total, West South Central	26,764	28,828	7.7
Total aged 35 to 54	6,543	7,849	20.0
Aged 35 to 39	2,108	2,387	13.2
Aged 40 to 44	1,837	2,164	17.8
Aged 45 to 49	1,427	1,846	29.3
Aged 50 to 54	1,170	1,453	24.2

(continued)

(continued from previous page)

	1990	1995	percent change
Total, West	53,046	57,596	8.6%
Total aged 35 to 54	13,450	16,117	19.8
Aged 35 to 39	4,436	4,973	12.1
Aged 40 to 44	3,848	4,500	17.0
Aged 45 to 49	2,881	3,787	31.4
Aged 50 to 54	2,285	2,857	25.1
Total, Mountain	13,716	15,645	14.1
Total aged 35 to 54	3,421	4,347	27.1
Aged 35 to 39	1,119	1,300	16.1
Aged 40 to 44	974	1,218	25.0
Aged 45 to 49	734	1,037	41.3
Aged 50 to 54	594	793	33.4
Total, Pacific	39,330	41,951	6.7
Total aged 35 to 54	10,029	11,770	17.4
Aged 35 to 39	3,317	3,673	10.7
Aged 40 to 44	2,874	3,282	14.2
Aged 45 to 49	2,148	2,750	28.1
Aged 50 to 54	1,690	2,064	22.1

Source: Bureau of the Census, Internet web site, http://www.census.gov

Middle-Aged Growing Faster in Some States Than in Others

Nevada and Colorado have the fastest growth in 35-to-54-year-olds.

The growth of the 35-to-54 age group by state is similar to that for the population as a whole, with rapid gains in the Mountain states and little growth in the Northeast. Between 1990 and 1995, the number of 35-to-54-year-olds grew fastest in Nevada (36 percent)and Colorado (30 percent). The slowest growth was recorded in New York (10 percent) and Rhode Island (11 percent).

In some states, the 35-to-54 age group grew much faster than the state population as a whole. In North Dakota the number of 35-to-54-year-olds grew 23 times faster than the state population as a whole—a 14 percent gain for 35-to-54-year-olds versus a tiny 0.6 percent for North Dakota's population as a whole. In Arizona, the growth of the 35-to-54 age group was less than twice as fast as that of the total state population (26 percent versus 15 percent), since much of Arizona's growth is from elderly retirees.

◆ In every state, the number of 40-to-44-year-olds grew faster than any other middle-aged group between 1990 and 1995. In the next five years, that growth will shift to the 50-to-54 age group while the number of 35-to-39-year-olds will shrink in many states.

State Populations, 1990 and 1995

(number of people aged 35 to 54 by state in 1990 and 1995, and percent change 1990-95; numbers in thousands)

	1990	1995	percent change
Total, United States	249,403	262,755	5.4%
Total aged 35 to 54	62,953	73,546	16.8
Aged 35 to 39	19,975	22,249	11.4
Aged 40 to 44	17,790	20,219	13.7
Aged 45 to 49	13,820	17,449	26.3
Aged 50 to 54	11,368	13,630	19.9
Total, Alabama	4,048	4,253	5.1
Total aged 35 to 54	1,012	1,171	15.7
Aged 35 to 39	309	342	10.7
Aged 40 to 44	282	319	13.1
Aged 45 to 49	226	283	25.5
Aged 50 to 54	196	228	16.2
Total, Alaska	553	604	9.1
Total aged 35 to 54	156	194	24.2
Aged 35 to 39	57	59	3.7
Aged 40 to 44	46	57	25.5
Aged 45 to 49	32	45	43.3
Aged 50 to 54	22	32	47.4
Total, Arizona	3,679	4,218	14.7
Total aged 35 to 54	874	1,103	26.3
Aged 35 to 39	281	336	19.7
Aged 40 to 44	246	303	22.8
Aged 45 to 49	190	260	36.7
Aged 50 to 54	156	204	30.9
Total, Arkansas	2,354	2,484	5.5
Total aged 35 to 54	573	660	15.2
Aged 35 to 39	170	187	10.0
Aged 40 to 44	159	177	11.2
Aged 45 to 49	132	161	22.2
Aged 50 to 54	112	135	20.5

(continued)

(continued from previous page)

	1990	1995	percent change
Total, California	29,904	31,589	5.6%
Total aged 35 to 54	7,506	8,657	15.3
Aged 35 to 39	2,487	2,760	11.0
Aged 40 to 44	2,139	2,396	12.0
Aged 45 to 49	1,604	1,997	24.5
Aged 50 to 54	1,275	1,504	18.0
Total, Colorado	3,304	3,747	13.4
Total aged 35 to 54	902	1,169	29.6
Aged 35 to 39	304	348	14.7
Aged 40 to 44	264	333	26.1
Aged 45 to 49	189	283	50.0
Aged 50 to 54	146	205	40.4
Total, Connecticut	3,289	3,275	-0.4
Total aged 35 to 54	869	956	10.0
Aged 35 to 39	267	290	8.8
Aged 40 to 44	247	256	3.7
Aged 45 to 49	200	227	13.4
Aged 50 to 54	156	183	17.5
Total, Delaware	669	717	7.2
Total aged 35 to 54	168	203	20.8
Aged 35 to 39	53	64	20.9
Aged 40 to 44	47	55	16.1
Aged 45 to 49	37	47	26.0
Aged 50 to 54	31	37	21.7
Total, District of Columbia	604	554	-8.2
Total aged 35 to 54	158	154	-2.4
Aged 35 to 39	52	47	-8.9
Aged 40 to 44	44	42	-4.5
Aged 45 to 49	34	36	6.2
Aged 50 to 54	28	29	2.6
Total, Florida	13,019	14,166	8.8
Total aged 35 to 54	3,087	3,725	20.7
Aged 35 to 39	952	1,116	17.2
Aged 40 to 44	855	1,009	18.0
Aged 45 to 49	690	881	27.8
Aged 50 to 54	590	719	21.8

(continued)

(continued from previous page)

	1990	*1995*	*percent change*
Total, Georgia	6,506	7,201	10.7%
Total aged 35 to 54	1,690	2,074	22.7
Aged 35 to 39	533	635	19.2
Aged 40 to 44	489	565	15.5
Aged 45 to 49	374	496	32.7
Aged 50 to 54	295	378	28.1
Total, Hawaii	1,113	1,187	6.6
Total aged 35 to 54	290	342	18.0
Aged 35 to 39	96	101	5.3
Aged 40 to 44	84	97	15.5
Aged 45 to 49	62	82	31.2
Aged 50 to 54	47	62	30.7
Total, Idaho	1,012	1,163	15.0
Total aged 35 to 54	249	316	27.1
Aged 35 to 39	80	91	14.6
Aged 40 to 44	70	90	27.6
Aged 45 to 49	54	76	40.1
Aged 50 to 54	45	59	33.0
Total, Illinois	11,448	11,830	3.3
Total aged 35 to 54	2,883	3,298	14.4
Aged 35 to 39	911	1,008	10.7
Aged 40 to 44	804	903	12.3
Aged 45 to 49	636	773	21.5
Aged 50 to 54	532	614	15.3
Total, Indiana	5,555	5,803	4.5
Total aged 35 to 54	1,407	1,638	16.5
Aged 35 to 39	438	488	11.2
Aged 40 to 44	393	451	14.5
Aged 45 to 49	312	390	24.9
Aged 50 to 54	263	310	18.1
Total, Iowa	2,780	2,842	2.2
Total aged 35 to 54	673	774	15.0
Aged 35 to 39	212	225	6.1
Aged 40 to 44	186	217	16.6
Aged 45 to 49	146	185	27.3
Aged 50 to 54	129	146	13.5

(continued)

(continued from previous page)

	1990	1995	percent change
Total, Kansas	2,481	2,565	3.4%
Total aged 35 to 54	600	700	16.7
Aged 35 to 39	196	213	8.5
Aged 40 to 44	168	198	17.5
Aged 45 to 49	128	164	28.0
Aged 50 to 54	107	125	16.9
Total, Kentucky	3,693	3,860	4.5
Total aged 35 to 54	940	1,090	15.9
Aged 35 to 39	290	318	9.5
Aged 40 to 44	265	298	12.5
Aged 45 to 49	207	265	27.6
Aged 50 to 54	177	209	17.9
Total, Louisiana	4,217	4,342	3.0
Total aged 35 to 54	1,021	1,168	14.4
Aged 35 to 39	328	348	6.1
Aged 40 to 44	285	324	13.9
Aged 45 to 49	222	277	24.8
Aged 50 to 54	187	219	17.5
Total, Maine	1,231	1,241	0.8
Total aged 35 to 54	321	369	14.7
Aged 35 to 39	103	109	6.7
Aged 40 to 44	93	103	10.2
Aged 45 to 49	69	90	29.6
Aged 50 to 54	56	67	18.6
Total, Maryland	4,798	5,042	5.1
Total aged 35 to 54	1,300	1,516	16.6
Aged 35 to 39	407	470	15.4
Aged 40 to 44	373	410	10.0
Aged 45 to 49	292	358	22.6
Aged 50 to 54	229	278	21.5
Total, Massachusetts	6,019	6,074	0.9
Total aged 35 to 54	1,523	1,720	13.0
Aged 35 to 39	485	526	8.4
Aged 40 to 44	438	467	6.5
Aged 45 to 49	336	411	22.2
Aged 50 to 54	264	317	20.1

(continued)

(continued from previous page)

	1990	*1995*	*percent change*
Total, Michigan	9,311	9,549	2.6%
Total aged 35 to 54	2,368	2,720	14.8
Aged 35 to 39	751	819	9.0
Aged 40 to 44	667	751	12.6
Aged 45 to 49	523	644	23.0
Aged 50 to 54	427	506	18.5
Total, Minnesota	4,387	4,610	5.1
Total aged 35 to 54	1,100	1,314	19.4
Aged 35 to 39	362	410	13.4
Aged 40 to 44	309	368	18.8
Aged 45 to 49	236	303	28.4
Aged 50 to 54	193	233	20.9
Total, Mississippi	2,577	2,697	4.7
Total aged 35 to 54	606	697	15.0
Aged 35 to 39	188	206	9.7
Aged 40 to 44	168	192	14.3
Aged 45 to 49	133	166	25.3
Aged 50 to 54	117	132	12.6
Total, Missouri	5,126	5,324	3.8
Total aged 35 to 54	1,265	1,466	15.9
Aged 35 to 39	391	444	13.4
Aged 40 to 44	350	398	13.7
Aged 45 to 49	284	345	21.5
Aged 50 to 54	240	280	16.7
Total, Montana	800	870	8.8
Total aged 35 to 54	209	256	22.3
Aged 35 to 39	68	71	5.3
Aged 40 to 44	59	74	23.9
Aged 45 to 49	45	63	40.4
Aged 50 to 54	37	48	29.1
Total, Nebraska	1,581	1,637	3.6
Total aged 35 to 54	380	445	16.9
Aged 35 to 39	124	134	7.7
Aged 40 to 44	107	126	17.6
Aged 45 to 49	81	105	30.6
Aged 50 to 54	69	80	16.4

(continued)

(continued from previous page)

	1990	1995	percent change
Total, Nevada	1,219	1,530	25.6%
Total aged 35 to 54	326	443	35.9
Aged 35 to 39	100	133	32.3
Aged 40 to 44	91	118	30.1
Aged 45 to 49	73	106	44.1
Aged 50 to 54	61	86	41.0
Total, New Hampshire	1,112	1,148	3.3
Total aged 35 to 54	298	348	16.9
Aged 35 to 39	98	112	15.1
Aged 40 to 44	87	96	9.8
Aged 45 to 49	64	81	26.3
Aged 50 to 54	49	59	20.6
Total, New Jersey	7,740	7,945	2.7
Total aged 35 to 54	2,042	2,318	13.5
Aged 35 to 39	624	703	12.8
Aged 40 to 44	577	621	7.6
Aged 45 to 49	465	550	18.4
Aged 50 to 54	376	443	17.7
Total, New Mexico	1,520	1,685	10.9
Total aged 35 to 54	375	465	24.0
Aged 35 to 39	122	139	14.7
Aged 40 to 44	107	131	22.2
Aged 45 to 49	80	111	38.9
Aged 50 to 54	67	84	25.9
Total, New York	18,002	18,136	0.7
Total aged 35 to 54	4,636	5,088	9.7
Aged 35 to 39	1,428	1,522	6.6
Aged 40 to 44	1,302	1,369	5.2
Aged 45 to 49	1,038	1,217	17.2
Aged 50 to 54	868	979	12.8
Total, North Carolina	6,657	7,195	8.1
Total aged 35 to 54	1,710	2,020	18.2
Aged 35 to 39	528	599	13.4
Aged 40 to 44	484	549	13.4
Aged 45 to 49	380	487	28.1
Aged 50 to 54	317	385	21.5

(continued)

(continued from previous page)

	1990	1995	percent change
Total, North Dakota	637	641	0.6%
Total aged 35 to 54	149	170	14.3
Aged 35 to 39	50	52	2.2
Aged 40 to 44	41	49	19.9
Aged 45 to 49	31	39	27.6
Aged 50 to 54	27	30	13.1
Total, Ohio	10,862	11,151	2.7
Total aged 35 to 54	2,753	3,136	13.9
Aged 35 to 39	858	938	9.3
Aged 40 to 44	776	862	11.1
Aged 45 to 49	600	753	25.4
Aged 50 to 54	518	583	12.5
Total, Oklahoma	3,147	3,278	4.2
Total aged 35 to 54	776	886	14.2
Aged 35 to 39	239	258	7.8
Aged 40 to 44	215	240	12.0
Aged 45 to 49	174	212	22.0
Aged 50 to 54	148	175	18.5
Total, Oregon	2,858	3,141	9.9
Total aged 35 to 54	772	943	22.0
Aged 35 to 39	250	263	5.1
Aged 40 to 44	226	271	19.8
Aged 45 to 49	167	235	41.0
Aged 50 to 54	130	174	34.3
Total, Pennsylvania	11,896	12,072	1.5
Total aged 35 to 54	2,973	3,384	13.8
Aged 35 to 39	926	1,003	8.3
Aged 40 to 44	832	933	12.1
Aged 45 to 49	655	810	23.8
Aged 50 to 54	559	638	14.1
Total, Rhode Island	1,005	990	-1.5
Total aged 35 to 54	245	271	10.5
Aged 35 to 39	79	84	6.6
Aged 40 to 44	70	74	6.5
Aged 45 to 49	53	64	19.1
Aged 50 to 54	43	49	13.3

(continued)

(continued from previous page)

	1990	1995	percent change
Total, South Carolina	3,499	3,673	5.0%
Total aged 35 to 54	885	1,029	16.2
Aged 35 to 39	277	300	8.2
Aged 40 to 44	251	283	12.4
Aged 45 to 49	196	250	27.8
Aged 50 to 54	161	196	21.9
Total, South Dakota	697	729	4.7
Total aged 35 to 54	159	190	19.8
Aged 35 to 39	53	57	9.1
Aged 40 to 44	43	55	25.4
Aged 45 to 49	33	44	31.6
Aged 50 to 54	29	34	16.9
Total, Tennessee	4,891	5,256	7.5
Total aged 35 to 54	1,274	1,505	18.2
Aged 35 to 39	388	435	12.3
Aged 40 to 44	359	410	14.2
Aged 45 to 49	286	367	28.2
Aged 50 to 54	241	293	21.8
Total, Texas	17,046	18,724	9.8
Total aged 35 to 54	4,173	5,135	23.1
Aged 35 to 39	1,370	1,594	16.3
Aged 40 to 44	1,179	1,422	20.7
Aged 45 to 49	900	1,196	32.9
Aged 50 to 54	724	924	27.6
Total, Utah	1,730	1,951	12.8
Total aged 35 to 54	366	452	23.4
Aged 35 to 39	125	139	11.9
Aged 40 to 44	102	129	25.8
Aged 45 to 49	77	104	34.6
Aged 50 to 54	62	80	29.0
Total, Vermont	565	585	3.6
Total aged 35 to 54	152	179	18.3
Aged 35 to 39	49	53	6.5
Aged 40 to 44	44	51	14.9
Aged 45 to 49	33	44	33.4
Aged 50 to 54	25	32	28.0

(continued)

(continued from previous page)

	1990	1995	percent change
Total, Virginia	6,214	6,618	6.5%
Total aged 35 to 54	1,662	1,956	17.7
Aged 35 to 39	519	591	13.9
Aged 40 to 44	478	530	10.8
Aged 45 to 49	371	470	26.5
Aged 50 to 54	293	365	24.6
Total, Washington	4,901	5,431	10.8
Total aged 35 to 54	1,306	1,635	25.2
Aged 35 to 39	426	490	14.9
Aged 40 to 44	379	461	21.7
Aged 45 to 49	283	392	38.4
Aged 50 to 54	217	292	34.5
Total, West Virginia	1,792	1,828	2.0
Total aged 35 to 54	466	524	12.5
Aged 35 to 39	141	142	0.1
Aged 40 to 44	132	146	10.2
Aged 45 to 49	101	133	31.5
Aged 50 to 54	91	103	13.8
Total, Wisconsin	4,902	5,123	4.5
Total aged 35 to 54	1,207	1,433	18.8
Aged 35 to 39	389	435	11.8
Aged 40 to 44	339	401	18.0
Aged 45 to 49	260	338	30.0
Aged 50 to 54	218	260	19.1
Total, Wyoming	453	480	5.9
Total aged 35 to 54	120	142	19.0
Aged 35 to 39	41	41	0.6
Aged 40 to 44	34	42	23.1
Aged 45 to 49	25	34	36.2
Aged 50 to 54	20	26	27.6

Source: Bureau of the Census, Internet web site, http://www.census.gov

Boomers to Move South and West

Twenty-one states will be retirement hot spots for boomers.

As the baby-boom generation ages, it will carry the youth market into older age groups. By 2020, when the youngest boomers are aged 65 to 74, boomers will account for 59 percent of the entire 65-and-older age group. While they will have left the mid-youth market behind, they will create the late-youth market within the sixty- and seventysomething age groups.

Between 1993 and 2020, the population aged 65 or older will grow by 63 percent, according to projections by the Census Bureau. As millions of boomers leave the work force and head to retirement areas, the elderly population will grow much faster in some states than in others. Overall, the growth rate of the 65-plus population will exceed the national rate in 21 states, including Arizona, Georgia, North Carolina, and Washington. Fully 19 states will have more than 1 million people aged 65 or older in 2020, up from only 9 states today.

♦ In states with below-average growth in the 65-plus age group, the elderly who remain will be older, less healthy, and less affluent than those who moved elsewhere.

♦ States with above-average growth in the 65-plus population will attract active, affluent retirees. As aging boomers spend their hard-earned wealth, retirement areas in these fortunate states will experience rapid economic growth.

Projections of the Population Aged 65 or Older by State, 1993 to 2020

(number of persons aged 65 or older by state, 1993 and 2020; percent change, 1993-2020; numbers in thousands)

	1993	2020	percent change
United States	32,792	53,350	62.7%
Alabama	545	874	60.4
Alaska	26	54	107.7
Arizona	529	1,121	111.9
Arkansas	362	580	60.2
California	3,303	6,622	100.5
Colorado	357	743	108.1
Connecticut	462	630	36.4
District of Columbia	77	87	13.0
Delaware	87	146	67.8
Florida	2,539	4,982	96.2
Georgia	695	1,419	104.2
Hawaii	137	262	91.2
Idaho	130	246	89.2
Illinois	1,479	1,952	32.0
Indiana	728	1,048	44.0
Iowa	436	546	25.2
Kansas	353	517	46.5
Kentucky	482	729	51.2
Louisiana	487	741	52.2
Maine	170	256	50.6
Massachusetts	842	1,109	31.7
Maryland	549	929	69.2
Michigan	1,171	1,579	34.8
Minnesota	568	918	61.6
Mississippi	329	514	56.2
Missouri	741	1,072	44.7
Montana	113	174	54.0
North Carolina	865	1,633	88.8
North Dakota	94	117	24.5
New Hampshire	134	237	76.9
New Jersey	1,071	1,480	38.2
New Mexico	178	350	96.6
New York	2,388	3,028	26.8

(continued)

(continued from previous page)

	1993	2020	percent change
Nebraska	229	317	38.4%
Nevada	155	333	114.8
Ohio	1,480	1,986	34.2
Oklahoma	440	661	50.2
Oregon	418	724	73.2
Pennsylvania	1,908	2,303	20.7
Rhode Island	155	195	25.8
South Carolina	426	788	85.0
South Dakota	105	142	35.2
Tennessee	651	1,129	73.4
Texas	1,835	3,640	98.4
Utah	165	334	102.4
Virginia	712	1,319	85.3
Vermont	69	110	59.4
West Virginia	278	342	23.0
Washington	612	1,245	103.4
Wisconsin	676	1,013	49.9
Wyoming	51	74	45.1

Source: Bureau of the Census, 65+ in the United States, Current Population Reports, P23-190, 1996

2

Families and Households

♦ Most households headed by 35-to-54-year-olds are married couples.

♦ Gains are foreseen for every type of household among 45-to-54-year-olds as boomers inflate the age group.

♦ Household size should resume its long-term decline in a few years as boomers move out of their 30s and 40s.

♦ Millions of boomers are about to become the parents of teenagers, making them an important market for second phone lines, computer equipment, used cars, and much more.

♦ Although boomers typically have small families, a significant proportion have three or more children.

♦ Although female-headed families account for only 14 percent of all middle-aged households, they are the second-largest family household segment after married couples.

♦ Only 38 percent of black households headed by 35-to-54-year-olds are married couples.

♦ Although Hispanics will not outnumber blacks until after the turn of the century, Hispanic married couples outnumber black couples in the 35-to-54 age group.

Mid-Youth Is
Time of Stability

Most households headed by 35-to-54-year-olds are married couples.

In middle-age, the lifestyles of the baby-boom generation are more alike than they have ever been. More than 60 percent of households headed by people aged 35 to 54 are married couples, with the proportion peaking at 65 percent among 50-to-54-year-olds. Female-headed families comprise only 14 percent of households in this age group, ranging from a high of 16 percent among 35-to-39-year-olds to a low of 11 percent among 50-to-54-year-olds. Families headed by men are a tiny fraction of middle-aged households, accounting for just 3.6 percent.

Overall, only 16 percent of households headed by 35-to-54-year-olds are people who live alone. In this age group, there are more men (3.6 million) than women (3.0 million) who live alone.

♦ Among people who live alone, men outnumber women in the 35-to-44 age group by over 700,000. But single women begin to outnumber single men in the 50-to-54 age group. As boomers age into their 60s, women will increasingly outnumber men among those who live alone due to men's higher mortality rates.

Households by Type, 1994

(number and percent distribution of total households and households headed by persons aged 35 to 54, by type of household; numbers in thousands, 1994)

	total	35 to 54	35 to 39	40 to 44	45 to 49	50 to 54
Total households	97,107	39,130	11,795	10,498	9,221	7,616
Family households	68,490	31,081	9,402	8,401	7,285	5,993
Married couples	53,171	24,415	7,118	6,573	5,763	4,961
Female householder, no spouse present	12,406	5,463	1,898	1,472	1,264	829
Male householder, no spouse present	2,913	1,406	386	356	461	203
Nonfamily households	28,617	8,049	2,393	2,097	1,936	1,623
Female householder	16,155	3,552	872	863	950	867
Living alone	14,171	2,976	697	704	801	774
Male householder	12,462	4,497	1,521	1,234	986	756
Living alone	9,440	3,555	1,166	949	812	628
Total households	100.0%	100.0%	100.0%	100.0%	100.0%	100.0%
Family households	70.5	79.4	79.7	80.0	79.0	78.7
Married couples	54.8	62.4	60.3	62.6	62.5	65.1
Female householder, no husband present	12.8	14.0	16.1	14.0	13.7	10.9
Male householder, no wife present	3.0	3.6	3.3	3.4	5.0	2.7
Nonfamily households	29.5	20.6	20.3	20.0	21.0	21.3
Female householder	16.6	9.1	7.4	8.2	10.3	11.4
Living alone	14.6	7.6	5.9	6.7	8.7	10.2
Male householder	12.8	11.5	12.9	11.8	10.7	9.9
Living alone	9.7	9.1	9.9	9.0	8.8	8.2

Source: Bureau of the Census, Household and Family Characteristics: March 1994, *Current Population Reports, P20-483, 1995, and unpublished tables from the 1995 Current Population Survey*

Rapid Growth Forecast for Householders Aged 45 to 54

But the number of households headed by 35-to-44-year-olds will shrink.

Divergent paths lie ahead for middle-aged households as the enormous baby-boom generation passes through the 35-to-54 age group. Between 1995 and 2005, the number of households headed by 35-to-44-year-olds will drop slightly, while the number headed by people aged 45 to 54 will expand by 35 percent. The decline in the younger half of the age group is due to the aging of the baby-boom generation out of its 30s. The 45-to-54 age group will grow as the younger (and more numerous) half of the baby boom enters its late 40s and 50s.

Within the 35-to-44 age group, growth rates will differ by household type. The number of married couples will drop by more than 1 million, or 8 percent. In contrast, the number of male-headed households is projected to climb by 15 percent.

Gains are foreseen for every type of household among 45-to-54-year-olds as boomers inflate the age group. The smallest gain is projected for married couples (up 29 percent), while other types of households should grow by at least 40 percent during the decade.

♦ In producing its household projections, the Census Bureau assumes that marriage will continue to decline in popularity—even among the middle-aged who, typically, are most likely to be married.

Projections of Households by Type, 1995 and 2005

(number and percent distribution of households headed by persons aged 35 to 54 by type of household, 1995 and 2005; numerical and percent change, 1995-2005; numbers in thousands)

	1995		2005		change, 1995-2005	
	number	*percent*	*number*	*percent*	*number*	*percent*
Total, aged 35 to 44	22,756	100.0%	22,560	100.0%	-196	-0.9%
Family households	17,938	78.8	17,203	76.3	-735	-4.1
Married couples	13,766	60.5	12,714	56.4	-1,052	-7.6
Female householder, no spouse present	3,213	14.1	3,391	15.0	178	5.5
Male householder, no spouse present	959	4.2	1,098	4.9	139	14.5
Nonfamily households	4,819	21.2	5,357	23.7	538	11.2
Female householder	1,776	7.8	1,874	8.3	98	5.5
Living alone	1,459	6.4	1,539	6.8	80	5.5
Male householder	3,043	13.4	3,483	15.4	440	14.5
Living alone	2,392	10.5	2,738	12.1	346	14.5
Total, aged 45 to 54	17,723	100.0	23,924	100.0	6,201	35.0
Family households	14,039	79.2	18,570	77.6	4,531	32.3
Married couples	11,210	63.3	14,494	60.6	3,284	29.3
Female householder, no spouse present	2,147	12.1	3,070	12.8	923	43.0
Male householder, no spouse present	682	3.8	1,006	4.2	324	47.5
Nonfamily households	3,684	20.8	5,353	22.4	1,669	45.3
Female householder	1,807	10.2	2,584	10.8	777	43.0
Living alone	1,570	8.9	2,244	9.4	674	42.9
Male householder	1,877	10.6	2,769	11.6	892	47.5
Living alone	1,528	8.6	2,256	9.4	728	47.6

Source: Bureau of the Census, Projections of the Number of Households and Families in the United States: 1995 to 2010, *Current Population Reports, P25-1129, 1996*

Mid-Youth Households
Are Crowded

Household size peaks in the 35-to-39 age group.

The number of people in the average American household has been declining for decades as families have fewer children and more people live by themselves. Household size bottomed out in 1989 at 2.62 people, then began to increase slightly as the baby-boom generation had children. In 1994, the average American household contained 2.67 people.

Household size peaks in middle-age because that's when most people are married and have children. Overall, households headed by 35-to-54-year-olds had an average of 3.15 people in 1994. Household size is greatest for the 35-to-39 age group, with an average of 3.31 people.

Among households headed by 35-to-44-year-olds, the most common household size is four people, accounting for more than one in four households in the age group. But among 45-to-54-year-olds, two-person households are most common as children grow up and leave home.

◆ Household size should resume its long-term decline in a few years as boomers move out of their 30s and 40s.

Households by Size, 1994

(number and percent distribution of total households and households headed by persons aged 35 to 54, by size of household, 1994; numbers in thousands)

	total	35 to 54	35 to 39	40 to 44	45 to 54
Total households	97,107	39,130	11,795	10,498	16,837
One person	23,611	6,533	1,864	1,654	3,015
Two persons	31,211	9,129	2,038	2,099	4,992
Three persons	16,898	7,996	2,170	2,015	3,811
Four persons	15,073	8,991	3,313	2,698	2,980
Five persons	6,749	4,183	1,634	1,273	1,276
Six persons	2186	1,429	488	485	456
Seven or more persons	1379	869	288	275	306
Total households	100.0%	100.0%	100.0%	100.0%	100.0%
One person	24.3	16.7	15.8	15.8	17.9
Two persons	32.1	23.3	17.3	20.0	29.6
Three persons	17.4	20.4	18.4	19.2	22.6
Four persons	15.5	23.0	28.1	25.7	17.7
Five persons	7.0	10.7	13.9	12.1	7.6
Six persons	2.3	3.7	4.1	4.6	2.7
Seven or more persons	1.4	2.2	2.4	2.6	1.8
Average household size	2.67	3.15	3.31	3.30	2.95

Source: Bureau of the Census, Household and Family Characteristics: March 1994, *Current Population Reports, P20-483, 1995*

Most Mid-Youth Households Include Children

Even 45-to-54-year-olds are likely to have children at home.

Most Americans aged 35 to 54 live with children. Even among householders in their late 40s and early 50s, most have children at home.

Overall, 64 percent of households headed by 35-to-54-year-olds have children of any age at home, while just over half have children under age 18. The preschool market is one of the few no longer dominated by the baby-boom generation—only 15 percent of householders aged 35 to 54 have preschoolers at home, despite late childbearing by many boomers. Most mid-youth householders have school-aged children at home.

Sixty-nine percent of householders aged 35 to 39 have children under age 18 at home, as do 61 percent of 40-to-44-year-olds. While only one-third of householders aged 45 to 54 have children under age 18 at home, fully 51 percent live with children under age 25. These crowded nests are becoming more common because the falling incomes of young adults prevent many from setting up their own households.

♦ Millions of boomers are about to become the parents of teenagers. These "teenstage" parents will be an important market for second phone lines, computer equipment, used cars, college savings plans, and advice for navigating the teen years.

Households With Children at Home, 1994

(number and percent distribution of total households and households headed by persons aged 35 to 54, by age of own children in the home, 1994; numbers in thousands)

	total	35 to 54	35 to 39	40 to 44	45 to 54
Total households	97,107	39,130	11,795	10,498	16,837
With children of any age	44,108	24,830	8,300	7,111	9,419
With children <age 25	39,348	23,986	8,293	7,071	8,622
With children <age 18	34,018	20,047	8,078	6,380	5,589
With children <age 12	25,627	12,767	6,579	3,944	2,244
With children <age 6	15,909	5,735	3,614	1,549	572
With children <age 3	9,251	2,631	1,792	624	215
With children <age 1	3,265	823	567	192	64
With children aged 6 to 17	25,346	17,880	6,681	5,852	5,347
Total households	100.0%	100.0%	100.0%	100.0%	100.0%
With children of any age	45.4	63.5	70.4	67.7	55.9
With children <age 25	40.5	61.3	70.3	67.4	51.2
With children <age 18	35.0	51.2	68.5	60.8	33.2
With children <age 12	26.4	32.6	55.8	37.6	13.3
With children <age 6	16.4	14.7	30.6	14.8	3.4
With children <age 3	9.5	6.7	15.2	5.9	1.3
With children <age 1	3.4	2.1	4.8	1.8	0.4
With children aged 6 to 17	26.1	45.7	56.6	55.7	31.8

Note: Own children includes stepchildren and adopted children of the householder.
Source: Bureau of the Census, Household and Family Characteristics: March 1994, *Current Population Reports, P20-483, 1995*

Most Couples Have
at Least Two Children

Three children are common among 35-to-39-year-olds.

Although most boomers typically have small families, a significant proportion have three or more children. Over half of couples aged 35 to 39 have two or more children under age 18 at home. Those with three children at home are more numerous (25 percent) than those with only one (21 percent). Only 15 percent of 35-to-39-year-olds do not have any children under age 18 at home.

Married couples aged 40 to 44 are likely to have two children under age 18 (33 percent). Most couples aged 45 to 54 do not have any children in this age group at home—although many live with older children.

◆ In the next decade, the lifestyles of boomers will change dramatically as childrearing responsibilities end. By the age of 50, few will have dependent children to care for. Expect to see boomers breaking out of their cocoons and spending more time doing things away from home.

Married Couples by Presence and Number of Children, 1994

(number and percent distribution of total married couples and couples headed by 35-to-54-year-olds, by presence and number of own children under age 18 at home, 1994; numbers in thousands)

	total	35 to 54	35 to 39	40 to 44	45 to 54
Total married couples	53,171	24,415	7,118	6,573	10,724
Without children <18	28,113	8,703	1,053	1,539	6,111
With children <18	25,058	15,711	6,065	5,033	4,613
One	9,452	5,726	1,497	1,615	2,614
Two	10,188	6,397	2,801	2,197	1,399
Three or more	5,418	3,588	1,766	1,221	601
Total married couples	100.0%	100.0%	100.0%	100.0%	100.0%
Without children <18	52.9	35.6	14.8	23.4	57.0
With children <18	47.1	64.3	85.2	76.6	43.0
One	17.8	23.5	21.0	24.6	24.4
Two	19.2	26.2	39.4	33.4	13.0
Three or more	10.2	14.7	24.8	18.6	5.6

Note: Own children includes stepchildren and adopted children of the householder.
Source: Bureau of the Census, Household and Family Characteristics: March 1994, *Current Population Reports, P20-483, 1995*

Female-Headed Families Have Few Children

One child is most common, even among 35-to-39-year-olds.

Among 35-to-54-year-olds, most female-headed families are the result of divorce. Following a divorce, women are not likely to have additional children until they remarry. Consequently, middle-aged women who head families by themselves have fewer children than do married couples. Forty-one percent of couples aged 35 to 54 have two or more children under age 18 at home, but only 32 percent of female-headed families have that many children at home.

While the great majority of women aged 35 to 44 who head their own families have children under age 18 at home, the proportion falls to just 37 percent among those aged 45 to 54. Many of the women in the older age group have adult children at home, while some live with siblings or elderly parents.

♦ Although female-headed families account for only 14 percent of all middle-aged households, they are the second-largest household segment after married couples.

♦ The lifestyles of female family householders aged 35 to 44 differ from those of their counterparts aged 45 to 54. Single parents dominate the younger group, while adult interests and activities rule among the older group.

Female-Headed Families by Presence and Number of Children, 1994

(number and percent distribution of total female-headed families and families headed by 35-to-54-year-olds, by presence and number of own children under age 18 at home, 1994; numbers in thousands)

	total	35 to 54	35 to 39	40 to 44	45 to 54
Total female-headed families	12,406	5,463	1,898	1,472	2,093
Without children <18	4,759	1,827	165	348	1,314
With children <18	7,647	3,636	1,733	1,124	779
One	3,566	1,877	715	603	559
Two	2,531	1,149	620	360	169
Three or more	1,550	610	398	161	51
Total female-headed families	100.0%	100.0%	100.0%	100.0%	100.0%
Without children <18	38.4	33.4	8.7	23.6	62.8
With children <18	61.6	66.6	91.3	76.4	37.2
One	28.7	34.4	37.7	41.0	26.7
Two	20.4	21.0	32.7	24.5	8.1
Three or more	12.5	11.2	21.0	10.9	2.4

Note: Own children includes stepchildren and adopted children of the householder.
Source: Bureau of the Census, Household and Family Characteristics: March 1994, *Current Population Reports, P20-483, 1995*

Couples Dominate
White Households

Two out of three white households in the 35-to-54 age group are headed by married couples.

There is remarkably little variation within the 35-to-54 age group in the percentage of households headed by married couples. But there are sharp differences by age in the proportion of couples who have children under age 18 at home. While over half of couples aged 35 to 44 have dependent children, this proportion falls to just 28 percent among couples aged 45 to 54.

◆ Among households headed by whites aged 35 to 39, 11 percent are single-parent families headed by women. This proportion falls to just 4 percent among 45-to-54-year-olds.

◆ Although single-parent families have become more common among whites over the past few decades, they make up a tiny minority of white households in the 35-to-54 age group.

White Households by Type and Presence of Children, 1994

(number and percent distribution of total white households and white households headed by persons aged 35 to 54, by type of household and presence of own children under age 18 at home, 1994; numbers in thousands)

	total	35 to 54	35 to 39	40 to 44	45 to 54
Total households	82,387	32,842	9,770	8,748	14,324
Married couples	47,443	21,570	6,309	5,744	9,517
Without children <18	25,559	7,825	959	1,337	5,529
With children <18	21,884	13,745	5,350	4,407	3,988
Female householder, no spouse present	8,130	3,633	1,196	980	1,457
Without children <18	3,382	1,203	86	209	908
With children <18	4,748	2,430	1,110	771	549
Male householder, no spouse present	2,297	976	299	301	376
Without children <18	1,287	688	150	211	327
With children <18	1,010	288	149	90	49
Nonfamily households	24,518	6,663	1,966	1,723	2,974
Female householder	13,916	2,896	705	690	1,501
Male householder	10,602	3,767	1,261	1,033	1,473
Total households	100.0%	100.0%	100.0%	100.0%	100.0%
Married couples	57.6	65.7	64.6	65.7	66.4
Without children <18	31.0	23.8	9.8	15.3	38.6
With children <18	26.6	41.9	54.8	50.4	27.8
Female householder, no spouse present	9.9	11.1	12.2	11.2	10.2
Without children <18	4.1	3.7	0.9	2.4	6.3
With children <18	5.8	7.4	11.4	8.8	3.8
Male householder, no spouse present	2.8	3.0	3.1	3.4	2.6
Without children <18	1.6	2.1	1.5	2.4	2.3
With children <18	1.2	0.9	1.5	1.0	0.3
Nonfamily households	29.8	20.3	20.1	19.7	20.8
Female householder	16.9	8.8	7.2	7.9	10.5
Male householder	12.9	11.5	12.9	11.8	10.3

Note: Own children includes stepchildren and adopted children of the householder.
Source: Bureau of the Census, Household and Family Characteristics: March 1994, *Current Population Reports, P20-483, 1995*

Minority of Black Households Are Married Couples

Only 38 percent of black households headed by 35-to-54-year-olds are married couples.

Although married couples account for a minority of black households, couples outnumber single-parent families in the 35-to-54 age group overall. Thirty-eight percent of black households in this age group are headed by married couples, while 35 percent are female-headed families.

Within the 35-to-54 age group, however, household type varies by age. Among black householders aged 35 to 39, female-headed families are more numerous (43 percent of households) than married couples (31 percent). In the 40-to-44 age group, black couples begin to outnumber female-headed families, 39 to 33 percent. The gap grows in the 45-to-54 age group, with couples accounting for 42 percent of households and female-headed families for just 29 percent.

♦ While the mid-youth market among white households is overwhelmingly one of married couples, the black mid-youth market is more segmented, requiring careful targeting.

Black Households by Type and Presence of Children, 1994

(number and percent distribution of total black households and black households headed by persons aged 35 to 54, by type of household and presence of own children under age 18 at home, 1994; numbers in thousands)

	total	35 to 54	35 to 39	40 to 44	45 to 54
Total households	11,281	4,682	1,504	1,322	1,856
Married couples	3,714	1,768	465	520	783
Without children <18	1,790	624	68	144	412
With children <18	1,924	1,144	397	376	371
Female householder, no spouse present	3,825	1,616	643	440	533
Without children <18	1,195	526	69	125	332
With children <18	2,630	1,090	574	315	201
Male householder, no spouse present	450	178	70	45	63
Without children <18	212	78	22	26	30
With children <18	238	100	48	19	33
Nonfamily households	3,292	1,119	326	317	476
Female householder	1,840	526	115	151	260
Male householder	1,452	593	211	166	216
Total households	100.0%	100.0%	100.0%	100.0%	100.0%
Married couples	32.9	37.8	30.9	39.3	42.2
Without children <18	15.9	13.3	4.5	10.9	22.2
With children <18	17.1	24.4	26.4	28.4	20.0
Female householder, no spouse present	33.9	34.5	42.8	33.3	28.7
Without children <18	10.6	11.2	4.6	9.5	17.9
With children <18	23.3	23.3	38.2	23.8	10.8
Male householder, no spouse present	4.0	3.8	4.7	3.4	3.4
Without children <18	1.9	1.7	1.5	2.0	1.6
With children <18	2.1	2.1	3.2	1.4	1.8
Nonfamily households	29.2	23.9	21.7	24.0	25.6
Female householder	16.3	11.2	7.6	11.4	14.0
Male householder	12.9	12.7	14.0	12.6	11.6

Note: Own children includes stepchildren and adopted children of the householder.
Source: Bureau of the Census, Household and Family Characteristics: March 1994, *Current Population Reports, P20-483, 1995*

Couples With Children
Rank First Among Hispanics

Nuclear families are the most common household type among Hispanics aged 35 to 54.

Over half of households headed by Hispanics aged 35 to 44 are married couples with children under age 18 at home. This proportion drops to 34 percent among householders aged 45 to 54, but—unlike white households—the nuclear family remains the most common household type even in this older age group. Only 8 percent of Hispanic households headed by 35-to-39-year-olds are married couples without children at home. This proportion rises to 10 percent among those aged 40 to 44, and to 25 percent in the 45-to-54 age group.

Female-headed families are more common among Hispanic than white households. In the 35-to-39 age group, 22 percent of Hispanic households are female-headed families with children under age 18 at home. This proportion drops sharply in the older age groups, to just 9 percent of households headed by 45-to-54-year-olds.

♦ Because Hispanics have more children than non-Hispanics, Hispanic households remain child-centered well into middle-age. This makes the Hispanic mid-youth market "younger" than the non-Hispanic market.

Hispanic Households by Type and Presence of Children, 1994

(number and percent distribution of total Hispanic households and Hispanic households headed by persons aged 35 to 54, by type of household and presence of own children under age 18 at home, 1994; numbers in thousands)

	total	35 to 54	35 to 39	40 to 44	45 to 54
Total households	7,362	3,077	983	873	1,221
Married couples	4,033	1,857	591	554	712
Without children <18	1,424	469	78	91	300
With children <18	2,609	1,388	513	463	412
Female householder, no spouse present	1,498	647	225	168	254
Without children <18	492	205	12	44	149
With children <18	1,006	442	213	124	105
Male householder, no spouse present	410	149	51	39	59
Without children <18	235	69	16	19	34
With children <18	175	80	35	20	25
Nonfamily households	1,423	423	116	111	196
Female householder	676	163	29	46	88
Male householder	747	260	87	65	108
Total households	100.0%	100.0%	100.0%	100.0%	100.0%
Married couples	54.8	60.4	60.1	63.5	58.3
Without children <18	19.3	15.2	7.9	10.4	24.6
With children <18	35.4	45.1	52.2	53.0	33.7
Female householder, no spouse present	20.3	21.0	22.9	19.2	20.8
Without children <18	6.7	6.7	1.2	5.0	12.2
With children <18	13.7	14.4	21.7	14.2	8.6
Male householder, no spouse present	5.6	4.8	5.2	4.5	4.8
Without children <18	3.2	2.2	1.6	2.2	2.8
With children <18	2.4	2.6	3.6	2.3	2.0
Nonfamily households	19.3	13.7	11.8	12.7	16.1
Female householder	9.2	5.3	3.0	5.3	7.2
Male householder	10.1	8.4	8.9	7.4	8.8

Note: Own children includes stepchildren and adopted children of the householder.
Source: Bureau of the Census, Household and Family Characteristics: March 1994, *Current Population Reports, P20-483, 1995*

Most Middle-Aged Men
Head Families

About three out of four men aged 35 to 54 are family householders.

By the time men reach their mid-30s, most have settled down. Among men aged 35 to 39, fully 68 percent are family householders or spouses. This proportion rises to 72 percent among those aged 40 to 44 and to 78 percent among men aged 45 to 54.

Eight percent of men in the 35-to-39 age group still live with their parents. This is about double the proportion of women in this age group who still live with their parents.

Fourteen percent of men aged 35 to 39 head nonfamily households (meaning they live alone or with people to whom they aren't related), a share that drops slightly to 12 percent among men aged 45 to 54. Men are more likely to head nonfamily households than are women in the 35-to-39 age group, but by the 45-to-54 age group the proportions are about the same.

◆ Men are far more likely to live with their parents as young adults than are women, a tendency that continues through middle-age.

◆ While men become less likely to head nonfamily households through middle-age, women are more likely to live alone or with nonrelatives as they age.

Living Arrangements of Men, 1994

(number and percent distribution of total men and men aged 35 to 54 by living arrangement, 1994; numbers in thousands)

	total	35 to 54	35 to 39	40 to 44	45 to 54
Total men, number	91,222	34,997	10,892	9,651	14,454
Family householder or spouse	56,058	25,610	7,421	6,930	11,259
Child of householder	13,070	2,056	917	626	513
Other member of family household	4,026	991	350	275	366
Nonfamily householder	12,462	4,496	1,521	1,234	1,741
Other member, nonfamily household	5,503	1,813	667	583	563
Group quarters*	103	31	16	3	12
Total men, percent	100.0%	100.0%	100.0%	100.0%	100.0%
Family householder or spouse	61.5	73.2	68.1	71.8	77.9
Child of householder	14.3	5.9	8.4	6.5	3.5
Other member of family household	4.4	2.8	3.2	2.8	2.5
Nonfamily householder	13.7	12.8	14.0	12.8	12.0
Other member, nonfamily household	6.0	5.2	6.1	6.0	3.9
Group quarters*	0.1	0.1	0.1	0.0	0.1

* The Current Population Survey does not include people living in institutions such as prisons, the military, or college dormitories. It defines people living in group quarters as those in noninstitutional living arrangements that are not conventional housing units, such as rooming houses, staff quarters at a hospital, or halfway houses. Source: Bureau of the Census, Marital Status and Living Arrangements: March 1994, *Current Population Reports, P20-483, 1995*

Most Middle-Aged Women
Head Families

Over 80 percent are family householders or spouses.

Middle-aged women are even more likely to head families than are men. Over 80 percent of women aged 35 to 54 are family householders or spouses. No other living arrangement accounts for even 10 percent of women in this age group.

Few middle-aged women still live with their parents. In every age group, the share of women who live at home is just half that of men. Also in contrast to men, middle-aged women are increasingly likely to head nonfamily households as they age (meaning they live alone or with nonrelatives). The proportion rises from just 8 percent among women aged 35 to 39 to 12 percent among women aged 45 to 54.

♦ The rising proportion of middle-aged women who head nonfamily households is just the beginning of what eventually becomes the dominant household type among women in old age.

Living Arrangements of Women, 1994

(number and percent distribution of total women and women aged 35 to 54 by living arrangement, 1994; numbers in thousands)

	total	35 to 54	35 to 39	40 to 44	45 to 54
Total women, number	98,764	36,052	11,078	9,906	15,068
Family householder or spouse	65,514	29,720	9,191	8,247	12,282
Child of householder	8,813	968	434	263	271
Other member of family household	4,611	859	290	208	361
Nonfamily householder	16,150	3,552	872	863	1,817
Other member, nonfamily household	3,561	943	286	322	335
Group quarters*	115	10	5	3	2
Total women, percent	100.0%	100.0%	100.0%	100.0%	100.0%
Family householder or spouse	66.3	82.4	83.0	83.3	81.5
Child of householder	8.9	2.7	3.9	2.7	1.8
Other member of family household	4.7	2.4	2.6	2.1	2.4
Nonfamily householder	16.4	9.9	7.9	8.7	12.1
Other member, nonfamily household	3.6	2.6	2.6	3.3	2.2
Group quarters*	0.1	0.0	0.0	0.0	0.0

* The Current Population Survey does not include people living in institutions such as prisons, the military, or college dormitories. It defines people living in group quarters as those in noninstitutional living arrangements that are not conventional housing units, such as rooming houses, staff quarters at a hospital, or halfway houses. Source: Bureau of the Census, Marital Status and Living Arrangements: March 1994, *Current Population Reports, P20-483, 1995*

Few Americans Live Alone
in Middle Age

Just 12 percent of 35-to-54-year-olds live by themselves.

Middle-age is the stage of life when people are least likely to live alone, particularly in the 35-to-44 age group. Most 35-to-44-year-olds are married with children. The proportion of people who live alone bottoms out at 8.5 percent in this age group. Women aged 35 to 44 are less likely to live alone than men—7 versus 10 percent.

Lone living becomes somewhat more common among women in the 45-to-54 age group, rising to 11 percent as marriages dissolve due to divorce or death and as female-headed families become single-person households when children leave home.

Although middle-aged Americans are not likely to live alone, lone living is more common among 35-to-54-year-olds than it was a quarter-century ago. In 1970, just 7 percent of 35-to-54-year-olds lived by themselves. The increase in lone living has occurred for both men and women, with the greatest increase for men in the 35-to-44 age group.

◆ Although people aged 35 to 54 aren't likely to live alone, the proportion who do comprises a significant 10 percent of men aged 35 to 54 and women aged 45 to 54. The Census Bureau projects that the number of middle-aged people who live alone will continue to increase through the turn of the century.

People Who Live Alone, 1970 and 1994

(number and percent of total persons and persons aged 35 to 54 who live alone by age and sex, 1970 and 1994; numbers in thousands)

	1994		1970	
	number	*percent*	*number*	*percent*
Total persons	23,611	11.8%	10,851	7.3%
Aged 35 to 44	3,518	8.5	711	3.1
Aged 45 to 54	3,015	10.2	1,303	5.6
Total men	9,440	9.8	3,532	5.0
Aged 35 to 44	2,115	10.3	398	3.5
Aged 45 to 54	1,440	10.0	513	4.6
Total women	14,171	13.6	7,319	9.4
Aged 35 to 44	1,401	6.7	313	2.6
Aged 45 to 54	1,575	10.5	790	6.6

Source: Bureau of the Census, Marital Status and Living Arrangements: March 1994, *Current Population Reports, P20-484, 1996*

Most Mid-Youth Men and Women Are Married

Over 70 percent of 35-to-54-year-olds are married.

In middle-age, most people are married. The married proportion rises steadily for men through middle-age, from 70 percent among 35-to-39-year-olds to 79 percent of 45-to-54-year-olds. For women, the married proportion peaks in the 40-to-44 age group at 74 percent.

Fully 19 percent of men aged 35 to 39 have not married, a proportion that falls to just 8 percent by the 45-to-54 age group. Among women, the never-married share drops from 13 percent among 35-to-39-year-olds to just 6 percent among 45-to-54-year-olds.

The proportion of middle-aged people who are divorced is a substantial 12 percent among men and 15 percent among women. This figure includes only those who are currently divorced—not those who have ever been divorced. Fully 30 percent of middle-aged Americans have experienced divorce.

Widowhood among midlife men is rare. But a significant 5 percent of women in the 45-to-54 age group are widows, reflecting men's higher mortality rates.

♦ The mid-youth market is overwhelmingly a couples market, although many husbands and wives are in their second or even third marriages.

Marital Status by Sex, 1994

(number and percent distribution of total persons aged 15 or older and persons aged 35 to 54 by marital status and sex, 1994; numbers in thousands)

	total	*35 to 54*	*35 to 39*	*40 to 44*	*45 to 54*
Total women, number	104,032	36,052	11,078	9,906	15,068
Never married	24,645	3,221	1,420	909	892
Married	58,185	26,296	7,960	7,359	10,977
Divorced	11,073	5,549	1,563	1,492	2,494
Widowed	10,129	986	135	146	705
Total women, percent	100.0%	100.0%	100.0%	100.0%	100.0%
Never married	23.7	8.9	12.8	9.2	5.9
Married	55.9	72.9	71.9	74.3	72.8
Divorced	10.6	15.4	14.1	15.1	16.6
Widowed	9.7	2.7	1.2	1.5	4.7
Total men, number	96,768	34,997	10,892	9,651	14,454
Never married	30,228	4,534	2,094	1,255	1,185
Married	57,068	26,068	7,603	7,103	11,362
Divorced	7,250	4,196	1,164	1,262	1,770
Widowed	2,222	199	31	31	137
Total men, percent	100.0%	100.0%	100.0%	100.0%	100.0%
Never married	31.2	13.0	19.2	13.0	8.2
Married	59.0	74.5	69.8	73.6	78.6
Divorced	7.5	12.0	10.7	13.1	12.2
Widowed	2.3	0.6	0.3	0.3	0.9

Source: Bureau of the Census, Marital Status and Living Arrangements: March 1994, *Current Population Reports, P20-484, 1996*

Many Middle-Aged Blacks Are Single

Only slightly over half of blacks aged 35 to 54 are married.

The marital status of the middle-aged varies sharply by race. Among men and women aged 35 to 54, three out four whites and Hispanics are currently married. But among blacks, only 58 percent of men and 54 percent of women are married.

Behind the lower marriage rates among blacks is their growing propensity to postpone marriage altogether. Fully 26 percent of black men and 22 percent of black women aged 35 to 54 have never married. In contrast, the proportion never-married among white men and women is 12 and 7 percent, respectively.

Blacks are also more likely to be currently divorced than whites or Hispanics. Fully 20 percent of black women aged 35 to 54 are currently divorced, versus 15 percent of white and 14 percent of Hispanic women.

♦ The mid-youth market is highly segmented among blacks. While most middle-aged blacks are married, those who are divorced or never-married make up a significant share of the market.

Marital Status by Sex, Race, and Hispanic Origin 1994

(number and percent distribution of persons aged 35 to 54 by sex, marital status, race, and Hispanic origin, 1994; numbers in thousands)

	total	white	black	Hispanic
Total men, aged 35 to 54	36,459	29,829	3,691	2,939
Percent	100.0%	100.0%	100.0%	100.0%
Never married	13.0	11.5	26.1	15.1
Married	74.5	76.0	58.4	73.9
Divorced	12.0	12.0	14.1	10.0
Widowed	0.6	0.5	1.3	1.0
Total women, aged 35 to 54	36,052	30,001	4,389	2,974
Percent	100.0%	100.0%	100.0%	100.0%
Never married	8.9	7.1	21.8	10.0
Married	72.9	75.6	53.7	73.2
Divorced	15.4	14.9	20.2	13.6
Widowed	2.7	2.4	4.4	3.3

Note: Numbers will not add to total because Hispanics may be of any race and not all races are shown.
Source: Bureau of the Census, Marital Status and Living Arrangements: March 1994, *Current Population Reports, P20-484, 1996*

3

Income

♦ While 35-to-44-year-olds cut their discretionary spending sharply in many areas between 1990 and 1994, 45-to-54-year-olds cut back much less.

♦ The ranks of the rich are growing because the oversized baby-boom generation is beginning to reap the benefits of its education, work experience, and dual-income lifestyles.

♦ Among the 1.7 million households headed by 35-to-44-year-olds with incomes of $100,000 or more, nearly 90 percent are married couples.

♦ The median income of households headed by 45-to-54-year-olds was $47,261 in 1994, higher than that of any other age group.

♦ Although few black or Hispanic householders aged 35 to 54 have six-digit incomes, one in four has a household income of $50,000 or more.

♦ Since 1980, the median income of men aged 35 to 44 has fallen by 15 percent, after adjusting for inflation. The median income of all men fell by 4 percent during those years.

♦ Men aged 45 to 54 are the best-educated cohort in history—men with college degrees comprise the single largest segment of this age group.

♦ Poverty rates reach a low among people aged 45 to 54. With the enormous baby-boom generation entering this age group, public support for poverty programs has plummeted.

Divergent Income Trends for Middle-Aged

Household income is up for the older group, down for the younger.

Between 1990 and 1994, the median incomes of middle-aged householders fell slightly, after adjusting for inflation. Both 35-to-44-year-olds and 45-to-54-year-olds lost ground because of the recession.

A longer perspective presents a different story. The median income of householders aged 45 to 54 increased by 4.5 percent between 1980 and 1994—to $47,261, after adjusting for inflation. In contrast, the median income of householders aged 35 to 44 fell by 2 percent during those years, to $41,667.

Householders aged 45 to 54 typically have the highest incomes and their income peak is sharper today than in the past. In 1994, the median income of householders aged 45 to 54 was $5,600 greater than that of householders aged 35 to 44, up from a $2,700 gap in 1980.

◆ The rosier fortunes of 45-to-54-year-olds is evident in their spending patterns. While 35-to-44-year-olds cut their discretionary spending sharply in many areas, 45-to-54-year-olds cut back much less. Consequently, the older group is becoming more important in the marketplace, while the younger group is losing ground.

Median Income of Households, 1980 to 1994

(median income of total households and households headed by persons aged 35 to 54, 1980 to 1994; in 1994 dollars)

	total households	householders aged 35 to 54	
		35 to 44	45 to 54
1994	$32,264	$41,667	$47,261
1993	32,041	41,908	47,390
1992	32,361	42,097	46,938
1991	32,780	42,816	47,605
1990	33,952	43,723	47,535
1989	34,547	44,980	49,627
1988	34,106	45,793	47,871
1987	33,999	45,902	48,537
1986	33,665	44,334	48,219
1985	32,529	42,788	45,758
1984	31,972	42,482	44,953
1983	31,076	41,185	45,162
1982	31,270	40,878	43,383
1981	31,373	41,752	44,482
1980	31,891	42,546	45,236
Percent change			
1993-1994	0.7%	-0.6%	-0.3%
1990-1994	-5.0	-4.7	-0.6
1980-1994	1.2	-2.1	4.5

Source: Bureau of the Census, Internet web site, http://www.census.gov

Income Peaks
in Middle-Age

Householders in their late 40s and early 50s have the highest incomes.

Householders aged 35 to 54 had a median household income of $44,304 in 1994, far above the $32,264 national median. The reason for the higher incomes of 35-to-54-year-olds is that most households in this age group are headed by married couples and most married couples are two-earner. In addition, middle-aged householders are at the peak of their careers, when pay levels are highest.

Within the 35-to-54 age group, household incomes are highest among 45-to-54-year-olds, at about $47,000. One in eight households in this age group has a household income of $100,000 or more.

◆ When you hear about the growing gap between rich and poor in America, the "rich" they're talking about are baby boomers. The ranks of the rich are growing because the oversized baby-boom generation is beginning to reap the benefits of its education, work experience, and dual-income lifestyle. With demographic forces at play, the gap between rich and poor is not likely toshrink until boomers begin to retire and the affluent among them rejoin the middle class.

◆ Consumer businesses targeting the affluent should set their sites on the oldest boomers because that's where the money is. As the entire generation moves through its peak earning years, the affluent market should grow for more than a decade.

Income Distribution of Households, 1994

(number and percent distribution of total households and households headed by persons aged 35 to 54 by income, 1994; households in thousands as of 1995)

	total	35 to 54	35 to 39	40 to 44	45 to 49	50 to 54
Total households	98,990	40,504	11,947	10,967	9,807	7,783
Under $10,000	13,412	3,311	1,051	924	690	646
$10,000 to $19,999	17,371	4,312	1,476	1,058	970	808
$20,000 to $29,999	15,219	5,031	1,621	1,440	1,131	839
$30,000 to $39,999	12,985	5,420	1,769	1,533	1,207	911
$40,000 to $49,999	10,108	4,897	1,508	1,315	1,151	923
$50,000 to $59,999	7,917	4,077	1,245	1,174	922	736
$60,000 to $69,999	6,150	3,594	990	974	928	702
$70,000 to $79,999	4,362	2,647	642	800	677	528
$80,000 to $89,999	2,795	1,795	398	441	524	432
$90,000 to $99,999	2,089	1,249	295	289	397	268
$100,000 or more	6,581	4,172	952	1,022	1,208	990
Median income	$32,264	$44,304	$40,289	$43,666	$47,460	$46,974
Total households	100.0%	100.0%	100.0%	100.0%	100.0%	100.0%
Under $10,000	13.5	8.2	8.8	8.4	7.0	8.3
$10,000 to $19,999	17.5	10.6	12.4	9.6	9.9	10.4
$20,000 to $29,999	15.4	12.4	13.6	13.1	11.5	10.8
$30,000 to $39,999	13.1	13.4	14.8	14.0	12.3	11.7
$40,000 to $49,999	10.2	12.1	12.6	12.0	11.7	11.9
$50,000 to $59,999	8.0	10.1	10.4	10.7	9.4	9.5
$60,000 to $69,999	6.2	8.9	8.3	8.9	9.5	9.0
$70,000 to $79,999	4.4	6.5	5.4	7.3	6.9	6.8
$80,000 to $89,999	2.8	4.4	3.3	4.0	5.3	5.6
$90,000 to $99,999	2.1	3.1	2.5	2.6	4.0	3.4
$100,000 or more	6.6	10.3	8.0	9.3	12.3	12.7

Source: Bureau of the Census, unpublished tables from the 1995 Current Population Survey

Many 35-to-44-Year-Old Couples Are Affluent

The median income of couples in the 35-to-44 age group is well above average.

Among households headed by 35-to-44-year-olds, median income was $41,667 in 1994, well above the national median of $32,264. Married couples are the only household type in this age group with above-average incomes, however.

The median household income of couples aged 35 to 44 was $52,640 in 1994, versus a median of just $21,610 for female-headed families. The income of couples is far higher than that of female-headed families because most married couples are two-earner.

Men and women aged 35 to 44 who live alone have nearly equal incomes—$25,773 for women and $27,603 for men—evidence that women's incomes are catching up to men's.

◆ The affluent market is almost entirely one of married couples. Among the 1.7 million households headed by 35-to-44-year-olds with incomes of $100,000 or more, nearly 90 percent are married couples.

◆ Two out of three married couples in this age group are dual-earner. Most also have children at home. They lead busy, high-pressured lives, making them difficult to reach.

Income Distribution of Households by Type, 1994: Aged 35 to 44

(number and percent distribution of households headed by 35-to-44-year-olds by income and household type, 1994; households in thousands as of 1995)

| | | family households | | | nonfamily households | | | |
| | | | | | female householder | | male householder | |
	total	married couples	female hh no spouse present	male hh no spouse present	total	living alone	total	living alone
Total households	22,914	13,919	3,501	853	1,714	1,400	2,928	2,263
Under $10,000	1,975	413	800	90	288	267	384	354
$10,000 to $19,999	2,534	845	842	147	276	242	423	361
$20,000 to $29,999	3,061	1,338	614	151	349	312	610	500
$30,000 to $39,999	3,302	1,835	567	141	270	231	490	400
$40,000 to $49,999	2,823	1,902	262	115	201	141	341	260
$50,000 to $59,999	2,419	1,855	191	71	109	78	192	133
$60,000 to $69,999	1,964	1,613	66	52	57	33	175	97
$70,000 to $79,999	1,442	1,215	54	35	58	39	81	43
$80,000 to $89,999	839	705	34	15	33	12	49	29
$90,000 to $99,999	584	494	27	11	10	1	40	13
$100,000 or more	1,974	1,705	45	20	62	44	142	73
Median income	$41,667	$52,640	$21,610	$32,458	$27,848	$25,773	$30,714	$27,603
Total households	100.0%	100.0%	100.0%	100.0%	100.0%	100.0%	100.0%	100.0%
Under $10,000	8.6	3.0	22.9	10.6	16.8	19.1	13.1	15.6
$10,000 to $19,999	11.1	6.1	24.1	17.2	16.1	17.3	14.4	16.0
$20,000 to $29,999	13.4	9.6	17.5	17.7	20.4	22.3	20.8	22.1
$30,000 to $39,999	14.4	13.2	16.2	16.5	15.8	16.5	16.7	17.7
$40,000 to $49,999	12.3	13.7	7.5	13.5	11.7	10.1	11.6	11.5
$50,000 to $59,999	10.6	13.3	5.5	8.3	6.4	5.6	6.6	5.9
$60,000 to $69,999	8.6	11.6	1.9	6.1	3.3	2.4	6.0	4.3
$70,000 to $79,999	6.3	8.7	1.5	4.1	3.4	2.8	2.8	1.9
$80,000 to $89,999	3.7	5.1	1.0	1.8	1.9	0.9	1.7	1.3
$90,000 to $99,999	2.5	3.5	0.8	1.3	0.6	0.1	1.4	0.6
$100,000 or more	8.6	12.2	1.3	2.3	3.6	3.1	4.8	3.2

Source: Bureau of the Census, unpublished tables from the 1995 Current Population Survey

Couples Aged 45 to 54 Are Income Elite

Nearly one in five has an income of $100,000 or more.

The median income of households headed by 45-to-54-year-olds was $47,261 in 1994, higher than that of any other age group. Married couples aged 45 to 54 had a median income of $61,280 in 1994, nearly double the median income of households nationally. Among these couples, 18 percent had incomes of $100,000 or more.

Female-headed families in this age group have a median income of $28,997, which is relatively high for these typically low-income households. Many female family householders aged 45 to 54 have adult children in the home who contribute to the household's income. Women who live alone have the lowest incomes among 45-to-54-year-olds, just $21,427 in 1994.

♦ While millions of households lost ground economically during the past 15 years, those headed by 45-to-54-year-olds have seen their incomes grow. This age group has gained economic power relative to others.

♦ Married couples aged 45 to 54 are the heart of the affluent market. But most — even those with six-digit household incomes—would deny they are rich. Many feel pinched by mortgages, car payments, the costs of raising children, and the need to save for college and retirement. They work hard for their money and consider themselves to be very middle-class.

Income Distribution of Households by Type, 1994: Aged 45 to 54

(number and percent distribution of households headed by 45-to-54-year-olds by income and household type, 1994; households in thousands as of 1995)

| | | family households | | | nonfamily households | | | |
| | | | | | female householder | | male householder | |
	total	married couples	female hh no spouse present	male hh no spouse present	total	living alone	total	living alone
Total households	17,590	11,153	2,037	556	1,896	1,676	1,948	1,650
Under $10,000	1,336	264	295	39	413	400	326	315
$10,000 to $19,999	1,778	562	382	88	399	371	346	313
$20,000 to $29,999	1,970	778	376	92	383	348	341	295
$30,000 to $39,999	2,118	1,172	338	63	277	252	268	230
$40,000 to $49,999	2,074	1,390	265	72	167	145	181	159
$50,000 to $59,999	1,658	1,216	145	55	102	82	141	109
$60,000 to $69,999	1,630	1,303	97	56	43	30	133	96
$70,000 to $79,999	1,205	1,002	67	39	35	13	62	37
$80,000 to $89,999	956	868	16	12	20	8	39	25
$90,000 to $99,999	665	583	22	11	15	8	33	16
$100,000 or more	2,198	2,015	37	28	40	18	80	56
Median income	$47,261	$61,280	$28,997	$38,962	$22,728	$21,427	$28,593	$26,244
Total households	100.0%	100.0%	100.0%	100.0%	100.0%	100.0%	100.0%	100.0%
Under $10,000	7.6	2.4	14.5	7.0	21.8	23.9	16.7	19.1
$10,000 to $19,999	10.1	5.0	18.8	15.8	21.0	22.1	17.8	19.0
$20,000 to $29,999	11.2	7.0	18.5	16.5	20.2	20.8	17.5	17.9
$30,000 to $39,999	12.0	10.5	16.6	11.3	14.6	15.0	13.8	13.9
$40,000 to $49,999	11.8	12.5	13.0	12.9	8.8	8.7	9.3	9.6
$50,000 to $59,999	9.4	10.9	7.1	9.9	5.4	4.9	7.2	6.6
$60,000 to $69,999	9.3	11.7	4.8	10.1	2.3	1.8	6.8	5.8
$70,000 to $79,999	6.9	9.0	3.3	7.0	1.8	0.8	3.2	2.2
$80,000 to $89,999	5.4	7.8	0.8	2.2	1.1	0.5	2.0	1.5
$90,000 to $99,999	3.8	5.2	1.1	2.0	0.8	0.5	1.7	1.0
$100,000 or more	12.5	18.1	1.8	5.0	2.1	1.1	4.1	3.4

Source: Bureau of the Census, unpublished tables from the 1995 Current Population Survey

Black and Hispanic Incomes Are Below Average

Black and Hispanic household incomes barely peak in middle-age.

Even in the most affluent of age groups, the household incomes of blacks and Hispanics are well below the national average.

Among households headed by 35-to-54-year-olds, median income was $28,191 for blacks and $28,606 for Hispanics in 1994. This compares with a median of $32,264 for all households and $46,860 for white households in 1994.

Middle-aged blacks have lower household incomes than whites in part because few black households—even in this age group—are headed by married couples. Hispanic incomes are low because many are immigrants with little education.

Eleven percent of white householders aged 35 to 54 had incomes of $100,000 or more in 1994. Only about 4 percent of black and Hispanic households had incomes this high.

♦ The affluent market is dominated by whites. Among the 4 million householders aged 35 to 54 with incomes of $100,000 or more, 91 percent are white.

♦ Although few black or Hispanic householders aged 35 to 54 have six-digit incomes, one in four has a household income of $50,000 or more.

Household Income Distribution by Race and Hispanic Origin, 1994

(number and percent distribution of households headed by 35-to-54-year-olds by income, race, and Hispanic origin, 1994; households in thousands as of 1995)

	total	white	black	Hispanic
Total households, aged 35 to 54	40,504	33,774	4,996	3,182
Under $10,000	3,311	2,228	909	465
$10,000 to $19,999	4,312	3,161	917	615
$20,000 to $29,999	5,031	4,029	787	562
$30,000 to $39,999	5,420	4,558	621	450
$40,000 to $49,999	4,897	4,185	526	330
$50,000 to $59,999	4,077	3,544	397	240
$60,000 to $69,999	3,594	3,163	276	164
$70,000 to $79,999	2,647	2,363	181	125
$80,000 to $89,999	1,795	1,615	112	75
$90,000 to $99,999	1,249	1,115	79	45
$100,000 or more	4,172	3,811	194	111
Median income	$44,304	$46,860	$28,191	$28,606
Total households, aged 35 to 54	100.0%	100.0%	100.0%	100.0%
Under $10,000	8.2	6.6	18.2	14.6
$10,000 to $19,999	10.6	9.4	18.4	19.3
$20,000 to $29,999	12.4	11.9	15.8	17.7
$30,000 to $39,999	13.4	13.5	12.4	14.1
$40,000 to $49,999	12.1	12.4	10.5	10.4
$50,000 to $59,999	10.1	10.5	7.9	7.5
$60,000 to $69,999	8.9	9.4	5.5	5.2
$70,000 to $79,999	6.5	7.0	3.6	3.9
$80,000 to $89,999	4.4	4.8	2.2	2.4
$90,000 to $99,999	3.1	3.3	1.6	1.4
$100,000 or more	10.3	11.3	3.9	3.5

Note: Numbers will not add to total because Hispanics may be of any race and not all races are shown.
Source: Bureau of the Census, unpublished tables from the 1995 Current Population Survey

Incomes Down for
Mid-Youth Men

Men aged 35 to 44 have been hurt more than those aged 45 to 54.

Since 1980, the median income of men aged 35 to 44 has fallen by 15 percent, after adjusting for inflation—a loss of over $5,000. The median income of all men fell by 4 percent during those years.

Men aged 45 to 54 have fared better than those aged 35 to 44. The median income of the older men fell by only 3 percent between 1980 and 1994, after adjusting for inflation—a loss of $1,000. In 1980, the median income of men aged 45 to 54 was slightly below that of men aged 35 to 44. By 1994, the median income of men aged 45 to 54 was 14 percent greater than that of the younger men.

◆ Because men's incomes have been falling, the earnings of working women are becoming increasingly important to family well-being.

◆ The decline in men's incomes explains why Americans feel so economically insecure. Men are the primary breadwinners in most households, and a loss in men's incomes means a lower standard of living for many families.

Median Income of Men, 1980 to 1994

(median income of total men and men aged 35 to 54, 1980 to 1994; in 1994 dollars)

		men aged 35 to 54	
	total men	*35 to 44*	*45 to 54*
1994	$21,720	$30,707	$34,933
1993	21,642	31,119	34,003
1992	21,606	31,152	33,992
1991	22,272	31,883	34,579
1990	23,010	33,760	35,159
1989	23,775	35,182	37,005
1988	23,687	35,760	37,054
1987	23,203	35,279	37,164
1986	23,142	35,389	37,531
1985	22,466	34,926	35,597
1984	22,251	35,040	35,072
1983	21,770	33,389	34,393
1982	21,626	33,561	33,396
1981	22,161	34,734	34,578
1980	22,563	36,081	35,968
Percent change			
1993-1994	0.4%	-1.3%	2.7%
1990-1994	-5.6	-9.0	-0.6
1980-1994	-3.7	-14.9	-2.9

Source: Bureau of the Census, Internet web site, http://www.census.gov

Men's Incomes Rise
Through Middle-Age

Men aged 45 to 54 have the highest incomes.

The median income of men who work full-time peaks in the 45-to-54 age group, at just over $40,000 in 1994. This was nearly $9,000 more than the income of the average man who works full-time.

The median income of men aged 35 to 44 who work full-time was about $5,000 less than that of their older counterparts. As these men age into their late 40s, their incomes should grow with their job experience.

Three out of ten men aged 45 to 54 (including those who work full-time and those who don't) had an income of $50,000 or more in 1994. Six percent of men in this age group had an income of $100,000 or more, versus 3 percent of all men.

◆ Although earnings peak in middle-age, most men aged 35 to 54 have modest incomes. Two-earner couples, not highly paid men, are behind the affuence of mid-youth households.

Income Distribution of Men, 1994

(number and percent distribution of total men and men aged 35 to 54 by income, 1994; men in thousands as of 1995)

	total	35 to 54	35 to 39	40 to 44	45 to 49	50 to 54
Total men	97,704	35,994	11,041	9,931	8,504	6,518
Without income	6,450	893	300	285	174	134
With income	91,254	35,101	10,741	9,646	8,330	6,384
Under $10,000	20,703	4,286	1,394	1,222	882	788
$10,000 to $19,999	21,376	5,486	1,936	1,510	1,128	912
$20,000 to $29,999	16,097	6,188	2,025	1,785	1,325	1,053
$30,000 to $39,999	11,542	5,944	1,892	1,665	1,433	954
$40,000 to $49,999	7,399	4,350	1,296	1,189	1,070	795
$50,000 to $74,999	8,643	5,354	1,343	1,387	1,495	1,129
$75,000 to $99,999	2,616	1,631	416	409	469	337
$100,000 or more	2,878	1,862	439	478	528	417
Median income	$21,720	$32,416	$30,069	$31,425	$35,334	$34,093
Median income, year-round full-time workers	31,612	37,571	34,700	36,500	40,323	40,432
Percent of men who work year-round, full time	52.8%	74.9%	74.7%	74.5%	76.8%	73.2%
Total men	100.0%	100.0%	100.0%	100.0%	100.0%	100.0%
Without income	6.6	2.5	2.7	2.9	2.0	2.1
With income	93.4	97.5	97.3	97.1	98.0	97.9
Under $10,000	21.2	11.9	12.6	12.3	10.4	12.1
$10,000 to $19,999	21.9	15.2	17.5	15.2	13.3	14.0
$20,000 to $29,999	16.5	17.2	18.3	18.0	15.6	16.2
$30,000 to $39,999	11.8	16.5	17.1	16.8	16.9	14.6
$40,000 to $49,999	7.6	12.1	11.7	12.0	12.6	12.2
$50,000 to $74,999	8.8	14.9	12.2	14.0	17.6	17.3
$75,000 to $99,999	2.7	4.5	3.8	4.1	5.5	5.2
$100,000 or more	2.9	5.2	4.0	4.8	6.2	6.4

Source: Bureau of the Census, unpublished tables from the 1995 Current Population Survey

Among Men, Whites Make More Than Blacks

But gap shrinks among full-time workers.

The median income of black men aged 35 to 54 was just 62 percent as much as that of their white counterparts in 1994—$20,857 versus $33,737. One reason for this income gap is that relatively few black men work full-time. In the 35-to-54 age group, only 62 percent of black men—versus 77 percent of white men—work full time.

Among men aged 35 to 54 who work full-time, the median income of blacks is 73 percent as high as that of whites.

Hispanic men aged 35 to 54 make slightly less than their black counterparts, with a median income of $20,023 in 1994. But among full-time workers, the median income of Hispanic men is well below that of blacks—$24,189 versus $27,884. Although Hispanic men are more likely to work full-time than are blacks (66 versus 62 percent), black full-time workers earn more than Hispanic.

♦ White men aged 35 to 54 are much better educated than black or Hispanic men in that age group. This is one factor behind the higher incomes of whites. After controlling for educational differences, however, it's likely that an income gap would remain—the result of continuing discrimination in hiring and promotions.

Distribution of Men's Incomes by Race and Hispanic Origin, 1994

(number and percent distribution of men aged 35 to 54 by income, race, and Hispanic origin, 1994; men in thousands as of 1995)

	total	white	black	Hispanic
Total men, aged 35 to 54	35,994	30,538	3,829	2,993
Without income	893	575	246	122
With income	35,101	29,963	3,583	2,871
Under $10,000	4,286	3,221	838	642
$10,000 to $19,999	5,486	4,353	824	787
$20,000 to $29,999	6,188	5,242	674	614
$30,000 to $39,999	5,944	5,170	533	344
$40,000 to $49,999	4,350	3,890	306	205
$50,000 to $74,999	5,354	4,840	292	185
$75,000 to $99,999	1,631	1,509	61	55
$100,000 or more	1,862	1,739	54	40
Median income	$32,416	$33,737	$20,857	$20,023
Median income, year-round full-time workers	37,571	38,439	27,884	24,189
Percent of men who work year-round, full-time	74.9%	76.7%	61.8%	66.3%
Total men, aged 35 to 54	100.0%	100.0%	100.0%	100.0%
Without income	2.5	1.9	6.4	4.1
With income	97.5	98.1	93.6	95.9
Under $10,000	11.9	10.5	21.9	21.5
$10,000 to $19,999	15.2	14.3	21.5	26.3
$20,000 to $29,999	17.2	17.2	17.6	20.5
$30,000 to $39,999	16.5	16.9	13.9	11.5
$40,000 to $49,999	12.1	12.7	8.0	6.8
$50,000 to $74,999	14.9	15.8	7.6	6.2
$75,000 to $99,999	4.5	4.9	1.6	1.8
$100,000 or more	5.2	5.7	1.4	1.3

Note: Numbers will not add to total because Hispanics may be of any race and not all races are shown.
Source: Bureau of the Census, unpublished tables from the 1995 Current Population Survey

For Men Aged 35 to 44, Earnings Rise With Education

A bachelor's degree is worth thousands to 35-to-44-year-olds.

For those wondering whether the return to a college education is worth the cost, one glance at the accompanying table answers the question. Men with a college degree will recoup the money they spent getting a degree many times over.

Among men aged 35 to 44 who work full-time, those with a bachelor's degree had a median income of $50,797 in 1994. This was $20,000 more than the median income of men who went no further than high school. Fully 46 percent of full-time workers aged 35 to 44 with a bachelor's degree had an income of $50,000 or more in 1994, versus just 8 percent of their counterparts who went no further than high school.

◆ The returns to education keep rising as incomes grow for the well-educated and fall for those without college degrees. Men who graduate from college will earn enough to pay for their degree within a few years. The rest is gravy.

Earnings Distribution of Men Aged 35 to 44 by Education, 1994

(number and percent distribution of men aged 35 to 44 by earnings and education, 1994; men in thousands as of 1995)

	total	not a high school graduate	high school graduate	some college or assoc. degree	bachelor's degree or more
Total men, aged 35 to 44	20,972	2,594	6,872	5,631	5,874
Without earnings	1,690	587	652	288	164
With earnings	19,281	2,007	6,220	5,344	5,710
Under $10,000	2,082	604	700	488	291
$10,000 to $19,999	3,229	654	1,320	837	419
$20,000 to $29,999	3,772	406	1,595	1,148	623
$30,000 to $39,999	3,528	183	1,398	1,125	822
$40,000 to $49,999	2,403	103	637	840	823
$50,000 to $74,999	2,644	40	437	707	1,459
$75,000 to $99,999	795	19	95	121	560
$100,000 or more	829	-	37	80	713
Median earnings, total men	$31,118	$15,797	$26,167	$31,721	$47,837
Median earnings, year-round full-time workers	35,025	19,484	29,131	35,078	50,797
Percent of men who work year-round, full-time	74.6%	51.3%	73.1%	76.6%	84.6%
Total men, aged 35 to 44	100.0%	100.0%	100.0%	100.0%	100.0%
Without earnings	8.1	22.6	9.5	5.1	2.8
With earnings	91.9	77.4	90.5	94.9	97.2
Under $10,000	9.9	23.3	10.2	8.7	5.0
$10,000 to $19,999	15.4	25.2	19.2	14.9	7.1
$20,000 to $29,999	18.0	15.7	23.2	20.4	10.6
$30,000 to $39,999	16.8	7.1	20.3	20.0	14.0
$40,000 to $49,999	11.5	4.0	9.3	14.9	14.0
$50,000 to $74,999	12.6	1.5	6.4	12.6	24.8
$75,000 to $99,999	3.8	0.7	1.4	2.1	9.5
$100,000 or more	4.0	-	0.5	1.4	12.1

Source: Bureau of the Census, unpublished tables from the 1995 Current Population Survey

Incomes Peak for Educated 45-to-54-Year-Old Men

Men aged 45 to 54 are highly educated, and their incomes show it.

Over half of college-educated men aged 45 to 54 made more than $50,000 in 1994. Among their counterparts who went no further than high school, only 15 percent made this much money.

Nearly one in four college-educated men aged 45 to 54 had an income of $75,000 or more. Those who argue that college is no longer worth the expense should examine the statistics in the accompanying table. A college degree is the surest route to financial success in today's economy.

The median income of college-educated men aged 45 to 54 who work full-time was more than $21,000 greater than that of high school graduates and more than $30,000 greater than that of high school drop-outs.

◆ Men aged 45 to 54 are the best-educated cohort in history. Behind their high level of education was the Vietnam War, which many avoided by staying in school. Men with college degrees comprise the single largest segment of the 45-to-54 age group.

Earnings Distribution of Men Aged 45 to 54 by Education, 1994

(number and percent distribution of men aged 45 to 54 by earnings and education, 1994; men in thousands as of 1995)

	total	not a high school graduate	high school graduate	some college or assoc. degree	bachelor's degree or more
Total men, aged 45 to 54	15,022	2,087	4,351	3,674	4,910
Without earnings	1,505	554	510	277	164
With earnings	13,517	1,533	3,841	3,397	4,746
Under $10,000	1,149	298	355	282	214
$10,000 to $19,999	1,816	478	629	435	274
$20,000 to $29,999	2,353	381	872	645	455
$30,000 to $39,999	2,325	215	759	687	665
$40,000 to $49,999	1,865	87	567	561	649
$50,000 to $74,999	2,450	51	553	563	1,281
$75,000 to $99,999	778	17	71	133	557
$100,000 or more	782	5	37	90	651
Median earnings, total men	$35,651	$19,751	$30,523	$34,037	$51,030
Median earnings, year-round full-time workers	39,053	22,930	32,322	37,243	53,543
Percent of men who work year-round, full-time	75.2%	51.3%	72.4%	76.6%	84.4%
Total men, aged 45 to 54	100.0%	100.0%	100.0%	100.0%	100.0%
Without earnings	10.0	26.5	11.7	7.5	3.3
With earnings	90.0	73.5	88.3	92.5	96.7
Under $10,000	7.6	14.3	8.2	7.7	4.4
$10,000 to $19,999	12.1	22.9	14.5	11.8	5.6
$20,000 to $29,999	15.7	18.3	20.0	17.6	9.3
$30,000 to $39,999	15.5	10.3	17.4	18.7	13.5
$40,000 to $49,999	12.4	4.2	13.0	15.3	13.2
$50,000 to $74,999	16.3	2.4	12.7	15.3	26.1
$75,000 to $99,999	5.2	0.8	1.6	3.6	11.3
$100,000 or more	5.2	-	0.9	2.4	13.3

Source: Bureau of the Census, unpublished tables from the 1995 Current Population Survey

Incomes of Mid-Youth Women Have Soared

The rise in median income has been fastest for women aged 45 to 54.

In contrast to the decline in men's incomes since 1980, women's incomes have soared. Among all women, median income grew by 29 percent, with an even greater increase for women aged 35 to 54.

Behind the rapid rise in the median income of women is the increasing proportion of women who work. In 1980, only 65 percent of women aged 35 to 44 were in the labor force. By 1994, 77 percent were working. The median income of women in this age group rose by 39 percent between 1980 and 1994. Among women aged 45 to 54, median income rose by an even larger 48 percent, to $17,051 in 1994.

Despite these rapid income gains, the median income of women remains much lower than that of men because women are more likely to work part-time.

◆ In the 35-to-44 age group, women's income gains have not quite made up for the losses in men's incomes over the past 15 years. While the median income of men aged 35 to 44 fell by more than $5,300 between 1980 and 1994, after adjusting for inflation, the median income of women in this age group grew by a smaller $4,500.

◆ In the 45-to-54 age group, women's income gains have far surpassed men's losses. While women's median income grew by $5,500 between 1980 and 1994, after adjusting for inflation, men's incomes fell by just $1,000.

Median Income of Women, 1980 to 1994

(median income of total women and women aged 35 to 54, 1980 to 1994; in 1994 dollars)

	total women	women aged 35 to 54	
		35 to 44	45 to 54
1994	$11,466	$16,189	$17,051
1993	11,329	16,250	16,742
1992	11,317	16,286	16,745
1991	11,399	16,458	16,021
1990	11,418	16,445	16,135
1989	11,502	16,499	15,708
1988	11,130	15,717	15,058
1987	10,821	15,649	14,694
1986	10,290	14,960	14,035
1985	9,940	14,152	13,249
1984	9,797	13,637	12,699
1983	9,403	13,183	12,209
1982	9,126	12,171	11,629
1981	8,977	12,115	11,564
1980	8,859	11,642	11,530
Percent change			
1993-1994	1.2%	-0.4%	1.8%
1990-1994	0.4	-1.6	5.7
1980-1994	29.4	39.1	47.9

Source: Bureau of the Census, Internet web site, http://www.census.gov

No Peak in Incomes of Mid-Youth Women

The median incomes of women who work full-time is about the same, regardless of age.

Unlike men, women's incomes do not show a distinct peak in middle-age. The median income of women aged 50 to 54 who work full-time is just $2,272 greater than that of all women who work full-time. In contrast, the median income of men aged 50 to 54 who work full-time is $8,820 greater than that of all male full-time workers.

Women in the 50-to-54 age group in 1994 were members of the "Swing" generation preceding the baby boom. Swing women are less educated than boomer women and more likely to regard their work as "just a job" rather than a career, according to the Virginia Slims Opinion Poll. Consequently, their incomes are relatively low. As career-oriented baby-boom women enter this age group, the incomes of women aged 50 to 54 will rise, creating a more distinct income peak for women in middle-age.

◆ While the incomes of women in middle age will rise, they will never equal those of men because a significant number of women drop out of the labor force while their children are young. Their fewer years on the job mean lower incomes.

Income Distribution of Women, 1994

(number and percent distribution of total women and women aged 35 to 54 by income, 1994; women in thousands as of 1995)

	total	35 to 54	35 to 39	40 to 44	45 to 49	50 to 54
Total women	105,028	37,034	11,200	10,163	8,813	6,858
Without income	9,881	2,237	632	600	503	502
With income	95,147	34,797	10,568	9,563	8,310	6,356
Under $10,000	42,771	11,577	3,702	3,150	2,585	2,140
$10,000 to $19,999	24,170	8,417	2,640	2,222	1,958	1,597
$20,000 to $29,999	13,612	6,249	1,885	1,773	1,546	1,045
$30,000 to $39,999	7,231	3,979	1,123	1,111	1,020	725
$40,000 to $49,999	3,490	2,160	553	650	584	373
$50,000 to $74,999	2,780	1,713	438	492	458	325
$75,000 to $99,999	542	354	116	81	83	74
$100,000 or more	552	345	111	81	76	77
Median income	$11,466	$16,590	$15,635	$16,882	$17,813	$16,147
Median income, year-round full-time workers	23,265	25,811	25,327	26,177	26,176	25,537
Percent of women who work year-round, full-time	32.5%	48.2%	46.9%	48.2%	50.6%	47.1%
Total women	100.0%	100.0%	100.0%	100.0%	100.0%	100.0%
Without income	9.4	6.0	5.6	5.9	5.7	7.3
With income	90.6	94.0	94.4	94.1	94.3	92.7
Under $10,000	40.7	31.3	33.1	31.0	29.3	31.2
$10,000 to $19,999	23.0	22.7	23.6	21.9	22.2	23.3
$20,000 to $29,999	13.0	16.9	16.8	17.4	17.5	15.2
$30,000 to $39,999	6.9	10.7	10.0	10.9	11.6	10.6
$40,000 to $49,999	3.3	5.8	4.9	6.4	6.6	5.4
$50,000 to $74,999	2.6	4.6	3.9	4.8	5.2	4.7
$75,000 to $99,999	0.5	1.0	1.0	0.8	0.9	1.1
$100,000 or more	0.5	0.9	1.0	0.8	0.9	1.1

Source: Bureau of the Census, unpublished tables from the 1995 Current Population Survey

Little Variation in Women's Incomes by Race

White women have the highest incomes, but not by much.

The median income of white women aged 35 to 54 who work full-time was $26,369 in 1994, about $4,000 higher than the median income of their black or Hispanic counterparts. Slightly fewer than half of white women in this age group work full-time, versus 51 percent of black women. Hispanic women are much less likely to work full-time, with only 40 percent doing so in 1994.

White women aged 35 to 54 have higher incomes than black or Hispanic women in this age group because they are better educated. Employers are paying a premium for educated workers.

Seven percent of white women aged 35 to 54 had an income of $50,000 or more in 1994, versus 5 percent of black and 2 percent of Hispanic women.

♦ Until black and Hispanic women catch up to white women in educational attainment, their incomes will remain below those of whites.

Distribution by Women's Incomes by Race and Hispanic Origin, 1994

(number and percent distribution of women aged 35 to 54 by income, race, and Hispanic origin, 1994; women in thousands as of 1995)

	total	white	black	Hispanic
Total women, aged 35 to 54	37,034	30,815	4,555	3,139
Without income	2,237	1,773	329	463
With income	34,797	29,042	4,227	2,675
Under $10,000	11,577	9,658	1,356	1,167
$10,000 to $19,999	8,417	6,840	1,209	747
$20,000 to $29,999	6,249	5,232	781	408
$30,000 to $39,999	3,979	3,396	426	179
$40,000 to $49,999	2,160	1,824	235	102
$50,000 to $74,999	1,713	1,483	164	56
$75,000 to $99,999	354	303	27	6
$100,000 or more	345	306	30	13
Median income, total women	$16,590	$16,817	$15,713	$11,476
Median income, year-round full-time workers	25,811	26,369	22,474	22,435
Percent of women who work year-round, full-time	48.2%	47.7%	51.4%	39.5%
Total women, aged 35 to 54	100.0%	100.0%	100.0%	100.0%
Without income	6.0	5.8	7.2	14.7
With income	94.0	94.2	92.8	85.2
Under $10,000	31.3	31.3	29.8	37.2
$10,000 to $19,999	22.7	22.2	26.5	23.8
$20,000 to $29,999	16.9	17.0	17.1	13.0
$30,000 to $39,999	10.7	11.0	9.4	5.7
$40,000 to $49,999	5.8	5.9	5.2	3.2
$50,000 to $74,999	4.6	4.8	3.6	1.8
$75,000 to $99,999	1.0	1.0	0.6	0.2
$100,000 or more	0.9	1.0	0.7	0.4

Note: Numbers will not add to total because Hispanics may be of any race and not all races are shown.
Source: Bureau of the Census, unpublished tables from the 1995 Current Population Survey

Education Boosts Earnings
of Women Aged 35 to 44

College-educated 35-to-44-year-olds earn far more than those with less education.

The median earnings of college-educated women aged 35 to 44 who work full-time was nearly $17,000 greater than that of their female counterparts who went no further than high school—$36,742 versus $20,083 in 1994. Behind this earnings gap is the premium employers pay for well-educated workers. Fully 15 percent of women aged 35 to 44 with bachelor's degrees earned $50,000 or more in 1994, versus fewer than 1 percent of women in this age group who stopped with a high school diploma.

College-educated women aged 35 to 44 are also more likely to work full-time than those with less education. Among those with bachelor's degrees, 54 percent work full-time. This compares with 47 percent of those with a high school diploma and just 28 percent of those who did not graduate from high school.

◆ College-educated women aged 35 to 44 who work full-time earn only 72 percent as much as their male counterparts—$36,742 versus $50,797 in 1994. Many women in this age group spent several years out of the labor force while their children were young. Their fewer years on the job account, in part, for their lower earnings.

Earnings Distribution of Women Aged 35 to 44 by Education, 1994

(number and percent distribution of women aged 35 to 44 by earnings and education, 1994; women in thousands as of 1995)

	total	not a high school graduate	high school graduate	some college or assoc. degree	bachelor's degree or more
Total women, aged 35 to 44	21,363	2,336	7,230	6,399	5,398
Without earnings	4,432	1,009	1,617	1,009	797
With earnings	16,931	1,326	5,613	5,391	4,602
Under $10,000	4,629	699	1,820	1,439	671
$10,000 to $19,999	4,589	444	1,931	1,535	682
$20,000 to $29,999	3,438	136	1,183	1,200	921
$30,000 to $39,999	2,072	35	447	735	853
$40,000 to $49,999	1,128	6	173	297	652
$50,000 to $74,999	757	5	45	154	556
$75,000 to $99,999	154	1	11	15	127
$100,000 or more	163	-	3	18	142
Median earnings, total women	$17,990	$9,348	$14,602	$18,113	$30,209
Median earnings, year-round full-time workers	24,704	13,266	20,083	24,240	36,742
Percent of women who work year-round, full-time	47.5%	28.2%	47.0%	49.6%	54.0%
Total women, aged 35 to 44	100.0%	100.0%	100.0%	100.0%	100.0%
Without earnings	20.7	43.2	22.4	15.8	14.8
With earnings	79.3	56.8	77.6	84.2	85.3
Under $10,000	21.7	29.9	25.2	22.5	12.4
$10,000 to $19,999	21.5	19.0	26.7	24.0	12.6
$20,000 to $29,999	16.1	5.8	16.4	18.8	17.1
$30,000 to $39,999	9.7	1.5	6.2	11.5	15.8
$40,000 to $49,999	5.3	0.3	2.4	4.6	12.1
$50,000 to $74,999	3.5	0.2	0.6	2.4	10.3
$75,000 to $99,999	0.7	0.0	0.2	0.2	2.4
$100,000 or more	0.8	-	0.0	0.3	2.6

Source: Bureau of the Census, unpublished tables from the 1995 Current Population Survey

Most Educated Women
Aged 45 to 54 Work Full-Time

The earnings of college-educated women are much higher than the earnings of those with less education.

In 1994, 57 percent of college-educated women aged 45 to 54 worked full-time. Women in this age group are more likely to work full-time than are those aged 35 to 44 because the younger women are more likely to have young children at home, which prevents many of them from working full-time.

The median earnings of college-educated women aged 45 to 54 who work full-time was $36,470 in 1994, fully $16,000 higher than that of their female counterparts who stopped with a high school diploma. Sixteen percent of college-educated women aged 45 to 54 earned $50,000 or more in 1994.

◆ As career-oriented baby-boom women entirely fill this age group in the next few years, the earnings of the college-educated will rise faster than those of the less educated. Consequently, the gap in women's earings by education will widen.

Earnings Distribution of Women Aged 45 to 54 by Education, 1994

(number and percent distribution of women aged 45 to 54 by earnings and education, 1994; women in thousands as of 1995)

	total	not a high school graduate	high school graduate	some college or assoc. degree	bachelor's degree or more
Total women, aged 45 to 54	15,672	2,135	5,617	4,223	3,697
Without earnings	3,475	947	1,345	718	465
With earnings	12,196	1,187	4,272	3,505	3,232
Under $10,000	2,977	550	1,148	796	484
$10,000 to $19,999	3,371	434	1,566	967	404
$20,000 to $29,999	2,475	139	911	849	573
$30,000 to $39,999	1,666	41	385	506	734
$40,000 to $49,999	860	17	143	236	464
$50,000 to $74,999	648	4	78	123	444
$75,000 to $99,999	97	3	17	20	58
$100,000 or more	102	-	23	8	71
Median earnings, total women	$19,086	$10,745	$16,137	$19,709	$31,362
Median earnings, year-round full-time workers	24,903	14,728	20,259	25,044	36,470
Percent of women who work year-round, full-time	49.1%	28.9%	49.0%	52.8%	56.5%
Total women, aged 45 to 54	100.0%	100.0%	100.0%	100.0%	100.0%
Without earnings	22.2	44.4	23.9	17.0	12.6
With earnings	77.8	55.6	76.1	83.0	87.4
Under $10,000	19.0	25.8	20.4	18.8	13.1
$10,000 to $19,999	21.5	20.3	27.9	22.9	10.9
$20,000 to $29,999	15.8	6.5	16.2	20.1	15.5
$30,000 to $39,999	10.6	1.9	6.9	12.0	19.9
$40,000 to $49,999	5.5	0.8	2.5	5.6	12.6
$50,000 to $74,999	4.1	0.2	1.4	2.9	12.0
$75,000 to $99,999	0.6	0.1	0.3	0.5	1.6
$100,000 or more	0.7	-	0.4	0.2	1.9

Source: Bureau of the Census, unpublished tables from the 1995 Current Population Survey

Poverty Unlikely
Among Middle-Aged

But Hispanics are more likely to be poor than whites or blacks.

While 14.5 percent of all Americans were poor in 1994, the poverty rate among people aged 35 to 44 was a smaller 11 percent. Only 8 percent of people aged 45 to 54 were poor.

Poverty rates for middle-aged women are about 2 percentage points higher than those for middle-aged men. There is more variation in poverty rates by race and Hispanic origin. While only 6 percent of whites aged 45 to 54 are poor, 17 percent of blacks and 19 percent of Hispanics live in poverty.

Among 35-to-44-year-olds, fully 27 percent of Hispanic women are poor. This compares with just 10 percent of white women and 9 percent of white men in this age group.

◆ Poverty rates reach a low among people aged 45 to 54. With the enormous baby-boom generation entering this age group, public support for poverty programs has plummeted.

People in Poverty by Sex, Race, and Hispanic Origin, 1994

(number and percent of total persons and persons aged 35 to 54 in poverty, by sex, race, and Hispanic origin, 1994; persons in thousands as of 1995)

	total	*white*	*black*	*Hispanic*
Total persons in poverty	38,059	25,379	10,196	8,416
Aged 35 to 44	4,467	3,022	1,136	889
Aged 45 to 54	2,381	1,675	537	438
Total females in poverty	21,744	14,460	5,980	4,527
Aged 35 to 44	2,539	1,681	692	522
Aged 45 to 54	1,348	940	317	255
Total males in poverty	16,316	10,919	4,216	3,889
Aged 35 to 44	1,929	1,342	443	367
Aged 45 to 54	1,033	735	221	183
Total persons in poverty	14.5%	11.7%	30.6%	30.7%
Aged 35 to 44	10.6	8.6	21.9	23.0
Aged 45 to 54	7.8	6.4	16.8	19.3
Total females in poverty	16.3	13.1	33.7	33.4
Aged 35 to 44	11.9	9.6	24.7	26.6
Aged 45 to 54	8.6	7.1	18.1	21.7
Total males in poverty	12.8	10.3	27.0	28.0
Aged 35 to 44	9.2	7.6	18.5	19.3
Aged 45 to 54	6.9	5.7	15.3	16.8

Note: Numbers will not add to total because Hispanics may be of any race and not all races are shown.
Source: Bureau of the Census, unpublished tables from the 1995 Current Population Survey

4

Wealth and Spending

♦ For householders aged 35 to 54, homeownership rates have fallen over the past ten years.

♦ Among householders aged 35 to 44, net worth is below average, at $29,587 in 1993. But householders aged 45 to 54 have a net worth of $57,755 and more than a third of them have a net worth of $100,000 or more.

♦ Home equity accounts for the largest share of net worth among middle-aged householders—the value of this asset was $35,000 for those aged 35 to 44 and $50,000 for 45-to-54-year-olds.

♦ Householders aged 35 to 44 spend well above average on day care and babysitting, computer hardware and software for nonbusiness use, children's apparel, fees for recreational lessons, toys and playground equipment, athletic gear, and encyclopedias.

♦ Householders aged 45 to 54 are the biggest spenders. They spend much more than average on household furnishings, food away from home, clothes, transportation, entertainment, personal care products and services, and education.

Homeownership Down in 35-to-54 Age Group

But the trends vary by household type.

In the past ten years, the nation's homeownership rate has grown by a paltry 0.8 percentage points, from 63.9 to 64.7 percent. But for householders aged 35 to 54, homeownership rates have fallen. The decline ranges from a tiny 0.5 percent for those aged 50 to 54, to a significant 3.3 percent for those aged 35 to 39.

Fully 80 percent of married couples aged 35 to 44 owned their home in 1995, as did 87 percent of couples aged 45 to 54. Since 1985, homeownership rates fell slightly for younger couples and rose slightly for older ones.

Homeownership rates fell for female-headed families in the 35-to-44 age group and for male-headed families in both the 35-to-44 and 45-to-54 age groups. In contrast, homeownership rates rose for men and women aged 35 to 54 who live alone.

♦ Because they were there first, 45-to-54-year-olds have fared better than 35-to-44-year-olds in the housing market, an advantage that will continue into the forseeable future. The oldest boomers are likely to recoup the equity in their homes when they sell upon retirement, while younger boomers may lose ground.

Homeownership Rates, 1985 and 1995

(percent of total households and households headed by persons aged 35 to 54 who own their home by household type, 1995 and 1985, percentage point change in homeownership, 1985-95)

	total			married couples			female-headed families		
	1995	1985	percentage point change	1995	1985	percentage point change	1995	1985	percentage point change
Total households	64.7%	63.9%	0.8%	79.6%	78.2%	1.4%	45.1%	45.8%	-0.7%
Aged 35 to 44	65.2	68.1	-2.9	79.8	80.9	-1.1	42.4	45.1	-2.7
Aged 45 to 54	75.2	75.9	-0.7	87.1	86.3	0.8	59.8	59.6	0.2
Aged 35 to 39	62.1	65.4	-3.3	77.0	78.6	-1.6	37.5	40.5	-3.0
Aged 40 to 44	68.6	71.4	-2.8	82.8	83.6	-0.8	47.9	50.4	-2.5
Aged 45 to 49	73.7	74.3	-0.6	86.2	85.1	1.1	57.1	56.2	0.9
Aged 50 to 54	77.0	77.5	-0.5	88.1	87.5	0.6	64.2	63.8	0.4

	male-headed families			men living alone			women living alone		
	1995	1985	percentage point change	1995	1985	percentage point change	1995	1985	percentage point change
Total households	55.3%	57.8%	-2.5%	43.8%	38.8%	5.0%	55.4%	51.3%	4.1%
Aged 35 to 44	54.4	61.3	-6.9	40.8	39.4	1.4	42.0	38.7	3.3
Aged 45 to 54	66.4	70.7	-4.3	47.0	42.3	4.7	55.6	52.8	2.8
Aged 35 to 39	51.3	59.4	-8.1	39.2	38.4	0.8	40.3	36.7	3.6
Aged 40 to 44	57.5	63.1	-5.6	42.7	40.9	1.8	43.7	41.1	2.6
Aged 45 to 49	64.6	68.0	-3.4	46.6	41.0	5.6	52.5	49.2	3.3
Aged 50 to 54	69.0	73.7	-4.7	47.6	43.5	4.1	58.6	55.6	3.0

Source: Bureau of the Census, Internet web site, http://www.census.gov

Net Worth Rises in Middle-Age

Peak in net worth comes later, however.

In middle-age, most households reach an important milestone. They make the transition from being poorer than average to richer than average.

Among householders aged 35 to 44, net worth is below average, at $29,587 in 1993. Twelve percent of these householders had zero or negative net worth, slightly greater than the 11.5 percent of all households with zero or negative net worth. But fortunes improve among 45-to-54-year-olds as earnings increase, children's expenses diminish, and retirement savings expand. The net worth of householders in this age group was $57,755 in 1993. Only 8 percent had zero or negative net worth, while more than one-third had a net worth of $100,000 or more.

By household type, married couples have the greatest net worth. Only 6 percent of couples aged 35 to 54 had zero or negative net worth, while one-third had a net worth of $100,000 or more. In contrast, 20 percent of female-headed families aged 35 to 54 had no net worth and only 13 percent had a net worth of $100,000 or more.

◆ As boomers enter the 45-to-54 age group, their savings and net worth should expand rapidly. Boomer investing should keep the stock market heading in a generally upward direction for many years.

Distribution of Net Worth for Households, 1993

(percent distribution of net worth and median net worth for total households and households headed by 35-to-54-year-olds, 1993)

| | total | householders aged 35 to 54 | | | | |
		35 to 44	45 to 54	married couples	male householders	female householders
Total	100.0%	100.0%	100.0%	100.0%	100.0%	100.0%
Zero or negative	11.5	12.2	8.2	6.4	13.4	20.0
$1 to $4,999	13.7	14.1	9.4	7.1	19.3	21.5
$5,000 to $9,999	6.3	6.7	4.7	4.4	8.1	8.3
$10,000 to $24,999	10.8	12.6	8.9	10.6	11.5	11.7
$25,000 to $49,999	12.2	14.6	13.5	14.7	14.3	12.7
$50,000 to $99,999	16.5	16.9	19.6	21.0	13.8	12.6
$100,000 to $249,999	18.5	15.8	22.6	23.2	12.9	9.5
$250,000 to $499,999	6.9	5.3	8.6	8.6	4.7	2.6
$500,000 or more	3.6	1.9	4.5	3.9	1.9	1.0
Median net worth	$37,587	$29,587	$57,755	$61,874	$18,426	$8,405

Source: Bureau of the Census, Internet web site, http://www.census.gov

Homes Are Biggest
Asset of Middle-Aged

Home equity overshadows all other assets in net worth calculations.

Home equity accounts for the largest share of net worth among middle-aged householders. Sixty-four percent of householders aged 35 to 44 and 75 percent of those aged 45 to 54 owned a home in 1993. The value of this asset amounted to $35,000 for the younger householders and $50,000 for the older ones.

The most commonly held asset among Americans of all ages is equity in a motor vehicle. Nine out of ten householders aged 35 to 54 owned a car, with a median equity of between $5,000 and $6,500. Interest-earning assets at financial institutions are the second most commonly held asset (owned by over 70 percent), but with even less value than motor vehicles—a median of $2,000 to $3,000 in 1993.

◆ In 1993, the average householder aged 35 to 44 had only $9,900 in an IRA or KEOGH account, while those aged 45 to 54 had $14,900. Those values are probably larger today and should continue to grow as boomers save for retirement.

Median Value of Assets Owned by Households, 1993

(median value of assets for those owning asset and percent owning asset, for total households and households headed by 35-to-54-year-olds, by household type, 1993)

	total	householders aged 35 to 54				
		35 to 44	45 to 54	married couples	male householders	female householders
Median value of asset						
Interest-earning assets at financial institutions	$2,999	$1,998	$2,999	$2,799	$1,999	$1,199
Other interest-earning assets	12,998	7,363	9,999	8,999	7,999	8,000
Regular checking accounts	499	498	492	495	498	290
Stocks and mutual fund shares	6,960	4,700	5,800	4,900	7,900	4,500
Equity in business or profession	7,000	7,533	9,500	9,800	3,800	1,500
Equity in motor vehicles	5,140	5,343	6,483	7,345	3,666	3,342
Equity in own home	46,669	34,968	49,991	44,940	33,645	30,536
Rental property equity	29,300	27,500	38,000	34,526	29,000	14,666
Other real estate equity	19,415	17,500	23,000	19,000	18,000	16,000
U.S. savings bonds	775	575	825	700	900	475
IRA or KEOGH accounts	12,985	9,900	14,900	12,985	10,136	7,800
Percent owning asset						
Interest-earning assets at financial institutions	71.1%	71.0%	73.0%	79.5%	62.7%	57.7%
Other interest-earning assets	8.6	7.2	9.7	9.6	7.3	5.2
Regular checking accounts	45.9	48.6	52.4	54.7	40.7	44.5
Stocks and mutual fund shares	20.9	20.4	25.6	27.5	17.1	13.0
Equity in business or profession	10.8	14.0	16.2	19.0	12.4	5.6
Equity in motor vehicles	85.7	89.2	90.5	96.1	83.6	76.8
Equity in own home	64.3	64.3	74.5	81.1	50.1	47.4
Rental property equity	8.4	7.6	10.8	11.0	7.4	4.5
Other real estate equity	9.3	8.9	13.2	13.2	9.3	4.8
U.S. savings bonds	18.5	22.5	22.8	28.0	14.9	13.3
IRA or KEOGH accounts	23.1	24.0	31.4	31.8	23.0	17.1

Source: Bureau of the Census, Internet web site, http://www.census.gov

Pension Coverage Common Among Mid-Youth Workers

Over half of workers in their 40s are vested.

Among the nation's 106 million workers in 1993, 40 percent were vested in a pension—meaning they will eventually collect a retirement income from an employer. Over half of workers in their 40s and 50s are vested in a pension, as are 45 percent of those in their 30s.

More than 80 percent of baby-boom workers whose employers offer a pension plan participate in it. But only 66 percent of employees in their 30s and 71 percent of those in their 40s work for a company that provides pension benefits.

Though pension coverage is widespread, many pensions today are no longer the traditional "defined benefit" plans in which employees receive a predetermined amount based on length of service and salary. Instead, an increasing number of plans are "defined contribution," requiring employees to contribute to the plan. The amount they receive in retirement will depend on how much they save.

♦ While most baby-boom workers are covered by a pension, many will receive little pension income in retirement because they do not contribute much to their defined contribution pension plan.

Pension Coverage by Age, 1993

(total number of workers, percent working for an employer that sponsors a pension, percent participating in a pension, percent participating among those whose employer sponsors a pension, and percent of all workers vested in a pension, by age, 1993; numbers in thousands)

	total	sponsorship rate	participation rate	sponsored participation rate	vesting rate
Total workers	105,815	62.1%	47.1%	75.9%	40.3%
Aged 16 to 20	6,634	32.2	3.5	11.0	1.6
Aged 21 to 30	26,359	56.6	33.8	59.8	25.8
Aged 31 to 40	31,047	65.8	52.7	80.1	45.0
Aged 41 to 50	23,459	70.6	61.5	87.1	54.5
Aged 51 to 60	13,164	66.8	59.3	88.8	53.3
Aged 61 to 64	2,781	62.4	51.3	82.3	47.7
Aged 65 or older	2,371	46.1	29.0	63.0	26.6

Source: Employee Benefit Research Institute, Baby Boomers in Retirement: What Are Their Prospects?, *EBRI Issue Brief Number 151, 1994*

Spending Fell
Between 1989 and 1994

Householders aged 35 to 44 cut their spending sharply.

Between 1989 and 1994, householders aged 35 to 44 cut their spending by 12 percent, after adjusting for inflation. This compares with a 4 percent decline in spending for householders aged 45 to 54 and a 5 percent decline for all households as the recession cut incomes.

Although the spending of householders aged 35 to 44 fell in every category, the biggest cuts were for discretionary items. After adjusting for inflation, householders aged 35 to 44 spent 20 percent less on apparel in 1994 than in 1989, 25 percent less on food away from home, 24 percent less on alcohol, and 28 percent less on cash transfers and contributions. Spending fell the least on health care, food at home, and housing.

Householders aged 45 to 54 also spent less in 1994 than in 1989 on nearly every category of goods and services, after adjusting for inflation. While their spending cuts were not as deep as those made by householders aged 35 to 44, they too cut spending the most on discretionary items. They spent 19 percent less on food away from home in 1994 than in 1989, 19 percent less on tobacco, and 18 percent less on alcohol.

◆ Even if spending levels rebound, mid-youth consumers are likely to remain cautious. Job losses have made many baby boomers nervous. Until boomers boost their savings to a new comfort level, they will not spend as freely as they once did.

Average Spending of Households, 1989 and 1994

(average before-tax income and average annual spending of total consumer units and consumer units aged 35 to 54, 1994 and 1989; percent change in spending, 1989-94; in 1994 dollars)

	total consumer units*			35 to 44			45 to 54		
	1994	1989	percent change	1994	1989	percent change	1994	1989	percent change
Average before-tax income of consumer unit	**$36,838**	**$37,419**	**-1.6%**	**$46,217**	**$48,902**	**-5.5%**	**$49,627**	**$50,160**	**-1.1%**
Average spending of consumer unit, total	**31,751**	**33,239**	**-4.5**	**37,588**	**42,536**	**-11.6**	**41,444**	**43,114**	**-3.9**
Food	4,411	4,962	-11.1%	5,367	6,247	-14.1%	5,614	6,407	-12.4%
Food at home	2,712	2,857	-5.1	3,336	3,559	-6.3	3,319	3,562	-6.8
Food away from home	1,698	2,106	-19.3	2,031	2,688	-24.5	2,295	2,846	-19.4
Alcoholic beverages	278	339	-18.1	296	387	-23.6	292	354	-17.6
Housing	10,106	10,289	-1.8	12,274	13,066	-6.1	12,457	12,779	-2.5
Apparel and services	1,644	1,891	-13.1	2,054	2,566	-20.0	2,262	2,404	-5.9
Transportation	6,044	6,200	-2.5	6,796	7,882	-13.8	7,893	8,137	-3.0
Health care	1,755	1,682	4.3	1,616	1,621	-0.3	1,855	1,660	11.7
Entertainment	1,567	1,702	-7.9	2,025	2,487	-18.6	2,104	2,210	-4.8
Personal care products and services	397	437	-9.3	457	521	-12.3	507	545	-7.0
Reading	165	188	-12.2	184	226	-18.5	204	228	-10.7
Education	460	439	4.8	483	590	-18.2	882	877	0.6
Tobacco products and smoking supplies	259	312	-17.1	319	379	-15.7	327	402	-18.6
Miscellaneous	749	769	-2.6	908	1,059	-14.3	1,071	1,028	4.2
Cash transfers and contributions	960	1,076	-10.7	788	1,091	-27.8	1,436	1,663	-13.6
Personal insurance and pensions	2,957	2,955	0.1	4,022	4,413	-8.9	4,539	4,422	2.6

* The Bureau of Labor Statistics uses consumer units rather than households as the sampling unit in the Consumer Expenditure Survey.
Note: For the definition of consumer units, see the glossary.
Source: Bureau of Labor Statistics, 1994 and 1989 Consumer Expenditure Surveys

Householders Aged 35 to 44 Spend More Than Average

Spending is especially high on children's goods and services.

In 1994, households headed by 35-to-44-year-olds spent $37,588—18 percent more than the average household. Because many of these households include children, spending is especially high on the products and services children need and want.

Householders aged 35 to 44 spend 22 percent more than average on food. Spending is even higher on bread and crackers, frozen fruit juices, peanut butter, potato chips, and school lunches.

Spending on day care and babysitting by householders aged 35 to 44 is nearly twice as high as that of the average household. Also well above average is spending on computer hardware and software for nonbusiness use, children's apparel, fees for recreational lessons, toys and playground equipment, athletic gear, and encyclopedias.

♦ Children's wants and needs are the key to this consumer market. Although householders aged 35 to 44 have cut their spending sharply, they still spend a lot on their children.

Note: The Consumer Expenditure Survey, on which the spending tables are based, presents average spending data for all households in a segment, not just for purchasers of an item. When examining the spending data that follow, it is important to remember that by including purchasers and nonpurchasers in the calculation of the average, the average spending amount is diluted for items that are not purchased universally. For categories purchased by few consumers, the average spending figures are less revealing than the indexes. For universally purchased items such as soaps and detergents, the average spending figures give a more accurate picture of actual spending.

Average and Indexed Spending of Householders Aged 35 to 44, 1994

(average annual spending of total consumer units and average annual and indexed spending of consumer units headed by 35-to-44-year-olds, 1994)

	average spending of total consumer units	consumer units headed by 35-to-44-year-olds	
		average spending	indexed spending*
Number of consumer units (in thousands)	**102,210**	**22,825.00**	**-**
Average before-tax income	**$36,838.00**	**$46,217.00**	**125**
Total average annual spending	**31,750.63**	**37,587.69**	**118**
FOOD	**$4,410.52**	**$5,366.69**	**122**
Food at home	**2,712.05**	**3,336.05**	**123**
Cereals and bakery products	428.68	535.66	125
Cereals and cereal products	161.74	210.32	130
Flour	7.60	8.07	106
Prepared flour mixes	12.79	15.87	124
Ready-to-eat and cooked cereals	98.27	130.51	133
Rice	15.43	20.41	132
Pasta, cornmeal, other cereal products	27.65	35.47	128
Bakery products	266.93	325.34	122
Bread	76.22	87.07	114
White bread	37.65	46.07	122
Bread, other than white	38.57	40.99	106
Crackers and cookies	62.56	78.94	126
Cookies	42.97	54.33	126
Crackers	19.59	24.62	126
Frozen and refrigerated bakery products	21.56	25.52	118
Other bakery products	106.59	133.80	126
Biscuits and rolls	35.96	44.42	124
Cakes and cupcakes	31.19	41.00	131
Bread and cracker products	4.72	6.82	144
Sweetrolls, coffee cakes, doughnuts	21.92	24.61	112
Pies, tarts, turnovers	12.80	16.94	132
Meats, poultry, fish, and eggs	732.45	918.57	125
Beef	226.76	290.71	128
Ground beef	88.45	113.80	129
Roast	39.41	49.00	124
Chuck roast	12.26	14.33	117
Round roast	14.84	17.46	118
Other roast	12.31	17.22	140

(continued)

(continued from previous page)

	average spending of total consumer units	consumer units headed by 35-to-44-year-olds	
		average spending	indexed spending*
Steak	$84.75	$104.59	123
Round steak	16.00	20.98	131
Sirloin steak	24.44	28.34	116
Other steak	44.31	55.28	125
Other beef	14.15	23.32	165
Pork	155.74	190.72	122
Bacon	22.78	25.21	111
Pork chops	39.32	50.44	128
Ham	36.88	45.31	123
Ham, not canned	34.16	41.37	121
Canned ham	2.72	3.94	145
Sausage	22.82	30.48	134
Other pork	33.93	39.27	116
Other meats	93.95	118.72	126
Frankfurters	18.76	24.17	129
Lunch meats (cold cuts)	65.66	82.16	125
Bologna, liverwurst, salami	23.73	29.74	125
Other lunchmeats	41.93	52.42	125
Lamb, organ meats and others	9.53	12.38	130
Lamb and organ meats	9.35	12.20	130
Mutton, goat and game	0.18	0.18	100
Poultry	136.58	175.35	128
Fresh and frozen chickens	107.89	139.65	129
Fresh and frozen whole chicken	29.56	38.08	129
Fresh and frozen chicken parts	78.33	101.57	130
Other poultry	28.69	35.70	124
Fish and seafood	89.43	108.57	121
Canned fish and seafood	15.03	18.67	124
Fresh fish and shellfish	51.26	63.08	123
Frozen fish and shellfish	23.15	26.82	116
Eggs	30.00	34.50	115
Dairy products	288.92	360.38	125
Fresh milk and cream	127.13	156.85	123
Fresh milk, all types	118.94	146.88	123
Cream	8.19	9.97	122
Other dairy products	161.79	203.54	126
Butter	11.65	13.66	117
Cheese	81.83	104.89	128

(continued)

(continued from previous page)

	average spending of total consumer units	consumer units headed by 35-to-44-year-olds	
		average spending	indexed spending*
Ice cream and related products	$47.64	$58.47	123
Miscellaneous dairy products	20.66	26.52	128
Fruits and vegetables	436.57	507.28	116
Fresh fruits	133.02	149.84	113
Apples	25.37	33.02	130
Bananas	29.66	30.97	104
Oranges	16.36	17.00	104
Citrus fruits, excl. oranges	10.96	11.62	106
Other fresh fruits	50.67	57.23	113
Fresh vegetables	134.89	159.77	118
Potatoes	28.01	32.93	118
Lettuce	17.38	19.63	113
Tomatoes	21.01	25.52	121
Other fresh vegetables	68.50	81.69	119
Processed fruits	93.08	106.44	114
Frozen fruits and fruit juices	16.28	20.76	128
Frozen orange juice	9.49	11.07	117
Frozen fruits	1.60	1.58	99
Frozen fruit juices	5.19	8.11	156
Canned fruit	14.23	14.03	99
Dried fruit	5.89	5.59	95
Fresh fruit juices	17.90	19.81	111
Canned and bottled fruit juices	38.78	46.24	119
Processed vegetables	75.57	91.23	121
Frozen vegetables	24.83	33.87	136
Canned and dried vegetables and juices	50.74	57.37	113
Canned beans	10.44	11.85	114
Canned corn	6.81	8.24	121
Other canned and dried vegetables	27.05	30.58	113
Frozen vegetable juices	0.23	0.36	157
Fresh and canned vegetable juices	6.21	6.33	102
Other food at home	825.43	1,014.15	123
Sugar and other sweets	105.25	127.30	121
Candy and chewing gum	62.32	74.78	120
Sugar	18.31	23.26	127
Artificial sweeteners	3.39	3.42	101
Jams, preserves, other sweets	21.23	25.84	122
Fats and oils	79.25	95.56	121
Margarine	14.16	14.88	105

(continued)

(continued from previous page)

	average spending of total consumer units	consumer units headed by 35-to-44-year-olds	
		average spending	indexed spending*
Fats and oils	$23.09	$26.81	116
Salad dressings	23.75	29.35	124
Nondairy cream and imitation milk	6.56	8.08	123
Peanut butter	11.70	16.45	141
Miscellaneous foods	361.62	462.21	128
Frozen prepared foods	66.14	77.10	117
Frozen meals	21.43	22.96	107
Other frozen prepared foods	44.71	54.14	121
Canned and packaged soups	29.55	35.14	119
Potato chips, nuts, and other snacks	74.07	104.04	140
Potato chips and other snacks	58.18	87.63	151
Nuts	15.89	16.42	103
Condiments and seasonings	79.74	104.00	130
Salt, spices and other seasonings	19.30	23.69	123
Olives, pickles, relishes	10.16	13.42	132
Sauces and gravies	36.43	49.39	136
Baking needs and misc. products	13.85	17.49	126
Other canned/packaged prepared foods	112.12	141.94	127
Prepared salads	10.97	14.00	128
Prepared desserts	7.99	9.14	114
Baby food	28.11	32.94	117
Miscellaneous prepared foods	65.05	85.86	132
Nonalcoholic beverages	232.89	279.78	120
Cola	89.45	113.08	126
Other carbonated drinks	38.89	47.06	121
Coffee	43.01	41.32	96
Roasted coffee	29.13	29.82	102
Instant and freeze-dried coffee	13.88	11.51	83
Noncarb. fruit flavored drinks incl. non-frozen lemonade	21.86	32.31	148
Tea	16.25	18.02	111
Nonalcoholic beer	0.66	0.63	95
Other nonalcoholic beverages	22.77	27.35	120
Food prepared by cu on out-of-town trips	46.41	49.30	106
Food away from home	**1,698.46**	**2,030.64**	**120**
Meals at restaurants, carry-outs, other	1,306.21	1,589.57	122
Lunch	451.76	595.07	132
Dinner	651.79	746.26	114

(continued)

(continued from previous page)

	average spending of total consumer units	consumer units headed by 35-to-44-year-olds	
		average spending	indexed spending*
Snacks and nonalcoholic beverages	$101.72	$135.93	134
Breakfast and brunch	100.95	112.32	111
Board (including at school)	50.72	36.25	71
Catered affairs	56.09	38.27	68
Food on out-of-town trips	207.89	213.92	103
School lunches	53.76	133.68	249
Meals as pay	23.79	18.95	80
ALCOHOLIC BEVERAGES	**278.03**	**295.99**	**106**
At home	**165.13**	**183.64**	**111**
Beer and ale	99.68	112.23	113
Whiskey	13.68	9.01	66
Wine	36.41	45.29	124
Other alcoholic beverages	15.35	17.10	111
Away from home	**112.91**	**112.35**	**100**
Beer and ale	38.56	36.65	95
Wine	15.79	16.36	104
Other alcoholic beverages	27.96	28.57	102
Alcoholic beverages purchased on trips	30.61	30.76	100
HOUSING	**10,106.32**	**12,274.21**	**121**
Shelter	**5,686.26**	**7,172.65**	**126**
Owned dwellings**	3,491.71	4,963.34	142
Mortgage interest and charges	1,918.71	3,288.54	171
Mortgage interest	1,822.54	3,159.77	173
Interest paid, home equity loan	44.51	62.72	141
Interest paid, home equity line of credit	51.11	64.29	126
Prepayment penalty charges	0.55	1.77	322
Property taxes	921.61	1,020.58	111
Maintenance, repairs, insurance, and other expenses	651.39	654.23	100
Homeowners and related insurance	207.71	224.73	108
Fire and extended coverage	5.95	5.64	95
Homeowners insurance	201.76	219.08	109
Ground rent	37.79	40.38	107
Maintenance and repair services	313.66	278.11	89
Painting and papering	44.00	40.81	93
Plumbing and water heating	36.33	27.64	76

(continued)

(continued from previous page)

	average spending of total consumer units	consumer units headed by 35-to-44-year-olds	
		average spending	indexed spending*
Heat, air conditioning, electrical work	$55.27	$47.39	86
Roofing and gutters	50.96	31.04	61
Other repair and maintenance services	108.66	103.47	95
Repair and replacement of hard surface flooring	16.78	25.91	154
Repair of built-in appliances	1.67	1.86	111
Maintenance and repair materials	71.89	97.28	135
Paint, wallpaper, and supplies	18.40	25.52	139
Tools and equipment for painting and wallpapering	1.98	2.74	138
Plumbing supplies and equipment	8.59	10.34	120
Electrical supplies, heating/ cooling equipment	5.12	4.49	88
Material for hard surface flooring, repair and replacement	5.01	8.01	160
Material and equipment for roofing and gutters	5.36	7.98	149
Plaster, paneling, siding, windows, doors, screens, awnings	11.75	20.22	172
Patio, walk, fence, driveway, masonry, brick, stucco materials	0.47	0.83	177
Material for landscape maintenance	1.47	1.61	110
Miscellaneous supplies and equipment	13.73	15.53	113
Material for insulation, other maintenance and repair	9.37	11.00	117
Material to finish basement, remodel rooms, etc. (owner)	4.37	4.54	104
Property management and security	20.16	13.60	67
Property management	12.17	9.33	77
Management and upkeep services for security	7.99	4.27	53
Parking	0.18	0.13	72
Rented dwellings	1,799.39	1,841.31	102
Rent	1,728.66	1,767.88	102
Rent as pay	42.90	41.31	96
Maintenance, repairs, insurance, and other expenses	27.84	32.12	115
Tenant's insurance	8.99	15.74	175

(continued)

(continued from previous page)

	average spending of total consumer units	consumer units headed by 35-to-44-year-olds	
		average spending	indexed spending*
Maintenance and repair services	$10.13	$7.54	74
Repair or maintenance services	9.07	7.05	78
Repair and replacement of hard surface flooring	0.94	0.42	45
Repair of built-in appliances	0.12	0.06	50
Maintenance and repair materials	8.72	8.84	101
Paint, wallpaper, and supplies	1.85	1.33	72
Tools and equipment for painting and wallpapering	0.20	0.14	70
Plaster, paneling, roofing, gutters, etc.	1.13	1.27	112
Patio, walk, fence, driveway, masonry, brick, stucco materials	0.08	0.06	75
Plumbing supplies and equipment	0.69	0.71	103
Electrical supplies, heating/ cooling equipment	1.14	2.27	199
Miscellaneous supplies and equipment	2.90	2.53	87
Material for insulation, other maintenance and repair	0.99	0.52	53
Material for additions, finishing basements, remodeling rooms	1.40	0.72	51
Construction materials for jobs not started	0.51	1.28	251
Material for hard surface flooring	0.46	0.25	54
Material for landscape maintenance	0.26	0.28	108
Other lodging	395.16	368.00	93
Owned vacation homes	117.35	98.85	84
Mortgage interest and charges	41.73	51.68	124
Mortgage interest	38.43	51.25	133
Interest paid, home equity loan	0.49	0.29	59
Interest paid, home equity line of credit	2.81	0.14	5
Property taxes	49.87	36.23	73
Maintenance, insurance, and other expenses	25.75	10.93	42
Homeowners and related insurance	7.33	5.58	76
Homeowners insurance	7.04	5.32	76
Fire and extended coverage	0.29	0.26	90
Ground rent	3.27	0.25	8
Maintenance and repair services	10.66	2.39	22

(continued)

(continued from previous page)

	average spending of total consumer units	consumer units headed by 35-to-44-year-olds	
		average spending	indexed spending*
Maintenance and repair materials	$1.24	$0.10	8
Property management and security	3.20	2.60	81
Property management	2.30	1.83	80
Management and upkeep services for security	0.90	0.77	86
Parking	0.05	0.01	20
Housing while attending school	60.57	40.07	66
Lodging on out-of-town trips	217.24	229.08	105
Utilities, fuels, and public services	**2,188.56**	**2,427.76**	**111**
Natural gas	282.73	288.31	102
Natural gas (renter)	59.46	67.03	113
Natural gas (owner)	221.05	220.91	100
Natural gas (vacation)	2.22	0.36	16
Electricity	861.50	990.13	115
Electricity (renter)	207.36	239.73	116
Electricity (owner)	646.50	747.66	116
Electricity (vacation)	7.63	2.75	36
Fuel oil and other fuels	97.97	98.19	100
Fuel oil	59.72	50.08	84
Fuel oil (renter)	6.19	7.07	114
Fuel oil (owner)	52.90	42.37	80
Fuel oil (vacation)	0.63	0.65	103
Coal	1.46	2.49	171
Coal (renter)	0.46	0.98	213
Coal (owner)	1.00	1.51	151
Bottled/tank gas	30.20	37.70	125
Gas (renter)	3.89	6.85	176
Gas (owner)	23.38	26.29	112
Gas (vacation)	2.93	4.56	156
Wood and other fuels	6.59	7.92	120
Wood and other (renter)	0.64	0.89	139
Wood and other (owner)	5.78	7.03	122
Telephone services	689.82	766.33	111
Telephone services in home city, excl. mobile car phones	676.16	749.27	111
Telephone services for mobile car phones	13.66	17.06	125
Water and other public services	256.53	284.80	111

(continued)

(continued from previous page)

	average spending of total consumer units	consumer units headed by 35-to-44-year-olds	
		average spending	indexed spending*
Water and sewerage maintenance	$183.05	$204.52	112
Water/sewerage maintenance (renter)	25.86	31.80	123
Water/sewerage maintenance (owner)	155.80	172.23	111
Water/sewerage maintenance (vacation)	1.38	0.50	36
Trash and garbage collection	72.27	78.92	109
Trash and garbage collection (renter)	9.05	12.38	137
Trash and garbage collection (owner)	61.75	65.62	106
Trash and garbage collection (vacation)	1.46	0.93	64
Septic tank cleaning	1.22	1.35	111
Septic tank cleaning (renter)	0.01	-	-
Septic tank cleaning (owner)	1.20	1.31	109
Household operations	**490.15**	**673.38**	**137**
Personal services	229.80	412.34	179
Babysitting/child care in own home	47.24	93.00	197
Babysitting/child care in someone else's home	32.71	48.39	148
Care for elderly, invalids, handicapped, etc.	19.25	14.46	75
Day care centers, nursery and preschools	130.60	256.49	196
Other household services	260.35	261.04	100
Housekeeping services	85.14	81.51	96
Gardening, lawn care service	69.26	49.22	71
Water softening service	2.68	3.49	130
Household laundry and drycleaning (nonclothing), not coin-operated	1.80	1.17	65
Coin-operated household laundry and dry cleaning (nonclothing)	5.34	5.33	100
Termite/pest control maintenance	6.84	10.72	157
Other home services	19.44	22.28	115
Termite/pest control products	0.27	0.35	130
Moving, storage, and freight express	26.91	32.06	119
Appliance repair, including service center	14.21	13.58	96
Reupholstering and furniture repair	10.19	8.48	83
Repairs/rentals of lawn, garden equipment, hand or power tools, other hh equip.	8.09	5.09	63
Appliance rental	1.57	2.82	180
Rental of office equipment for nonbusiness use	0.27	0.09	33

(continued)

(continued from previous page)

	average spending of total consumer units	consumer units headed by 35-to-44-year-olds	
		average spending	indexed spending*
Repair of miscellaneous household equip. and furnishings	$6.91	$22.52	326
Repair of computer systems for nonbusiness use	1.42	2.35	165
Housekeeping supplies	**393.32**	**435.33**	**111**
Laundry and cleaning supplies	109.37	139.77	128
Soaps and detergents	62.00	79.91	129
Other laundry cleaning products	47.37	59.86	126
Other household products	173.91	197.50	114
Cleansing and toilet tissue, paper towels and napkins	55.89	67.31	120
Miscellaneous household products	73.73	88.86	121
Lawn and garden supplies	44.29	41.33	93
Postage and stationery	110.05	98.06	89
Stationery, stationery supplies, giftwrap	58.09	59.77	103
Postage	51.96	38.29	74
Household furnishings and equipment	**1,348.04**	**1,565.08**	**116**
Household textiles	99.52	101.52	102
Bathroom linens	12.63	15.21	120
Bedroom linens	48.69	49.32	101
Kitchen and dining room linens	6.87	8.10	118
Curtains and draperies	18.55	17.87	96
Slipcovers, decorative pillows	1.93	2.45	127
Sewing materials for household items	9.84	7.20	73
Other linens	0.99	1.37	138
Furniture	318.43	399.40	125
Mattress and springs	41.64	54.72	131
Other bedroom furniture	51.84	74.00	143
Sofas	78.50	90.16	115
Living room chairs	33.00	35.24	107
Living room tables	14.61	20.50	140
Kitchen and dining room furniture	48.70	66.90	137
Infants' furniture	6.12	5.10	83
Outdoor furniture	11.11	14.06	127
Wall units, cabinets and other furniture	32.92	38.73	118
Floor coverings	119.76	100.02	84
Wall-to-wall carpet (renter)	2.34	0.46	20

(continued)

(continued from previous page)

	average spending of total consumer units	consumer units headed by 35-to-44-year-olds	
		average spending	indexed spending*
Wall-to-wall carpet, installed (renter)	$1.94	$0.19	10
Wall-to-wall carpet, not installed carpet squares (renter)	0.40	0.27	68
Wall-to-wall carpet (replacement) (owner)	35.11	42.00	120
Wall-to-wall carpet, not installed (replacement), carpet squares (owner)	2.03	3.33	164
Wall-to-wall carpet, installed (replacement) (owner)	33.07	38.66	117
Room-size rugs and other floor covering, nonpermanent	82.31	57.57	70
Major appliances	148.95	160.03	107
Dishwashers (built-in), garbage disposals, range hoods (renter)	0.68	0.16	24
Dishwashers (built-in), garbage disposals, range hoods (owner)	10.34	10.40	101
Refrigerators and freezers (renter)	6.92	4.49	65
Refrigerators and freezers (owner)	39.28	39.24	100
Washing machines (renter)	5.98	6.37	107
Washing machines (owner)	14.04	21.03	150
Clothes dryers (renter)	3.98	4.41	111
Clothes dryers (owner)	8.96	12.57	140
Cooking stoves, ovens (renter)	2.29	1.27	55
Cooking stoves, ovens (owner)	21.32	18.87	89
Microwave ovens (renter)	3.13	4.12	132
Microwave ovens (owner)	6.15	5.49	89
Portable dishwasher (renter)	0.06	0.29	483
Portable dishwasher (owner)	0.66	0.42	64
Window air conditioners (renter)	2.63	3.14	119
Window air conditioners (owner)	4.49	2.61	58
Electric floor cleaning equipment	13.44	20.90	156
Sewing machines	3.21	3.18	99
Miscellaneous household appliances	1.40	1.06	76
Small appliances, misc. housewares	80.76	89.06	110
Housewares	57.18	59.14	103
Plastic dinnerware	1.50	2.08	139
China and other dinnerware	10.72	11.93	111
Flatware	4.95	5.28	107
Glassware	8.07	4.15	51
Silver serving pieces	1.67	0.81	49

(continued)

(continued from previous page)

	average spending of total consumer units	consumer units headed by 35-to-44-year-olds	
		average spending	indexed spending*
Other serving pieces	$1.60	$2.12	133
Nonelectric cookware	14.19	14.45	102
Tableware, nonelectric kitchenware	14.48	18.32	127
Small appliances	23.57	29.92	127
Small electric kitchen appliances	17.27	21.52	125
Portable heating and cooling equipment	6.30	8.40	133
Miscellaneous household equipment	580.63	715.04	123
Window coverings	13.52	20.70	153
Infants' equipment	6.78	6.65	98
Laundry and cleaning equipment	10.48	11.09	106
Outdoor equipment	5.20	7.40	142
Clocks	4.76	10.27	216
Lamps and lighting fixtures	34.97	26.44	76
Other household decorative items	125.25	161.50	129
Telephones and accessories	38.87	35.81	92
Lawn and garden equipment	48.56	61.76	127
Power tools	13.16	14.91	113
Small miscellaneous furnishings	1.95	0.38	19
Hand tools	10.48	21.92	209
Indoor plants and fresh flowers	49.35	55.03	112
Closet and storage items	7.85	6.53	83
Rental of furniture	4.12	3.37	82
Luggage	7.70	10.38	135
Computers and computer hardware, nonbusiness use	112.01	166.20	148
Computer software and accessories, nonbusiness use	19.31	34.86	181
Telephone answering devices	3.87	5.56	144
Calculators	2.18	2.83	130
Business equipment for home use	4.93	6.50	132
Other hardware	20.66	7.83	38
Smoke alarms (owner)	0.81	0.68	84
Smoke alarms (renter)	0.15	0.22	147
Other household appliances (renter)	6.25	5.45	87
Other household appliances (owner)	1.33	2.30	173
Misc. household equipment and parts	26.12	28.45	109
APPAREL AND SERVICES	**1,644.03**	**2,053.51**	**125**
Men and boys	**394.67**	**516.94**	**131**

(continued)

(continued from previous page)

	average spending of total consumer units	consumer units headed by 35-to-44-year-olds	
		average spending	indexed spending*
Men, aged 16 or older	$304.52	$326.01	107
Suits	31.94	43.33	136
Sportcoats and tailored jackets	12.96	11.23	87
Coats and jackets	26.57	19.66	74
Underwear	11.96	13.44	112
Hosiery	9.55	11.10	116
Nightwear	2.61	4.65	178
Accessories	27.69	27.28	99
Sweaters and vests	14.33	14.63	102
Active sportswear	11.70	14.88	127
Shirts	75.18	71.52	95
Pants	60.44	75.77	125
Shorts and shorts sets	14.22	12.88	91
Uniforms	3.36	4.37	130
Costumes	2.03	1.27	63
Boys, aged 2 to 15	90.15	190.93	212
Coats and jackets	6.28	14.24	227
Sweaters	2.60	4.25	163
Shirts	20.60	41.24	200
Underwear	4.04	10.73	266
Nightwear	1.78	1.48	83
Hosiery	3.23	8.90	276
Accessories	6.93	11.32	163
Suits, sportcoats, and vests	5.02	12.77	254
Pants	21.03	41.82	199
Shorts and shorts sets	9.66	23.88	247
Uniforms and active sportswear	7.63	17.36	228
Costumes	1.35	2.94	218
Women and girls	**651.83**	**810.26**	**124**
Women, aged 16 or older	552.01	590.45	107
Coats and jackets	51.10	47.03	92
Dresses	76.08	60.74	80
Sportcoats and tailored jackets	4.47	6.51	146
Sweaters and vests	35.23	37.40	106
Shirts, blouses, and tops	92.00	99.22	108
Skirts	22.91	28.84	126
Pants	57.78	72.22	125
Shorts and shorts sets	24.25	26.97	111

(continued)

(continued from previous page)

	average spending of total consumer units	consumer units headed by 35-to-44-year-olds	
		average spending	indexed spending*
Active sportswear	$23.62	$31.21	132
Sleepwear	25.57	29.10	114
Undergarments	27.72	33.77	122
Hosiery	24.60	28.43	116
Suits	36.11	34.56	96
Accessories	47.23	50.68	107
Uniforms	1.34	2.06	154
Costumes	2.00	1.71	86
Girls, aged 2 to 15	99.81	219.81	220
Coats and jackets	7.75	17.41	225
Dresses and suits	13.82	28.20	204
Shirts, blouses, and sweaters	23.96	56.62	236
Skirts and pants	16.29	34.89	214
Shorts and shorts sets	9.02	18.75	208
Active sportswear	7.15	16.35	229
Underwear and sleepwear	7.59	15.11	199
Hosiery	5.17	11.25	218
Accessories	4.08	9.92	243
Uniforms	1.95	3.85	197
Costumes	3.06	7.47	244
Children under age 2	**79.85**	**96.93**	**121**
Coats, jackets, and snowsuits	2.72	3.18	117
Dress and outerwear	21.37	21.00	98
Underwear	46.65	61.97	133
Nightwear and loungewear	3.85	4.64	121
Accessories	5.26	6.14	117
Footwear	**253.65**	**319.69**	**126**
Men's	80.57	94.91	118
Boys'	33.02	58.21	176
Women's	114.13	110.08	96
Girls'	25.93	56.49	218
Other apparel products and services	**264.03**	**309.68**	**117**
Material for making clothes	6.85	8.03	117
Sewing patterns and notions	2.32	2.29	99
Watches	23.41	40.48	173
Jewelry	103.30	111.53	108
Shoe repair and other shoe services	2.97	3.63	122

(continued)

(continued from previous page)

	average spending of total consumer units	consumer units headed by 35-to-44-year-olds	
		average spending	indexed spending*
Coin-operated apparel laundry and dry cleaning	$36.01	$37.42	104
Alteration, repair, and tailoring of apparel and accessories	6.73	5.76	86
Clothing rental	3.70	3.02	82
Watch and jewelry repair services	5.51	5.17	94
Apparel laundry, dry cleaning, not coin-operated	72.44	91.50	126
Clothing storage	0.81	0.84	104
TRANSPORTATION	**6,044.16**	**6,796.44**	**112**
Vehicle purchases (net outlay)	**2,724.66**	**2,984.15**	**110**
Cars and trucks, new	1,390.51	1,504.00	108
New cars	749.71	674.92	90
New trucks	640.80	829.08	129
Cars and trucks, used	1,289.97	1,412.10	109
Used cars	863.70	842.84	98
Used trucks	426.27	569.26	134
Other vehicles	44.18	68.05	154
New motorcycles	23.80	44.68	188
Used motorcycles	20.38	23.37	115
Gasoline and motor oil	**985.91**	**1,192.62**	**121**
Gasoline	878.15	1,078.97	123
Diesel fuel	9.23	8.47	92
Gasoline on out-of-town trips	86.21	90.94	105
Gasohol	0.15	0.44	293
Motor oil	11.31	12.88	114
Motor oil on out-of-town trips	0.87	0.92	106
Other vehicle expenses	**1,952.54**	**2,248.15**	**115**
Vehicle finance charges	235.30	298.69	127
Automobile finance charges	137.45	158.06	115
Truck finance charges	86.14	127.74	148
Motorcycle and plane finance charges	0.97	1.35	139
Other vehicle finance charges	10.74	11.54	107
Maintenance and repairs	680.27	780.25	115
Coolant, additives, brake, transmission fluids	6.11	7.36	120
Tires	86.89	106.80	123

(continued)

	average spending of total consumer units	consumer units headed by 35-to-44-year-olds	
		average spending	indexed spending*
Parts, equipment, and accessories	$112.58	$100.69	89
Vehicle audio equipment, excluding labor	5.11	5.23	102
Vehicle products	4.78	4.90	103
Misc. auto repair, servicing	33.27	28.66	86
Body work and painting	34.63	46.90	135
Clutch, transmission repair	44.21	53.49	121
Drive shaft and rear-end repair	5.69	6.74	118
Brake work	42.05	50.20	119
Repair to steering or front-end	17.98	21.54	120
Repair to engine cooling system	22.08	24.34	110
Motor tune-up	41.69	50.57	121
Lube, oil change, and oil filters	38.53	42.28	110
Front-end alignment, wheel balance and rotation	9.54	11.75	123
Shock absorber replacement	6.59	7.10	108
Brake adjustment	3.69	4.48	121
Gas tank repair, replacement	2.23	2.20	99
Repair tires and other repair work	26.87	31.05	116
Vehicle air conditioning repair	15.00	12.69	85
Exhaust system repair	19.74	24.10	122
Electrical system repair	30.22	36.79	122
Motor repair, replacement	65.90	92.06	140
Auto repair service policy	4.87	8.34	171
Vehicle insurance	689.64	771.39	112
Vehicle rental, leases, licenses, and other charges	347.34	397.83	115
Leased and rented vehicles	200.82	230.89	115
Rented vehicles	37.56	45.73	122
Auto rental	5.99	9.03	151
Auto rental, out-of-town trips	24.44	24.91	102
Truck rental	1.54	1.25	81
Truck rental, out-of-town trips	4.32	7.30	169
Aircraft rental	0.17	0.43	253
Motorcycle rental, out-of-town trips	0.10	0.15	150
Aircraft rental, out-of-town trips	1.01	2.66	263
Leased vehicles	163.26	185.17	113
Car lease payments	109.24	110.37	101
Cash downpayment (car lease)	13.22	8.58	65

(continued)

(continued from previous page)

	average spending of total consumer units	consumer units headed by 35-to-44-year-olds	
		average spending	indexed spending*
Termination fee (car lease)	$0.37	$1.03	278
Truck lease payments	36.55	57.42	157
Cash downpayment (truck lease)	3.86	7.77	201
Termination fee (truck lease)	0.03	-	-
State and local registration	79.21	89.88	113
Drivers' license	6.96	8.02	115
Vehicle inspection	8.36	10.04	120
Parking fees	25.59	31.98	125
Parking fees in home city, excluding residence	22.49	29.08	129
Parking fees, out-of-town trips	3.10	2.90	94
Tolls	9.34	11.14	119
Tolls on out-of-town trips	4.63	4.44	96
Towing charges	4.96	4.87	98
Automobile service clubs	7.47	6.56	88
Public transportation	381.05	371.51	97
Airline fares	249.48	239.83	96
Intercity bus fares	11.34	10.59	93
Intracity mass transit fares	47.65	62.18	130
Local trans. on out-of-town trips	10.35	9.11	88
Taxi fares on trips	6.08	5.35	88
Taxi fares	7.70	9.18	119
Intercity train fares	16.24	14.89	92
Ship fares	31.13	18.69	60
School bus	1.07	1.69	158
HEALTH CARE	**1,754.74**	**1,615.96**	**92**
Health insurance	**814.95**	**689.29**	**85**
Commercial health insurance	262.44	300.98	115
Blue Cross/Blue Shield	160.50	139.96	87
Health maintenance plans (HMO's)	122.81	162.32	132
Medicare payments	153.65	18.49	12
Commercial Medicare supplements/ other health insurance	115.55	67.53	58
Medical services	**571.04**	**627.21**	**110**
Physician's services	163.63	197.58	121
Dental services	188.04	231.08	123
Eye care services	29.51	30.52	103

(continued)

(continued from previous page)

	average spending of total consumer units	consumer units headed by 35-to-44-year-olds	
		average spending	indexed spending*
Services by professionals other than physicians	$31.92	$36.60	115
Lab tests, x-rays	24.95	22.61	91
Hospital room	47.81	51.51	108
Hospital services other than room	59.54	42.31	71
Care in convalescent or nursing home	13.49	1.46	11
Repair of medical equipment	0.03	-	-
Other medical care services	12.12	13.55	112
Drugs	**285.78**	**213.24**	**75**
Non-prescription drugs	76.19	70.56	93
Prescription drugs	209.58	142.69	68
Medical supplies	**82.98**	**86.22**	**104**
Eyeglasses and contact lenses	50.99	57.96	114
Hearing aids	0.73	-	-
Topicals and dressings	22.94	22.95	100
Medical equipment for general use	2.53	1.54	61
Supportive/convalescent medical equipment	3.83	2.16	56
Rental of medical equipment	0.68	1.25	184
Rental of supportive, convalescent medical equipment	1.28	0.35	27
ENTERTAINMENT	**1,566.93**	**2,024.72**	**129**
Fees and admissions	**439.11**	**574.34**	**131**
Recreation expenses, out of town trips	20.93	25.55	122
Social, recreation, civic club membership	84.23	88.92	106
Fees for participant sports	73.54	89.02	121
Participant sports, out-of-town trips	26.99	34.11	126
Movie, theater, opera, ballet	76.23	93.04	122
Movie, other admissions, out-of-town trips	36.38	42.49	117
Admission to sporting events	32.42	48.76	150
Admission to sports events, out-of-town trips	12.13	14.16	117
Fees for recreational lessons	55.31	112.72	204
Other entertainment services, out-of-town trips	20.93	25.55	122
Television, radio, and sound equipment	**533.16**	**669.08**	**125**
Televisions	370.56	433.07	117
Community antenna or cable TV	209.60	224.97	107
Black and white TV	1.79	-	-

(continued)

(continued from previous page)

	average spending of total consumer units	consumer units headed by 35-to-44-year-olds	
		average spending	indexed spending*
Color TV, console	$24.03	$26.86	112
Color TV, portable/table model	53.02	63.07	119
VCR's and video disc players	32.24	41.24	128
Video cassettes, tapes, and discs	21.90	30.64	140
Video game hardware and software	19.21	34.90	182
Repair of TV, radio, and sound equipment	8.43	10.87	129
Rental of televisions	0.33	0.52	158
Radios and sound equipment	162.60	236.01	145
Radios	9.21	5.61	61
Tape recorders and players	6.05	13.73	227
Sound components/component systems	30.28	46.70	154
Miscellaneous sound equipment	1.18	3.52	298
Sound equipment accessories	4.75	5.45	115
Compact disc, tape, record, and video mail order clubs	12.08	15.93	132
Records, CDs, audio tapes, needles	36.16	48.91	135
Rental of VCR, radio, sound equipment	0.36	0.42	117
Musical instruments and accessories	17.02	24.36	143
Rental and repair of musical instruments	1.92	4.74	247
Rental of video cassettes, tapes, films, and discs	43.58	66.64	153
Pets, toys, and playground equipment	**288.73**	**388.78**	**135**
Pets	165.03	209.59	127
Pet food	75.80	90.63	120
Pet purchase, supplies, and medicines	26.15	33.81	129
Pet services	15.53	21.47	138
Veterinary services	47.56	63.69	134
Toys, games, hobbies, and tricycles	121.11	175.67	145
Playground equipment	2.59	3.52	136
Other entertainment equipment, supplies, and services	**305.92**	**392.51**	**128**
Unmotored recreational vehicles	27.76	16.50	59
Boats without motor and boat trailer	5.13	11.55	225
Trailers and other attachable campers	22.63	4.95	22
Motorized recreational vehicles	81.56	97.46	119
Motorized campers	16.55	-	-
Other motorized recreational vehicles	22.84	48.94	214
Boats with motor	42.17	48.51	115

(continued)

(continued from previous page)

	average spending of total consumer units	consumer units headed by 35-to-44-year-olds	
		average spending	indexed spending*
Rental of recreational vehicles	$2.33	$4.52	194
Rental of noncamper trailer	0.11	0.17	155
Boat and trailer rental, out-of-town trips	0.80	1.06	133
Rental of campers on out-of-town trips	0.35	1.27	363
Rental of other vehicles on out-of-town trips	0.66	0.71	108
Rental of boat	0.08	0.34	425
Rental of motorized camper	0.19	0.87	458
Rental of other RVs	0.14	0.09	64
Outboard motors	1.79	0.45	25
Docking and landing fees	5.59	7.72	138
Sports, recreation, and exercise equipment	107.91	161.48	150
Athletic gear, game tables, and exercise equipment	51.01	81.02	159
Bicycles	13.36	23.36	175
Camping equipment	3.23	4.52	140
Hunting and fishing equipment	18.99	22.89	121
Winter sports equipment	5.08	7.10	140
Water sports equipment	6.03	9.50	158
Other sports equipment	8.44	9.78	116
Rental and repair of sports equipment	1.77	3.31	187
Photographic equipment, supplies, and services	70.55	89.67	127
Film	19.61	25.36	129
Other photographic supplies	0.36	0.30	83
Film processing	27.15	33.65	124
Repair and rental of photographic equip.	0.32	0.61	191
Photographic equipment	12.50	13.30	106
Photographer fees	10.60	16.46	155
Fireworks	1.58	1.69	107
Souvenirs	0.51	0.28	55
Visual goods	1.77	4.93	279
Pinball and electronic video games	4.58	7.83	171
PERSONAL CARE PRODUCTS AND SERVICES	**396.66**	**456.86**	**115**
Personal care products	**219.22**	**247.11**	**113**
Hair care products	46.35	52.56	113
Nonelectric articles for the hair	6.36	8.01	126

(continued)

(continued from previous page)

	average spending of total consumer units	consumer units headed by 35-to-44-year-olds	
		average spending	indexed spending*
Wigs and hairpieces	$0.83	$0.41	49
Oral hygiene products, articles	23.10	26.36	114
Shaving needs	12.07	14.22	118
Cosmetics, perfume, and bath preparation	99.46	99.77	100
Deodorant, feminine hygiene products, misc.	26.87	40.99	153
Electric personal care appliances	4.18	4.79	115
Personal care services	**177.45**	**209.74**	**118**
Personal care services/female	87.44	93.97	107
Personal care services/male	89.89	115.68	129
Repair of personal care appliances	0.12	0.09	75
READING	**164.80**	**184.04**	**112**
Newspapers, subscription	52.48	48.94	93
Newspapers, non-subscription	17.83	20.37	114
Magazines, subscription	24.59	25.12	102
Magazines, non-subscription	12.19	14.66	120
Newsletters	0.11	-	-
Books purchased through book clubs	10.51	12.54	119
Books not purchased through book clubs	45.85	60.25	131
Encyclopedia and other reference book sets	1.23	2.15	175
EDUCATION	**459.88**	**482.69**	**105**
College tuition	271.59	182.01	67
Elementary/high school tuition	64.79	131.17	202
Other school tuition	14.46	17.36	120
Other school expenses including rentals	18.85	27.65	147
School books, supplies, equipment for college	38.29	26.34	69
School books, supplies, equipment for elementary/high school	9.51	23.04	242
School books, supplies, equipment for day care, nursery, other	3.34	5.02	150
School supplies, etc., unspecified	39.04	70.10	180
TOBACCO PRODUCTS AND SMOKING SUPPLIES	**258.55**	**319.27**	**123**
Cigarettes	236.05	297.39	126
Other tobacco products	21.06	19.55	93
Smoking accessories	1.44	2.33	162

(continued)

	average spending of total consumer units	consumer units headed by 35-to-44-year-olds	
		average spending	indexed spending*
MISCELLANEOUS EXPENSES	**$748.51**	**$907.62**	**121**
Miscellaneous fees, pari-mutuel losses	44.69	58.34	131
Legal fees	112.87	153.25	136
Funeral expenses	85.75	51.80	60
Safe deposit box rental	5.69	4.62	81
Checking accounts, other			
bank service charges	26.49	35.77	135
Cemetery lots, vaults, and maintenance fees	18.48	11.93	65
Accounting fees	43.06	39.01	91
Miscellaneous personal services	22.50	32.26	143
Finance charges, except mortgage			
and vehicles	205.23	286.45	140
Occupational expenses	84.96	110.55	130
Expenses for other properties	93.52	118.43	127
Interest paid, home equity line			
of credit (other property)	0.42	-	-
Credit card memberships	92.98	5.23	6
CASH CONTRIBUTIONS	**960.31**	**787.66**	**82**
Cash contributions to non-cu member,			
incl. students, alimony, child support	265.01	271.84	103
Gifts of cash, stocks and bonds			
to non-cu member	206.25	52.98	26
Contributions to charities	90.33	91.31	101
Contributions to church	363.85	343.51	94
Contributions to educational organizations	21.24	18.12	85
Contributions to political organizations	7.17	4.92	69
Other contributions	6.45	4.99	77
PERSONAL INSURANCE			
AND PENSIONS	**2,957.19**	**4,022.04**	**136**
Life and other personal			
insurances except health	**397.69**	**439.10**	**110**
Life, endowment, annuity,			
other personal insurance	380.59	425.43	112
Other nonhealth insurance	17.11	13.67	80
Pensions and Social Security	**2,559.49**	**3,582.93**	**140**
Deductions for government retirement	70.79	76.37	108
Deductions for railroad retirement	4.53	6.64	147

(continued)

(continued from previous page)

	average spending of total consumer units	consumer units headed by 35-to-44-year-olds	
		average spending	indexed spending*
Deductions for private pensions	$273.66	$392.83	144
Non-payroll deposit to retirement plans	298.11	347.36	117
Deductions for Social Security	1,912.40	2,759.73	144
GIFTS*	**1,007.51**	**843.30**	**84**
Food	**84.05**	**62.95**	**75**
Cakes and cupcakes	2.44	2.77	114
Candy and chewing gum	9.86	11.19	113
Potato chips and other snacks	2.04	2.87	141
Board (including at school)	27.35	18.93	69
Catered affairs	18.48	6.07	33
Housing	**262.20**	**220.20**	**84**
Housekeeping supplies	37.84	33.71	89
Other household products	8.28	8.17	99
Miscellaneous household products	4.99	5.27	106
Lawn and garden supplies	2.14	1.32	62
Postage and stationery	27.69	24.51	89
Stationery, stationery supplies, giftwraps	22.27	22.28	100
Postage	5.42	2.23	41
Household textiles	15.73	10.75	68
Bathroom linens	2.56	2.36	92
Bedroom linens	10.39	5.69	55
Appliances and misc. housewares	26.36	18.37	70
Major appliances	5.46	3.16	58
Small appliances and misc. housewares	20.90	15.21	73
China and other dinnerware	3.43	2.18	64
Glassware	4.29	2.09	49
Nonelectric cookware	2.54	1.03	41
Tableware, nonelectric kitchenware	3.07	3.40	111
Small electric kitchen appliances	3.79	3.43	91
Miscellaneous household equipment	65.40	69.41	106
Lamps and lighting fixtures	3.66	0.22	6
Other household decorative items	24.59	32.69	133
Lawn and garden equipment	2.30	5.03	219
Indoor plants and flowers	16.77	16.55	99
Computers and computer hardware, nonbusiness use	5.60	6.10	109

(continued)

(continued from previous page)

	average spending of total consumer units	consumer units headed by 35-to-44-year-olds	
		average spending	indexed spending*
Other housing	$116.87	$87.95	75
Repair or maintenance services	5.00	4.45	89
Housing while attending school	36.93	26.62	72
Lodging on out-of-town trips	2.49	2.01	81
Electricity (renter)	9.95	5.62	56
Telephone services in home city, excl. mobile car phone	12.04	7.89	66
Day-care centers, nursery, and preschools	12.40	14.23	115
Housekeeping services	5.52	3.52	64
Gardening, lawn care services	2.48	1.16	47
Moving, storage, freight express	2.29	2.18	95
Sofas	2.72	1.27	47
Kitchen, dining room furniture	2.26	0.60	27
Infants' furniture	2.18	1.25	57
Apparel and services	**246.23**	**240.95**	**98**
Males, aged 2 or older	64.05	63.02	98
Men's coats and jackets	4.46	5.18	116
Men's accessories	5.71	4.55	80
Men's sweaters and vests	3.26	1.99	61
Men's active sportswear	2.24	1.84	82
Men's shirts	15.44	17.26	112
Men's pants	5.72	6.14	107
Boys' shirts	4.95	3.67	74
Boys' accessories	2.02	1.95	97
Boys' pants	3.73	3.40	91
Boys' shorts and short sets	2.07	3.16	153
Females, aged 2 or older	93.94	98.14	104
Women's coats and jackets	10.55	4.97	47
Women's dresses	9.92	8.00	81
Women's vests and sweaters	6.44	8.59	133
Women's shirts, tops, blouses	14.50	20.63	142
Women's pants	5.12	9.47	185
Women's active sportswear	3.30	4.01	122
Women's sleepwear	5.85	4.78	82
Women's undergarments	2.30	1.64	71
Women's suits	2.42	1.62	67
Women's accessories	10.27	10.76	105

(continued)

(continued from previous page)

	average spending of total consumer units	consumer units headed by 35-to-44-year-olds	
		average spending	indexed spending*
Girls' dresses and suits	$3.23	$2.59	80
Girls' shirts, blouses, sweaters	6.04	7.16	119
Girls' skirts and pants	2.23	1.82	82
Children under age 2	34.90	36.81	105
Infant dresses, outerwear	13.81	11.62	84
Infant underwear	14.38	18.64	130
Infant nightwear, loungewear	2.50	2.46	98
Infant accessories	2.78	2.67	96
Other apparel products and services	53.33	42.98	81
Jewelry and watches	25.94	20.82	80
Watches	3.40	3.76	111
Jewelry	22.54	17.06	76
All other apparel products and services	27.40	22.16	81
Men's footwear	8.18	6.69	82
Boys' footwear	4.83	3.21	66
Women's footwear	7.59	6.06	80
Girls' footwear	4.94	4.52	91
Transportation	**56.11**	**36.31**	**65**
New cars	7.43	-	-
Used cars	11.40	3.42	30
Gasoline on out-of-town trips	13.14	12.53	95
Airline fares	9.19	9.06	99
Ship fares	4.74	4.07	86
Health care	**34.69**	**34.90**	**101**
Physicians services	2.66	3.67	138
Dental services	3.43	3.96	115
Hospital room	3.66	15.89	434
Hospital service other than room	3.68	3.37	92
Care in convalescent or nursing home	11.30	0.66	6
Prescription drugs	2.28	1.59	70
Entertainment	**83.57**	**83.72**	**100**
Toys, games, hobbies, tricycles	32.48	33.86	104
Other entertainment	51.08	49.85	98
Movie, other admission, out-of-town trips	7.27	6.34	87
Admission to sports events, out-of-town trips	2.42	2.11	87
Fees for recreational lessons	4.96	3.38	68

(continued)

(continued from previous page)

	average spending of total consumer units	consumer units headed by 35-to-44-year-olds	
		average spending	indexed spending*
Community antenna or cable TV	$2.81	$2.08	74
Color TV, portable/table model	2.01	2.32	115
VCRs, video disc players	2.67	1.80	67
Video game hardware and software	2.00	3.46	173
Radios	4.70	2.36	50
Sound components and component systems	2.05	3.61	176
Veterinary services	3.48	2.74	79
Athletic gear, game tables, and exercise equipment	3.46	6.39	185
Education	**114.09**	**66.17**	**58**
College tuition	86.94	46.37	53
Elementary, high school tuition	6.43	3.93	61
Other schools tuition	3.09	0.89	29
Other school expenses including rentals	4.72	3.44	73
School books, supplies, equipment for college	6.56	3.26	50
School supplies, etc., unspecified	5.32	6.40	120
All other gifts	126.58	98.10	78
Gifts of out-of-town trip expenses	49.51	34.03	69
Other gifts	**77.06**	**64.08**	**83**

The index compares the average spending of consumer units headed by 35-to-44-year-olds with the average spending of all consumer units by dividing the spending of 35-to-44-year-olds by average total spending in each category and multiplying by 100. An index of 100 means that the spending of 35-to-44-year-olds in that category equals average spending. An index of 132 means that the spending of 35-to-44-year-olds is 32 percent above average, while an index of 75 means that the spending of 35-to-44-year-olds is 25 percent below average.

** This figure does not include the amount paid for mortgage principle, which is considered an asset.

*** Expenditures on gifts are also included in the preceding product and service categories. Food spending, for example, includes the amount spent on food gifts. Only gift categories with average spending of $2.00 or more by the average consumer unit are shown.

Note: The Bureau of Labor Statistics uses consumer units rather than households as the sampling unit in the Consumer Expenditure Survey. For the definition of consumer units, see the glossary. Expenditures listed for items in a given category may not add to the total for that category because the listing is incomplete. (-) means the sample is too small to make a reliable estimate.

Source: Bureau of Labor Statistics, unpublished tables from the 1994 Consumer Expenditure Survey

Spending Peaks in the 45-to-54 Age Group

This age group is an increasingly important consumer market.

Householders aged 45 to 54 spent $41,444 in 1994, 31 percent more than the average household. They are the biggest spenders among all age groups. The spending of householders aged 45 to 54 has become increasingly important over the past few years because of the reduction in spending by householders aged 35 to 44. In 1989, householders aged 45 to 54 spent just $578 more than those aged 35 to 44. By 1994, they spent fully $3,856 more.

Householders aged 45 to 54 spend 27 percent more than the average household on food. They are especially big spenders on steak, butter, fresh fruit juices, roasted coffee, and restaurant meals.

Because few of these householders have young children at home, they spend less than average on babysitting services and day care. But they spend much more than average on household furnishings as they fix up their homes after their children are gone.

Overall, this age group spends more than any other on food away from home, clothes, transportation, entertainment, personal care products and services, and education.

♦ While many advertisers still chase the young adult market, the action has moved into the mid-youth market. Consumers aged 45 to 54 are the biggest spenders on most products and services.

Note: The Consumer Expenditure Survey, on which the spending tables are based, presents average spending data for all households in a segment, not just for purchasers of an item. When examining the spending data that follow, it is important to remember that by including purchasers and nonpurchasers in the calculation of the average, the average spending amount is diluted for items that are not purchased universally. For categories purchased by few consumers, the average spending figures are less revealing than the indexes. For universally purchased items such as soaps and detergents, the average spending figures give a more accurate picture of actual spending.

Average and Indexed Spending of Householders Aged 45 to 54, 1994

(average annual spending of total consumer units and average annual and indexed spending of consumer units headed by 45-to-54-year-olds, 1994)

	average spending of total consumer units	consumer units headed by 45-to-54-year-olds	
		average spending	indexed spending*
Number of consumer units (in thousands)	**102,210**	**17,812**	**-**
Average before-tax income	**$36,838.00**	**$49,627.00**	**135**
Total average annual spending	**31,750.63**	**41,443.60**	**131**
FOOD	**$4,410.52**	**$5,614.35**	**127**
Food at home	**2,712.05**	**3,319.26**	**122**
Cereals and bakery products	428.68	511.68	119
Cereals and cereal products	161.74	188.24	116
Flour	7.60	8.48	112
Prepared flour mixes	12.79	14.06	110
Ready-to-eat and cooked cereals	98.27	110.69	113
Rice	15.43	19.17	124
Pasta, cornmeal, other cereal products	27.65	35.85	130
Bakery products	266.93	323.43	121
Bread	76.22	91.60	120
White bread	37.65	41.81	111
Bread, other than white	38.57	49.79	129
Crackers and cookies	62.56	70.43	113
Cookies	42.97	48.79	114
Crackers	19.59	21.64	110
Frozen and refrigerated bakery products	21.56	28.37	132
Other bakery products	106.59	133.03	125
Biscuits and rolls	35.96	48.38	135
Cakes and cupcakes	31.19	37.04	119
Bread and cracker products	4.72	5.81	123
Sweetrolls, coffee cakes, doughnuts	21.92	29.03	132
Pies, tarts, turnovers	12.80	12.77	100
Meats, poultry, fish, and eggs	732.45	935.68	128
Beef	226.76	296.63	131
Ground beef	88.45	105.78	120
Roast	39.41	55.91	142
Chuck roast	12.26	13.27	108
Round roast	14.84	22.76	153
Other roast	12.31	19.88	161

(continued)

(continued from previous page)

	average spending of total consumer units	consumer units headed by 45-to-54-year-olds	
		average spending	indexed spending*
Steak	$84.75	$121.02	143
Round steak	16.00	25.43	159
Sirloin steak	24.44	33.54	137
Other steak	44.31	62.05	140
Other beef	14.15	13.93	98
Pork	155.74	187.54	120
Bacon	22.78	26.05	114
Pork chops	39.32	50.41	128
Ham	36.88	42.03	114
Ham, not canned	34.16	40.79	119
Canned ham	2.72	1.23	45
Sausage	22.82	24.24	106
Other pork	33.93	44.81	132
Other meats	93.95	119.48	127
Frankfurters	18.76	21.22	113
Lunch meats (cold cuts)	65.66	85.10	130
Bologna, liverwurst, salami	23.73	28.79	121
Other lunchmeats	41.93	56.31	134
Lamb, organ meats and others	9.53	13.17	138
Lamb and organ meats	9.35	13.17	141
Mutton, goat and game	0.18	-	-
Poultry	136.58	182.81	134
Fresh and frozen chickens	107.89	144.05	134
Fresh and frozen whole chicken	29.56	38.65	131
Fresh and frozen chicken parts	78.33	105.40	135
Other poultry	28.69	38.76	135
Fish and seafood	89.43	114.48	128
Canned fish and seafood	15.03	15.91	106
Fresh fish and shellfish	51.26	66.81	130
Frozen fish and shellfish	23.15	31.76	137
Eggs	30.00	34.75	116
Dairy products	288.92	338.21	117
Fresh milk and cream	127.13	145.14	114
Fresh milk, all types	118.94	135.38	114
Cream	8.19	9.77	119
Other dairy products	161.79	193.07	119
Butter	11.65	17.42	150
Cheese	81.83	93.85	115

(continued)

(continued from previous page)

	average spending of total consumer units	consumer units headed by 45-to-54-year-olds	
		average spending	indexed spending*
Ice cream and related products	$47.64	$56.15	118
Miscellaneous dairy products	20.66	25.64	124
Fruits and vegetables	436.57	521.56	119
Fresh fruits	133.02	163.72	123
Apples	25.37	30.89	122
Bananas	29.66	35.82	121
Oranges	16.36	22.25	136
Citrus fruits, excl. oranges	10.96	12.44	114
Other fresh fruits	50.67	62.32	123
Fresh vegetables	134.89	162.72	121
Potatoes	28.01	33.86	121
Lettuce	17.38	21.36	123
Tomatoes	21.01	24.53	117
Other fresh vegetables	68.50	82.97	121
Processed fruits	93.08	108.73	117
Frozen fruits and fruit juices	16.28	17.73	109
Frozen orange juice	9.49	10.47	110
Frozen fruits	1.60	1.42	89
Frozen fruit juices	5.19	5.84	113
Canned fruit	14.23	14.24	100
Dried fruit	5.89	8.03	136
Fresh fruit juices	17.90	25.19	141
Canned and bottled fruit juices	38.78	43.55	112
Processed vegetables	75.57	86.40	114
Frozen vegetables	24.83	27.22	110
Canned and dried vegetables and juices	50.74	59.17	117
Canned beans	10.44	11.74	112
Canned corn	6.81	7.89	116
Other canned and dried vegetables	27.05	31.87	118
Frozen vegetable juices	0.23	0.31	135
Fresh and canned vegetable juices	6.21	7.37	119
Other food at home	825.43	1,012.13	123
Sugar and other sweets	105.25	127.28	121
Candy and chewing gum	62.32	79.89	128
Sugar	18.31	21.99	120
Artificial sweeteners	3.39	3.92	116
Jams, preserves, other sweets	21.23	21.48	101
Fats and oils	79.25	90.96	115
Margarine	14.16	14.74	104

(continued)

(continued from previous page)

	average spending of total consumer units	consumer units headed by 45-to-54-year-olds	
		average spending	indexed spending*
Fats and oils	$23.09	$27.48	119
Salad dressings	23.75	29.94	126
Nondairy cream and imitation milk	6.56	8.24	126
Peanut butter	11.70	10.57	90
Miscellaneous foods	361.62	424.56	117
Frozen prepared foods	66.14	86.77	131
Frozen meals	21.43	28.56	133
Other frozen prepared foods	44.71	58.20	130
Canned and packaged soups	29.55	32.10	109
Potato chips, nuts, and other snacks	74.07	95.10	128
Potato chips and other snacks	58.18	73.04	126
Nuts	15.89	22.06	139
Condiments and seasonings	79.74	96.50	121
Salt, spices and other seasonings	19.30	22.02	114
Olives, pickles, relishes	10.16	12.55	124
Sauces and gravies	36.43	45.12	124
Baking needs and misc. products	13.85	16.81	121
Other canned/packaged prepared foods	112.12	114.10	102
Prepared salads	10.97	13.80	126
Prepared desserts	7.99	8.97	112
Baby food	28.11	17.32	62
Miscellaneous prepared foods	65.05	74.01	114
Nonalcoholic beverages	232.89	296.67	127
Cola	89.45	117.44	131
Other carbonated drinks	38.89	44.94	116
Coffee	43.01	58.19	135
Roasted coffee	29.13	40.68	140
Instant and freeze-dried coffee	13.88	17.51	126
Noncarb. fruit flavored drinks incl. non-frozen lemonade	21.86	27.49	126
Tea	16.25	23.89	147
Nonalcoholic beer	0.66	0.26	39
Other nonalcoholic beverages	22.77	24.46	107
Food prepared by cu on out-of-town trips	46.41	72.66	157
Food away from home	**1,698.46**	**2,295.08**	**135**
Meals at restaurants, carry-outs, other	1,306.21	1,629.75	125
Lunch	451.76	563.23	125
Dinner	651.79	816.60	125

(continued)

(continued from previous page)

	average spending of total consumer units	consumer units headed by 45-to-54-year-olds	
		average spending	indexed spending*
Snacks and nonalcoholic beverages	$101.72	$122.75	121
Breakfast and brunch	100.95	127.16	126
Board (including at school)	50.72	153.10	302
Catered affairs	56.09	139.06	248
Food on out-of-town trips	207.89	284.02	137
School lunches	53.76	68.90	128
Meals as pay	23.79	20.25	85
ALCOHOLIC BEVERAGES	**278.03**	**291.67**	**105**
At home	**165.13**	**173.89**	**105**
Beer and ale	99.68	95.20	96
Whiskey	13.68	10.85	79
Wine	36.41	48.20	132
Other alcoholic beverages	15.35	19.64	128
Away from home	**112.91**	**117.78**	**104**
Beer and ale	38.56	36.17	94
Wine	15.79	17.09	108
Other alcoholic beverages	27.96	29.51	106
Alcoholic beverages purchased on trips	30.61	35.01	114
HOUSING	**10,106.32**	**12,457.33**	**123**
Shelter	**5,686.26**	**7,023.65**	**124**
Owned dwellings**	3,491.71	5,068.93	145
Mortgage interest and charges	1,918.71	2,971.91	155
Mortgage interest	1,822.54	2,793.18	153
Interest paid, home equity loan	44.51	85.72	193
Interest paid, home equity line of credit	51.11	92.97	182
Prepayment penalty charges	0.55	0.04	7
Property taxes	921.61	1,249.03	136
Maintenance, repairs, insurance, and other expenses	651.39	848.00	130
Homeowners and related insurance	207.71	306.88	148
Fire and extended coverage	5.95	9.59	161
Homeowners insurance	201.76	297.29	147
Ground rent	37.79	23.38	62
Maintenance and repair services	313.66	404.06	129
Painting and papering	44.00	61.40	140
Plumbing and water heating	36.33	50.85	140

(continued)

(continued from previous page)

	average spending of total consumer units	consumer units headed by 45-to-54-year-olds	
		average spending	indexed spending*
Heat, air conditioning, electrical work	$55.27	$48.89	88
Roofing and gutters	50.96	82.14	161
Other repair and maintenance services	108.66	131.09	121
Repair and replacement of			
hard surface flooring	16.78	27.73	165
Repair of built-in appliances	1.67	1.96	117
Maintenance and repair materials	71.89	94.62	132
Paint, wallpaper, and supplies	18.40	18.45	100
Tools and equipment for			
painting and wallpapering	1.98	1.98	100
Plumbing supplies and equipment	8.59	14.53	169
Electrical supplies, heating/			
cooling equipment	5.12	7.88	154
Material for hard surface flooring,			
repair and replacement	5.01	6.57	131
Material and equipment for			
roofing and gutters	5.36	6.13	114
Plaster, paneling, siding, windows,			
doors, screens, awnings	11.75	16.40	140
Patio, walk, fence, driveway,			
masonry, brick, stucco materials	0.47	0.47	100
Material for landscape maintenance	1.47	1.59	108
Miscellaneous supplies and equipment	13.73	20.60	150
Material for insulation, other			
maintenance and repair	9.37	17.20	184
Material to finish basement,			
remodel rooms, etc. (owner)	4.37	3.40	78
Property management and security	20.16	18.96	94
Property management	12.17	11.68	96
Management and upkeep			
services for security	7.99	7.28	91
Parking	0.18	0.10	56
Rented dwellings	1,799.39	1,318.48	73
Rent	1,728.66	1,253.60	73
Rent as pay	42.90	45.33	106
Maintenance, repairs, insurance,			
and other expenses	27.84	19.55	70
Tenant's insurance	8.99	6.82	76

(continued)

(continued from previous page)

	average spending of total consumer units	consumer units headed by 45-to-54-year-olds	
		average spending	indexed spending*
Maintenance and repair services	$10.13	$5.13	51
Repair or maintenance services	9.07	4.30	47
Repair and replacement of hard surface flooring	0.94	0.34	36
Repair of built-in appliances	0.12	0.49	408
Maintenance and repair materials	8.72	7.61	87
Paint, wallpaper, and supplies	1.85	1.88	102
Tools and equipment for painting and wallpapering	0.20	0.20	100
Plaster, paneling, roofing, gutters, etc.	1.13	2.16	191
Patio, walk, fence, driveway, masonry, brick, stucco materials	0.08	0.24	300
Plumbing supplies and equipment	0.69	1.26	183
Electrical supplies, heating/ cooling equipment	1.14	0.31	27
Miscellaneous supplies and equipment	2.90	0.40	14
Material for insulation, other maintenance and repair	0.99	0.18	18
Material for additions, finishing basements, remodeling rooms	1.40	0.22	16
Construction materials for jobs not started	0.51	-	-
Material for hard surface flooring	0.46	0.81	176
Material for landscape maintenance	0.26	0.34	131
Other lodging	395.16	636.23	161
Owned vacation homes	117.35	168.86	144
Mortgage interest and charges	41.73	81.87	196
Mortgage interest	38.43	80.51	209
Interest paid, home equity loan	0.49	1.08	220
Interest paid, home equity line of credit	2.81	0.28	10
Property taxes	49.87	55.40	111
Maintenance, insurance, and other expenses	25.75	31.60	123
Homeowners and related insurance	7.33	4.95	68
Homeowners insurance	7.04	4.87	69
Fire and extended coverage	0.29	0.08	28
Ground rent	3.27	0.61	19
Maintenance and repair services	10.66	19.12	179

(continued)

(continued from previous page)

	average spending of total consumer units	consumer units headed by 45-to-54-year-olds	
		average spending	indexed spending*
Maintenance and repair materials	$1.24	$4.86	392
Property management and security	3.20	1.98	62
Property management	2.30	1.06	46
Management and upkeep			
services for security	0.90	0.92	102
Parking	0.05	0.07	140
Housing while attending school	60.57	179.45	296
Lodging on out-of-town trips	217.24	287.92	133
Utilities, fuels, and public services	**2,188.56**	**2,603.42**	**119**
Natural gas	282.73	344.89	122
Natural gas (renter)	59.46	44.66	75
Natural gas (owner)	221.05	297.65	135
Natural gas (vacation)	2.22	2.57	116
Electricity	861.50	1,019.47	118
Electricity (renter)	207.36	150.38	73
Electricity (owner)	646.50	860.24	133
Electricity (vacation)	7.63	8.85	116
Fuel oil and other fuels	97.97	109.77	112
Fuel oil	59.72	60.56	101
Fuel oil (renter)	6.19	3.26	53
Fuel oil (owner)	52.90	57.18	108
Fuel oil (vacation)	0.63	0.12	19
Coal	1.46	3.37	231
Coal (renter)	0.46	0.97	211
Coal (owner)	1.00	2.40	240
Bottled/tank gas	30.20	34.17	113
Gas (renter)	3.89	2.79	72
Gas (owner)	23.38	29.09	124
Gas (vacation)	2.93	2.29	78
Wood and other fuels	6.59	11.67	177
Wood and other (renter)	0.64	0.42	66
Wood and other (owner)	5.78	10.55	183
Telephone services	689.82	819.06	119
Telephone services in home city,			
excl. mobile car phones	676.16	769.60	114
Telephone services for mobile car phones	13.66	22.46	164
Water and other public services	256.53	310.24	121

(continued)

(continued from previous page)

	average spending of total consumer units	consumer units headed by 45-to-54-year-olds	
		average spending	indexed spending*
Water and sewerage maintenance	$183.05	$222.14	121
Water/sewerage maintenance (renter)	25.86	18.57	72
Water/sewerage maintenance (owner)	155.80	202.34	130
Water/sewerage maintenance (vacation)	1.38	1.23	89
Trash and garbage collection	72.27	85.84	119
Trash and garbage collection (renter)	9.05	7.23	80
Trash and garbage collection (owner)	61.75	77.51	126
Trash and garbage collection (vacation)	1.46	1.10	75
Septic tank cleaning	1.22	2.25	184
Septic tank cleaning (renter)	0.01	0.02	200
Septic tank cleaning (owner)	1.20	2.23	186
Household operations	**490.15**	**416.27**	**85**
Personal services	229.80	102.33	45
Babysitting and child care in own home	47.24	33.59	71
Babysitting and child care in someone else's home	32.71	12.70	39
Care for elderly, invalids, handicapped, etc.	19.25	7.86	41
Day care centers, nursery and preschools	130.60	48.19	37
Other household services	260.35	313.93	121
Housekeeping services	85.14	123.78	145
Gardening, lawn care service	69.26	73.23	106
Water softening service	2.68	2.88	107
Household laundry and drycleaning (nonclothing), not coin-operated	1.80	2.20	122
Coin-operated household laundry and dry cleaning (nonclothing)	5.34	4.09	77
Termite/pest control maintenance	6.84	7.61	111
Other home services	19.44	16.33	84
Termite/pest control products	0.27	0.59	219
Moving, storage, and freight express	26.91	34.07	127
Appliance repair, including service center	14.21	18.24	128
Reupholstering and furniture repair	10.19	14.24	140
Repairs/rentals of lawn, garden equipment, hand or power tools, other hh equip.	8.09	6.05	75
Appliance rental	1.57	2.56	163
Rental of office equipment for nonbusiness use	0.27	0.23	85

(continued)

(continued from previous page)

	average spending of total consumer units	consumer units headed by 45-to-54-year-olds	
		average spending	indexed spending*
Repair of miscellaneous household equip. and furnishings	$6.91	$4.99	72
Repair of computer systems for nonbusiness use	1.42	2.83	199
Housekeeping supplies	**393.32**	**463.69**	**118**
Laundry and cleaning supplies	109.37	128.07	117
Soaps and detergents	62.00	77.82	126
Other laundry cleaning products	47.37	50.25	106
Other household products	173.91	208.63	120
Cleansing and toilet tissue, paper towels and napkins	55.89	65.12	117
Miscellaneous household products	73.73	88.92	121
Lawn and garden supplies	44.29	54.60	123
Postage and stationery	110.05	126.99	115
Stationery, stationery supplies, giftwrap	58.09	72.39	125
Postage	51.96	54.60	105
Household furnishings and equipment	**1,348.04**	**1,950.31**	**145**
Household textiles	99.52	161.41	162
Bathroom linens	12.63	17.21	136
Bedroom linens	48.69	68.86	141
Kitchen and dining room linens	6.87	12.80	186
Curtains and draperies	18.55	40.75	220
Slipcovers, decorative pillows	1.93	2.07	107
Sewing materials for household items	9.84	18.20	185
Other linens	0.99	1.52	154
Furniture	318.43	383.65	120
Mattress and springs	41.64	43.24	104
Other bedroom furniture	51.84	54.92	106
Sofas	78.50	106.74	136
Living room chairs	33.00	38.49	117
Living room tables	14.61	18.50	127
Kitchen and dining room furniture	48.70	50.18	103
Infants' furniture	6.12	7.09	116
Outdoor furniture	11.11	15.61	141
Wall units, cabinets and other furniture	32.92	48.89	149
Floor coverings	119.76	264.46	221
Wall-to-wall carpet (renter)	2.34	1.28	55

(continued)

	average spending of total consumer units	consumer units headed by 45-to-54-year-olds	
		average spending	indexed spending*
Wall-to-wall carpet, installed (renter)	$1.94	$0.78	40
Wall-to-wall carpet, not installed carpet squares (renter)	0.40	0.51	128
Wall-to-wall carpet (replacement) (owner)	35.11	65.72	187
Wall-to-wall carpet, not installed (replacement), carpet squares (owner)	2.03	2.43	120
Wall-to-wall carpet, installed (replacement) (owner)	33.07	63.29	191
Room-size rugs and other floor covering, nonpermanent	82.31	197.46	240
Major appliances	148.95	189.30	127
Dishwashers (built-in), garbage disposals, range hoods (renter)	0.68	0.91	134
Dishwashers (built-in), garbage disposals, range hoods (owner)	10.34	13.39	129
Refrigerators and freezers (renter)	6.92	9.04	131
Refrigerators and freezers (owner)	39.28	51.22	130
Washing machines (renter)	5.98	3.81	64
Washing machines (owner)	14.04	17.35	124
Clothes dryers (renter)	3.98	4.68	118
Clothes dryers (owner)	8.96	8.91	99
Cooking stoves, ovens (renter)	2.29	1.48	65
Cooking stoves, ovens (owner)	21.32	40.11	188
Microwave ovens (renter)	3.13	1.78	57
Microwave ovens (owner)	6.15	9.17	149
Portable dishwasher (renter)	0.06	-	-
Portable dishwasher (owner)	0.66	1.30	197
Window air conditioners (renter)	2.63	1.45	55
Window air conditioners (owner)	4.49	3.48	78
Electric floor cleaning equipment	13.44	14.14	105
Sewing machines	3.21	6.21	193
Miscellaneous household appliances	1.40	0.89	64
Small appliances, misc. housewares	80.76	97.24	120
Housewares	57.18	69.22	121
Plastic dinnerware	1.50	1.99	133
China and other dinnerware	10.72	14.78	138
Flatware	4.95	5.63	114
Glassware	8.07	5.11	63
Silver serving pieces	1.67	2.61	156

(continued)

(continued from previous page)

	average spending of total consumer units	consumer units headed by 45-to-54-year-olds	
		average spending	indexed spending*
Other serving pieces	$1.60	$2.00	125
Nonelectric cookware	14.19	19.70	139
Tableware, nonelectric kitchenware	14.48	17.40	120
Small appliances	23.57	28.02	119
Small electric kitchen appliances	17.27	21.08	122
Portable heating and cooling equipment	6.30	6.93	110
Miscellaneous household equipment	580.63	854.25	147
Window coverings	13.52	12.90	95
Infants' equipment	6.78	5.97	88
Laundry and cleaning equipment	10.48	17.11	163
Outdoor equipment	5.20	10.08	194
Clocks	4.76	5.34	112
Lamps and lighting fixtures	34.97	53.34	153
Other household decorative items	125.25	187.98	150
Telephones and accessories	38.87	74.40	191
Lawn and garden equipment	48.56	53.62	110
Power tools	13.16	15.07	115
Small miscellaneous furnishings	1.95	2.89	148
Hand tools	10.48	8.78	84
Indoor plants and fresh flowers	49.35	58.88	119
Closet and storage items	7.85	7.95	101
Rental of furniture	4.12	2.02	49
Luggage	7.70	11.44	149
Computers and computer hardware, nonbusiness use	112.01	167.49	150
Computer software and accessories, nonbusiness use	19.31	27.50	142
Telephone answering devices	3.87	4.99	129
Calculators	2.18	3.40	156
Business equipment for home use	4.93	5.39	109
Other hardware	20.66	78.81	381
Smoke alarms (owner)	0.81	1.39	172
Smoke alarms (renter)	0.15	0.09	60
Other household appliances (renter)	6.25	5.47	88
Other household appliances (owner)	1.33	1.31	98
Misc. household equipment and parts	26.12	30.64	117
APPAREL AND SERVICES	**1,644.03**	**2,262.02**	**138**
Men and boys	**394.67**	**572.96**	**145**

(continued)

(continued from previous page)

	average spending of total consumer units	consumer units headed by 45-to-54-year-olds	
		average spending	indexed spending*
Men, aged 16 or older	$304.52	$459.16	151
Suits	31.94	40.16	126
Sportcoats and tailored jackets	12.96	18.51	143
Coats and jackets	26.57	60.45	228
Underwear	11.96	16.70	140
Hosiery	9.55	11.44	120
Nightwear	2.61	0.99	38
Accessories	27.69	48.77	176
Sweaters and vests	14.33	18.50	129
Active sportswear	11.70	16.02	137
Shirts	75.18	101.49	135
Pants	60.44	84.55	140
Shorts and shorts sets	14.22	29.91	210
Uniforms	3.36	4.31	128
Costumes	2.03	7.36	363
Boys, aged 2 to 15	90.15	113.80	126
Coats and jackets	6.28	5.18	82
Sweaters	2.60	3.45	133
Shirts	20.60	26.50	129
Underwear	4.04	4.02	100
Nightwear	1.78	2.31	130
Hosiery	3.23	2.89	89
Accessories	6.93	8.75	126
Suits, sportcoats, and vests	5.02	3.94	78
Pants	21.03	36.62	174
Shorts and shorts sets	9.66	11.86	123
Uniforms and active sportswear	7.63	7.35	96
Costumes	1.35	0.94	70
Women and girls	**651.83**	**937.45**	**144**
Women, aged 16 or older	552.01	837.82	152
Coats and jackets	51.10	105.08	206
Dresses	76.08	104.66	138
Sportcoats and tailored jackets	4.47	7.79	174
Sweaters and vests	35.23	59.83	170
Shirts, blouses, and tops	92.00	143.35	156
Skirts	22.91	31.97	140
Pants	57.78	82.76	143
Shorts and shorts sets	24.25	49.48	204

(continued)

(continued from previous page)

	average spending of total consumer units	consumer units headed by 45-to-54-year-olds	
		average spending	indexed spending*
Active sportswear	$23.62	$24.76	105
Sleepwear	25.57	33.65	132
Undergarments	27.72	48.65	176
Hosiery	24.60	35.12	143
Suits	36.11	46.51	129
Accessories	47.23	57.80	122
Uniforms	1.34	2.01	150
Costumes	2.00	4.40	220
Girls, aged 2 to 15	99.81	99.63	100
Coats and jackets	7.75	7.57	98
Dresses and suits	13.82	13.72	99
Shirts, blouses, and sweaters	23.96	26.44	110
Skirts and pants	16.29	16.79	103
Shorts and shorts sets	9.02	7.81	87
Active sportswear	7.15	6.78	95
Underwear and sleepwear	7.59	7.41	98
Hosiery	5.17	4.19	81
Accessories	4.08	2.71	66
Uniforms	1.95	2.61	134
Costumes	3.06	3.60	118
Children under age 2	**79.85**	**57.30**	**72**
Coats, jackets, and snowsuits	2.72	2.92	107
Dress and outerwear	21.37	23.09	108
Underwear	46.65	21.60	46
Nightwear and loungewear	3.85	4.70	122
Accessories	5.26	4.99	95
Footwear	**253.65**	**347.64**	**137**
Men's	80.57	120.12	149
Boys'	33.02	51.01	154
Women's	114.13	162.59	142
Girls'	25.93	13.92	54
Other apparel products and services	**264.03**	**346.68**	**131**
Material for making clothes	6.85	9.33	136
Sewing patterns and notions	2.32	4.63	200
Watches	23.41	35.33	151
Jewelry	103.30	140.51	136
Shoe repair and other shoe services	2.97	4.00	135

(continued)

(continued from previous page)

	average spending of total consumer units	consumer units headed by 45-to-54-year-olds	
		average spending	indexed spending*
Coin-operated apparel laundry and dry cleaning	$36.01	$26.55	74
Alteration, repair, and tailoring of apparel and accessories	6.73	6.91	103
Clothing rental	3.70	7.95	215
Watch and jewelry repair services	5.51	8.12	147
Apparel laundry, dry cleaning, not coin-operated	72.44	103.05	142
Clothing storage	0.81	0.28	35
TRANSPORTATION	**6,044.16**	**7,893.20**	**131**
Vehicle purchases (net outlay)	**2,724.66**	**3,386.66**	**124**
Cars and trucks, new	1,390.51	1,724.48	124
New cars	749.71	834.14	111
New trucks	640.80	890.34	139
Cars and trucks, used	1,289.97	1,581.15	123
Used cars	863.70	1,065.84	123
Used trucks	426.27	515.30	121
Other vehicles	44.18	81.03	183
New motorcycles	23.80	47.55	200
Used motorcycles	20.38	33.48	164
Gasoline and motor oil	**985.91**	**1,294.59**	**131**
Gasoline	878.15	1,140.43	130
Diesel fuel	9.23	21.24	230
Gasoline on out-of-town trips	86.21	116.62	135
Gasohol	0.15	-	-
Motor oil	11.31	15.12	134
Motor oil on out-of-town trips	0.87	1.18	136
Other vehicle expenses	**1,952.54**	**2,719.71**	**139**
Vehicle finance charges	235.30	342.51	146
Automobile finance charges	137.45	204.50	149
Truck finance charges	86.14	115.13	134
Motorcycle and plane finance charges	0.97	0.91	94
Other vehicle finance charges	10.74	21.98	205
Maintenance and repairs	680.27	933.04	137
Coolant, additives, brake, transmission fluids	6.11	8.29	136
Tires	86.89	121.95	140

(continued)

(continued from previous page)

	average spending of total consumer units	consumer units headed by 45-to-54-year-olds	
		average spending	indexed spending*
Parts, equipment, and accessories	$112.58	$156.40	139
Vehicle audio equipment, excluding labor	5.11	5.52	108
Vehicle products	4.78	5.89	123
Misc. auto repair, servicing	33.27	58.34	175
Body work and painting	34.63	37.40	108
Clutch, transmission repair	44.21	71.57	162
Drive shaft and rear-end repair	5.69	6.77	119
Brake work	42.05	58.77	140
Repair to steering or front-end	17.98	25.47	142
Repair to engine cooling system	22.08	32.83	149
Motor tune-up	41.69	56.90	136
Lube, oil change, and oil filters	38.53	45.49	118
Front-end alignment, wheel balance and rotation	9.54	11.31	119
Shock absorber replacement	6.59	8.77	133
Brake adjustment	3.69	4.93	134
Gas tank repair, replacement	2.23	2.40	108
Repair tires and other repair work	26.87	33.32	124
Vehicle air conditioning repair	15.00	25.17	168
Exhaust system repair	19.74	23.79	121
Electrical system repair	30.22	44.18	146
Motor repair, replacement	65.90	81.33	123
Auto repair service policy	4.87	6.26	129
Vehicle insurance	689.64	934.76	136
Vehicle rental, leases, licenses, and other charges	347.34	509.40	147
Leased and rented vehicles	200.82	313.61	156
Rented vehicles	37.56	49.48	132
Auto rental	5.99	4.24	71
Auto rental, out-of-town trips	24.44	38.96	159
Truck rental	1.54	1.10	71
Truck rental, out-of-town trips	4.32	3.56	82
Aircraft rental	0.17	-	-
Motorcycle rental, out-of-town trips	0.10	0.17	170
Aircraft rental, out-of-town trips	1.01	1.45	144
Leased vehicles	163.26	264.13	162
Car lease payments	109.24	198.68	182
Cash downpayment (car lease)	13.22	30.32	229

(continued)

	average spending of total consumer units	consumer units headed by 45-to-54-year-olds	
		average spending	indexed spending*
Termination fee (car lease)	$0.37	$0.80	216
Truck lease payments	36.55	30.22	83
Cash downpayment (truck lease)	3.86	4.12	107
Termination fee (truck lease)	0.03	-	-
State and local registration	79.21	102.55	129
Drivers' license	6.96	9.46	136
Vehicle inspection	8.36	9.92	119
Parking fees	25.59	39.80	156
Parking fees in home city, excluding residence	22.49	35.59	158
Parking fees, out-of-town trips	3.10	4.21	136
Tolls	9.34	12.19	131
Tolls on out-of-town trips	4.63	5.81	125
Towing charges	4.96	6.18	125
Automobile service clubs	7.47	9.87	132
Public transportation	381.05	492.25	129
Airline fares	249.48	327.94	131
Intercity bus fares	11.34	13.92	123
Intracity mass transit fares	47.65	61.45	129
Local trans. on out-of-town trips	10.35	11.24	109
Taxi fares on trips	6.08	6.60	109
Taxi fares	7.70	5.97	78
Intercity train fares	16.24	19.00	117
Ship fares	31.13	43.98	141
School bus	1.07	2.16	202
HEALTH CARE	**1,754.74**	**1,854.98**	**106**
Health insurance	**814.95**	**772.43**	**95**
Commercial health insurance	262.44	347.91	133
Blue Cross/Blue Shield	160.50	155.39	97
Health maintenance plans (HMO's)	122.81	154.95	126
Medicare payments	153.65	37.67	25
Commercial Medicare supplements/ other health insurance	115.55	76.51	66
Medical services	**571.04**	**673.16**	**118**
Physician's services	163.63	173.70	106
Dental services	188.04	237.93	127
Eye care services	29.51	34.28	116

(continued)

(continued from previous page)

	average spending of total consumer units	consumer units headed by 45-to-54-year-olds	
		average spending	indexed spending*
Services by professionals other than physicians	$31.92	$52.42	164
Lab tests, x-rays	24.95	30.04	120
Hospital room	47.81	63.97	134
Hospital services other than room	59.54	61.86	104
Care in convalescent or nursing home	13.49	11.22	83
Repair of medical equipment	0.03	-	-
Other medical care services	12.12	7.74	64
Drugs	**285.78**	**290.61**	**102**
Non-prescription drugs	76.19	88.26	116
Prescription drugs	209.58	202.35	97
Medical supplies	**82.98**	**118.78**	**143**
Eyeglasses and contact lenses	50.99	76.34	150
Hearing aids	0.73	4.45	610
Topicals and dressings	22.94	28.24	123
Medical equipment for general use	2.53	3.93	155
Supportive/convalescent medical equipment	3.83	2.58	67
Rental of medical equipment	0.68	0.42	62
Rental of supportive, convalescent medical equipment	1.28	2.82	220
ENTERTAINMENT	**1,566.93**	**2,104.25**	**134**
Fees and admissions	**439.11**	**560.20**	**128**
Recreation expenses, out of town trips	20.93	27.96	134
Social, recreation, civic club membership	84.23	100.44	119
Fees for participant sports	73.54	69.23	94
Participant sports, out-of-town trips	26.99	40.55	150
Movie, theater, opera, ballet	76.23	97.37	128
Movie, other admissions, out-of-town trips	36.38	50.21	138
Admission to sporting events	32.42	37.44	115
Admission to sports events, out-of-town trips	12.13	16.74	138
Fees for recreational lessons	55.31	92.29	167
Other entertainment services, out-of-town trips	20.93	27.96	134
Television, radio, and sound equipment	**533.16**	**635.36**	**119**
Televisions	370.56	452.35	122
Community antenna or cable TV	209.60	254.50	121
Black and white TV	1.79	10.57	591

(continued)

(continued from previous page)

	average spending of total consumer units	consumer units headed by 45-to-54-year-olds	
		average spending	indexed spending*
Color TV, console	$24.03	$18.82	78
Color TV, portable/table model	53.02	59.29	112
VCR's and video disc players	32.24	49.47	153
Video cassettes, tapes, and discs	21.90	27.62	126
Video game hardware and software	19.21	21.53	112
Repair of TV, radio, and sound equipment	8.43	9.93	118
Rental of televisions	0.33	0.61	185
Radios and sound equipment	162.60	183.02	113
Radios	9.21	9.76	106
Tape recorders and players	6.05	3.78	62
Sound components/component systems	30.28	31.70	105
Miscellaneous sound equipment	1.18	1.95	165
Sound equipment accessories	4.75	1.50	32
Compact disc, tape, record, and video mail order clubs	12.08	13.94	115
Records, CDs, audio tapes, needles	36.16	44.09	122
Rental of VCR, radio, sound equipment	0.36	0.08	22
Musical instruments and accessories	17.02	19.68	116
Rental and repair of musical instruments	1.92	2.92	152
Rental of video cassettes, tapes, films, and discs	43.58	53.62	123
Pets, toys, and playground equipment	**288.73**	**389.26**	**135**
Pets	165.03	253.59	154
Pet food	75.80	123.49	163
Pet purchase, supplies, and medicines	26.15	39.09	149
Pet services	15.53	20.63	133
Veterinary services	47.56	70.38	148
Toys, games, hobbies, and tricycles	121.11	133.31	110
Playground equipment	2.59	2.36	91
Other entertainment equipment, supplies, and services	**305.92**	**519.43**	**170**
Unmotored recreational vehicles	27.76	80.01	288
Boats without motor and boat trailer	5.13	2.34	46
Trailers and other attachable campers	22.63	77.67	343
Motorized recreational vehicles	81.56	172.91	212
Motorized campers	16.55	34.32	207
Other motorized recreational vehicles	22.84	5.39	24
Boats with motor	42.17	133.21	316

(continued)

(continued from previous page)

	average spending of total consumer units	consumer units headed by 45-to-54-year-olds	
		average spending	indexed spending*
Rental of recreational vehicles	$2.33	$1.01	43
Rental of noncamper trailer	0.11	-	-
Boat and trailer rental, out-of-town trips	0.80	0.06	8
Rental of campers on out-of-town trips	0.35	0.22	63
Rental of other vehicles on out-of-town trips	0.66	0.56	85
Rental of boat	0.08	0.03	38
Rental of motorized camper	0.19	-	-
Rental of other RVs	0.14	0.14	100
Outboard motors	1.79	5.01	280
Docking and landing fees	5.59	11.31	202
Sports, recreation, and exercise equipment	107.91	152.10	141
Athletic gear, game tables, and exercise equipment	51.01	67.45	132
Bicycles	13.36	13.87	104
Camping equipment	3.23	3.93	122
Hunting and fishing equipment	18.99	29.10	153
Winter sports equipment	5.08	10.08	198
Water sports equipment	6.03	12.14	201
Other sports equipment	8.44	13.90	165
Rental and repair of sports equipment	1.77	1.63	92
Photographic equipment, supplies, and services	70.55	91.40	130
Film	19.61	23.78	121
Other photographic supplies	0.36	0.14	39
Film processing	27.15	33.05	122
Repair and rental of photographic equip.	0.32	0.71	222
Photographic equipment	12.50	16.34	131
Photographer fees	10.60	17.38	164
Fireworks	1.58	0.18	11
Souvenirs	0.51	0.79	155
Visual goods	1.77	1.18	67
Pinball and electronic video games	4.58	3.54	77
PERSONAL CARE PRODUCTS AND SERVICES	**396.66**	**507.01**	**128**
Personal care products	**219.22**	**311.64**	**142**
Hair care products	46.35	65.29	141
Nonelectric articles for the hair	6.36	11.60	182

(continued)

(continued from previous page)

	average spending of total consumer units	consumer units headed by 45-to-54-year-olds	
		average spending	indexed spending*
Wigs and hairpieces	$0.83	$1.14	137
Oral hygiene products, articles	23.10	29.08	126
Shaving needs	12.07	15.60	129
Cosmetics, perfume, and bath preparation	99.46	150.15	151
Deodorant, feminine hygiene products, misc.	26.87	33.67	125
Electric personal care appliances	4.18	5.12	122
Personal care services	**177.45**	**195.38**	**110**
Personal care services/female	87.44	86.19	99
Personal care services/male	89.89	109.05	121
Repair of personal care appliances	0.12	0.13	108
READING	**164.80**	**203.94**	**124**
Newspapers, subscription	52.48	59.79	114
Newspapers, non-subscription	17.83	22.57	127
Magazines, subscription	24.59	28.44	116
Magazines, non-subscription	12.19	15.57	128
Newsletters	0.11	-	-
Books purchased through book clubs	10.51	11.77	112
Books not purchased through book clubs	45.85	65.06	142
Encyclopedia and other reference book sets	1.23	0.73	59
EDUCATION	**459.88**	**882.31**	**192**
College tuition	271.59	548.31	202
Elementary/high school tuition	64.79	128.23	198
Other school tuition	14.46	31.44	217
Other school expenses including rentals	18.85	39.63	210
School books, supplies, equipment for college	38.29	68.60	179
School books, supplies, equipment for elementary/high school	9.51	11.98	126
School books, supplies, equipment for day care, nursery, other	3.34	4.96	149
School supplies, etc., unspecified	39.04	49.17	126
TOBACCO PRODUCTS AND SMOKING SUPPLIES	**258.55**	**327.04**	**126**
Cigarettes	236.05	301.49	128
Other tobacco products	21.06	23.49	112
1Smoking accessories	1.44	2.06	143

(continued)

(continued from previous page)

	average spending of total consumer units	consumer units headed by 45-to-54-year-olds	
		average spending	indexed spending*
MISCELLANEOUS EXPENSES	**$748.51**	**$1,070.71**	**143**
Miscellaneous fees, pari-mutuel losses	44.69	67.14	150
Legal fees	112.87	187.42	166
Funeral expenses	85.75	108.92	127
Safe deposit box rental	5.69	6.64	117
Checking accounts, other			
bank service charges	26.49	35.16	133
Cemetery lots, vaults, and maintenance fees	18.48	11.73	63
Accounting fees	43.06	47.23	110
Miscellaneous personal services	22.50	15.13	67
Finance charges, except mortgage			
and vehicles	205.23	293.79	143
Occupational expenses	84.96	171.84	202
Expenses for other properties	93.52	115.38	123
Interest paid, home equity line			
of credit (other property)	0.42	2.40	571
Credit card memberships	92.98	7.93	9
CASH CONTRIBUTIONS	**960.31**	**1,435.82**	**150**
Cash contributions to non-cu member,			
incl. students, alimony, child support	265.01	670.75	253
Gifts of cash, stocks and bonds			
to non-cu member	206.25	145.88	71
Contributions to charities	90.33	136.40	151
Contributions to church	363.85	431.14	118
Contributions to educational organizations	21.24	30.86	145
Contributions to political organizations	7.17	10.94	153
Other contributions	6.45	9.83	152
PERSONAL INSURANCE			
AND PENSIONS	**2,957.19**	**4538.97**	**153**
Life and other personal			
insurances except health	**397.69**	**590.19**	**148**
Life, endowment, annuity,			
other personal insurance	380.59	571.33	150
Other nonhealth insurance	17.11	18.86	110
Pensions and Social Security	**2,559.49**	**3948.78**	**154**
Deductions for government retirement	70.79	181.49	256
Deductions for railroad retirement	4.53	8.19	181

(continued)

(continued from previous page)

	average spending of total consumer units	consumer units headed by 45-to-54-year-olds	
		average spending	indexed spending*
Deductions for private pensions	$273.66	$475.94	174
Non-payroll deposit to retirement plans	298.11	490.58	165
Deductions for Social Security	1,912.40	2792.58	146
GIFTS*	**1,007.51**	**1,649.72**	**164**
Food	**84.05**	**175.97**	**209**
Cakes and cupcakes	2.44	4.43	182
Candy and chewing gum	9.86	12.47	126
Potato chips and other snacks	2.04	3.27	160
Board (including at school)	27.35	77.23	282
Catered affairs	18.48	40.39	219
Housing	**262.20**	**409.16**	**156**
Housekeeping supplies	37.84	45.17	119
Other household products	8.28	7.90	95
Miscellaneous household products	4.99	5.51	110
Lawn and garden supplies	2.14	1.28	60
Postage and stationery	27.69	33.18	120
Stationery, stationery supplies, giftwraps	22.27	30.02	135
Postage	5.42	3.16	58
Household textiles	15.73	23.94	152
Bathroom linens	2.56	4.94	193
Bedroom linens	10.39	13.02	125
Appliances and misc. housewares	26.36	38.66	147
Major appliances	5.46	10.34	189
Small appliances and misc. housewares	20.90	28.32	136
China and other dinnerware	3.43	5.67	165
Glassware	4.29	1.71	40
Nonelectric cookware	2.54	6.16	243
Tableware, nonelectric kitchenware	3.07	3.45	112
Small electric kitchen appliances	3.79	5.37	142
Miscellaneous household equipment	65.40	106.41	163
Lamps and lighting fixtures	3.66	6.15	168
Other household decorative items	24.59	38.41	156
Lawn and garden equipment	2.30	0.34	15
Indoor plants and flowers	16.77	31.09	185
Computers and computer hardware, nonbusiness use	5.60	10.17	182

(continued)

(continued from previous page)

	average spending of total consumer units	consumer units headed by 45-to-54-year-olds	
		average spending	indexed spending*
Other housing	$116.87	$194.98	167
Repair or maintenance services	5.00	1.60	32
Housing while attending school	36.93	114.78	311
Lodging on out-of-town trips	2.49	4.31	173
Electricity (renter)	9.95	8.70	87
Telephone services in home city, excl. mobile car phone	12.04	8.47	70
Day-care centers, nursery, and preschools	12.40	3.94	32
Housekeeping services	5.52	7.85	142
Gardening, lawn care services	2.48	2.01	81
Moving, storage, freight express	2.29	1.02	45
Sofas	2.72	5.44	200
Kitchen, dining room furniture	2.26	3.36	149
Infants' furniture	2.18	6.24	286
Apparel and services	**246.23**	**319.02**	**130**
Males, aged 2 or older	64.05	80.14	125
Men's coats and jackets	4.46	4.12	92
Men's accessories	5.71	6.41	112
Men's sweaters and vests	3.26	3.72	114
Men's active sportswear	2.24	3.43	153
Men's shirts	15.44	15.17	98
Men's pants	5.72	8.50	149
Boys' shirts	4.95	5.58	113
Boys' accessories	2.02	1.88	93
Boys' pants	3.73	8.98	241
Boys' shorts and short sets	2.07	2.13	103
Females, aged 2 or older	93.94	129.21	138
Women's coats and jackets	10.55	33.34	316
Women's dresses	9.92	11.82	119
Women's vests and sweaters	6.44	5.21	81
Women's shirts, tops, blouses	14.50	13.92	96
Women's pants	5.12	6.30	123
Women's active sportswear	3.30	4.88	148
Women's sleepwear	5.85	12.02	205
Women's undergarments	2.30	5.26	229
Women's suits	2.42	3.89	161
Women's accessories	10.27	5.39	52

(continued)

(continued from previous page)

	average spending of total consumer units	consumer units headed by 45-to-54-year-olds	
		average spending	indexed spending*
Girls' dresses and suits	$3.23	$2.83	88
Girls' shirts, blouses, sweaters	6.04	8.01	133
Girls' skirts and pants	2.23	2.93	131
Children under age 2	34.90	46.93	134
Infant dresses, outerwear	13.81	21.56	156
Infant underwear	14.38	14.08	98
Infant nightwear, loungewear	2.50	4.32	173
Infant accessories	2.78	4.38	158
Other apparel products and services	53.33	62.73	118
Jewelry and watches	25.94	22.27	86
Watches	3.40	5.27	155
Jewelry	22.54	17.00	75
All other apparel products and services	27.40	40.47	148
Men's footwear	8.18	11.74	144
Boys' footwear	4.83	11.29	234
Women's footwear	7.59	10.43	137
Girls' footwear	4.94	3.96	80
Transportation	**56.11**	**95.83**	**171**
New cars	7.43	9.63	130
Used cars	11.40	21.44	188
Gasoline on out-of-town trips	13.14	19.64	149
Airline fares	9.19	16.49	179
Ship fares	4.74	9.88	208
Health care	**34.69**	**44.81**	**129**
Physicians services	2.66	5.96	224
Dental services	3.43	7.22	210
Hospital room	3.66	0.43	12
Hospital service other than room	3.68	0.30	8
Care in convalescent or nursing home	11.30	10.51	93
Prescription drugs	2.28	5.51	242
Entertainment	**83.57**	**116.03**	**139**
Toys, games, hobbies, tricycles	32.48	43.67	134
Other entertainment	51.08	72.36	142
Movie, other admission, out-of-town trips	7.27	7.73	106
Admission to sports events, out-of-town trips	2.42	2.58	107
Fees for recreational lessons	4.96	13.32	269

(continued)

(continued from previous page)

	average spending of total consumer units	consumer units headed by 45-to-54-year-olds	
		average spending	indexed spending*
Community antenna or cable TV	$2.81	$2.14	76
Color TV, portable/table model	2.01	3.53	176
VCRs, video disc players	2.67	5.76	216
Video game hardware and software	2.00	2.60	130
Radios	4.70	0.87	19
Sound components and component systems	2.05	3.01	147
Veterinary services	3.48	3.92	113
Athletic gear, game tables, and exercise equipment	3.46	2.21	64
Education	**114.09**	**323.64**	**284**
College tuition	86.94	241.92	278
Elementary, high school tuition	6.43	21.18	329
Other schools tuition	3.09	14.10	456
Other school expenses including rentals	4.72	12.62	267
School books, supplies, equipment for college	6.56	23.36	356
School supplies, etc., unspecified	5.32	8.49	160
All other gifts	126.58	165.27	131
Gifts of out-of-town trip expenses	49.51	54.76	111
Other gifts	**77.06**	**110.50**	**143**

* The index compares the average spending of consumer units headed by 45-to-54-year-olds with the average spending of all consumer units by dividing the spending of 45-to-54-year-olds by average total spending in each category and multiplying by 100. An index of 100 means that the spending of 45-to-54-year-olds in that category equals average spending. An index of 132 means that the spending of 45-to-54-year-olds is 32 percent above average, while an index of 75 means that the spending of 45-to-54-year-olds is 25 percent below average.
** This figure does not include the amount paid for mortgage principle, which is considered an asset.
*** Expenditures on gifts are also included in the preceding product and service categories. Food spending, for example, includes the amount spent on food gifts. Only gift categories with average spending of $2.00 or more by the average consumer unit are shown.
Note: The Bureau of Labor Statistics uses consumer units rather than households as the sampling unit in the Consumer Expenditure survey. For the definition of consumer unit, see the Glossary. Expenditures listed for items in a given category may not add to the total for that category because the listing is incomplete. (-) means the sample is too small to make a reliable estimate.
Source: Bureau of Labor Statistics, unpublished tables from the 1994 Consumer Expenditure Survey

5

Labor Force

♦ In 1960, the labor force participation rate of men aged 35 to 44 was 56 percentage points higher than that of their female counterparts. By 1995, it was only 15 points higher.

♦ With white men accounting for slightly less than half—46 percent—of all workers aged 35 to 54, the typical worker in this age group is a woman or minority.

♦ Because people aged 35 to 54 are usually settled in their careers, unemployment rates are lower for this age group than for workers as a whole.

♦ Seven out of ten couples aged 35 to 54 are two-income.

♦ Among the 125 million employed Americans in 1995, 59 million were between the ages of 35 and 54—or 47 percent of the total.

♦ Workers aged 35 to 54 account for a majority of registered nurses, psychologists, actors and directors, architects, engineers, physicians, teachers, clergy, and lawyers.

♦ Among 35-to-54-year-olds, 9 percent are self-employed, accounting for 55 percent of the nation's self-employed.

♦ Women's labor force participation rates are projected to surpass 80 percent by 2005, while men's participation rates are projected to drop slightly.

Most Mid-Youth Men and Women Work

But men are less likely to work, while women are more likely.

Over the past three decades, the labor force participation rates of men and women aged 35 to 54 have moved in opposite directions. Men's rates have fallen while women's have increased sharply. Between 1960 and 1995, the labor force participation rate of women aged 35 to 44 grew by 36 percentage points, while that for women aged 45 to 54 gained 26 percentage points. In contrast, the labor force participation rate fell by 6 percentage points for men aged 35 to 44 and by 7 percentage points for men aged 45 to 54. As women went to work, more men could take time off to go to school or even stay home and care for their children.

Men and women aged 35 to 54 are more likely to work than is the population as a whole. Among all men aged 16 or older, 75 percent were in the labor force in 1995, far below the 92 percent rate for men aged 35 to 44. Among all women aged 16 or older, 59 percent were in the labor force, well below the 77 percent rate for women aged 35 to 44. Participation rates are lower for all men and women because millions of nonworking elderly are included in the population aged 16-plus.

◆ In 1960, the labor force participation rate of men aged 35 to 44 was 56 percentage points higher than that of their female counterparts. By 1995, it was only 15 points higher. As the labor force participation rates of men and women in middle-age converge, their lifestyles are becoming more alike, changing consumer behavior.

Labor Force Participation Rates by Sex, 1960 to 1995

(labor force participation rates for total persons aged 16 or older and for persons aged 35 to 54 by sex, selected years 1960 to 1995; percentage point change, 1960-95)

	1995	*1990*	*1980*	*1970*	*1960*	*percentage point change 1960-1995*
Total men aged 16 or older	75.0%	76.1%	78.2%	80.0%	83.4%	-8.4%
Aged 35 to 44	92.3	94.4	96.2	97.3	97.9	-5.6
Aged 45 to 54	88.8	90.7	92.1	94.9	96.1	-7.3
Total women aged 16 or older	58.9	57.5	51.2	42.6	36.5	22.4
Aged 35 to 44	77.2	76.5	65.0	49.9	41.5	35.7
Aged 45 to 54	74.4	71.2	59.6	53.7	48.6	25.8

Sources: Bureau of Labor Statistics, Employment and Earnings, *January 1996 and January 1991; and* Handbook of Labor Statistics, *Bulletin 2340, 1989*

White Men Have Highest Labor Force Rates

Over 90 percent of white men aged 35 to 54 work.

Among 35-to-54-year-olds, white men have the highest labor force participation rates, with at least 90 percent at work or looking for work. The lowest participation rates are found among Hispanic women—only 61 percent of those aged 45 to 54 were in the labor force in 1995.

The labor force participation rates of middle-aged Hispanic men are slightly below those of white men, while the rates for black men are far lower than the white rates. Only 79 percent of black men aged 45 to 54 are in the labor force, a rate not much higher than the 71 percent for their female counterparts. Among blacks, there are more women than men in the labor force.

◆ The typical middle-aged worker is no longer a white man. With white men accounting for slightly less than half—46 percent—of all workers aged 35 to 54, the typical worker in this age group is a woman or a minority.

Labor Force Participation Rates by Race and Hispanic Origin, 1995

(number and percent of total persons aged 16 or older and persons aged 35 to 54 in the civilian labor force, by sex, race, and Hispanic origin, 1995)

	white		black		Hispanic	
	number in labor force	*percent in labor force*	*number in labor force*	*percent in labor force*	*number in labor force*	*percent in labor force*
Total men, 16 or older	61,146	75.7%	7,183	69.0%	7,376	79.1%
Aged 35 to 44	16,414	93.4	1,987	84.1	1,795	91.3
Aged 45 to 54	11,730	90.0	1,148	78.5	965	85.6
Total women, 16 or older	50,804	59.0	7,634	59.5	4,891	52.6
Aged 35 to 44	13,697	77.6	2,178	77.3	1,318	65.9
Aged 45 to 54	10,074	75.2	1,256	70.5	706	60.5

Sources: Bureau of Labor Statistics, Employment and Earnings, *January 1996*

Few Mid-Youth Workers
Are Unemployed

Fewer than 4 percent of 35-to-54-year-olds were unemployed in 1995.

Because people aged 35 to 54 are usually settled in their careers, unemployment rates are lower for this age group than for workers as a whole. Overall, 5.6 percent of people aged 16 or older were working or looking for work in 1995, versus 3.9 percent of people aged 35 to 54. Within this age group, unemployment is highest for men and women aged 35 to 39, but still below the national rate.

Among middle-aged men, labor force participation rates are highest for those in the 35-to-39 age group, at 93 percent. The rate drops in each successive five-year age group, to just 86 percent among those aged 50 to 54. For middle-aged women, labor force participation rates peak in the 40-to-44 age group at 78 percent. By five-year age group, the gap in the labor force participation rates of men and women ranges narrowly from 13 to 16 percentage points.

◆ For companies marketing to mid-youth workers, it's important to note that there are almost as many women in the labor force as men—28 million versus 33 million. Women account for 47 percent of all workers in the 35-to-54 age group.

Employment Status by Sex, 1995

(number and percent of total persons aged 16 or older and persons aged 35 to 54 in the civilian labor force by sex and employment status, 1995; numbers in thousands)

	civilian, non-institutional population	civilian labor force			unemployed	
		total	percent of population	employed	number	percent of labor force
Total, aged 16 or older	198,584	132,304	66.6%	124,900	7,404	5.6%
Aged 35 to 54	73,228	60,974	83.3	58,580	2,394	3.9
Aged 35 to 44	42,254	35,751	84.6	34,201	1,549	4.3
Aged 45 to 54	30,974	25,223	81.4	24,379	845	3.4
Aged 35 to 39	22,105	18,633	84.3	17,769	863	4.6
Aged 40 to 44	20,149	17,118	85.0	16,432	686	4.0
Aged 45 to 49	17,498	14,668	83.8	14,165	503	3.4
Aged 50 to 54	13,476	10,555	78.3	10,214	342	3.2
Men, aged 16 or older	95,178	71,360	75.0	67,377	3,983	5.6
Aged 35 to 54	35,912	32,610	90.8	31,331	1,279	3.9
Aged 35 to 44	20,801	19,189	92.3	18,374	815	4.2
Aged 45 to 54	15,111	13,421	88.8	12,957	464	3.5
Aged 35 to 39	10,895	10,074	92.5	9,620	454	4.5
Aged 40 to 44	9,906	9,115	92.0	8,754	361	4.0
Aged 45 to 49	8,572	7,773	90.7	7,506	267	3.4
Aged 50 to 54	6,539	5,648	86.4	5,451	197	3.5
Women, aged 16 or older	103,406	60,944	58.9	57,523	3,421	5.6
Aged 35 to 54	37,316	28,363	76.0	27,248	1,116	3.9
Aged 35 to 44	21,453	16,562	77.2	15,828	735	4.4
Aged 45 to 54	15,863	11,801	74.4	11,420	381	3.2
Aged 35 to 39	11,210	8,559	76.3	8,149	410	4.8
Aged 40 to 44	10,243	8,003	78.1	7,679	325	4.1
Aged 45 to 49	8,926	6,894	77.2	6,658	236	3.4
Aged 50 to 54	6,937	4,907	70.7	4,762	145	3.0

Source: Bureau of Labor Statistics, Employment and Earnings, *January 1996*

Most Couples
Are Dual-Earners

Seven out of ten couples aged 35 to 54 are two-income.

Fully 17 million of the nation's 24 million middle-aged married couples are two-earner—71 percent of couples in the 35-to-54 age group. Fewer than 6 million couples with a householder aged 35 to 54 (23 percent) are traditional—meaning the husband works but not the wife.

Among middle-aged couples, the largest share of traditional couples is found in the 35-to-39 age group, at 27 percent. Many wives in their late 30s are at home caring for children. The dual-earner share of middle-aged couples is smallest in the 50-to-54 age group, at 67 percent. In 1994, this age group did not include baby boomers. As boomers age, the two-earner share of couples in their 50s will rise.

♦ With both spouses in the labor force, middle-aged couples are busy. Because no one specializes in household management, baby-boom couples spend less money than their older counterparts on cleaning supplies and other household products traditionally consumed by housewives.

Two-Income Couples, 1994

(number and percent distribution of total married couples and couples headed by persons aged 35 to 54 by labor force status of husband and wife, 1994; numbers in thousands)

	total couples	husband and wife in labor force	husband only in labor force	wife only in labor force	husband and wife not in labor force
Total couples	53,171	29,279	11,665	3,069	9,158
Total, aged 35 to 54	24,415	17,223	5,641	892	659
Aged 35 to 39	7,118	4,923	1,899	157	139
Aged 40 to 44	6,573	4,852	1,384	201	136
Aged 45 to 49	5,763	4,151	1,203	237	172
Aged 50 to 54	4,961	3,297	1,155	297	212
Total couples	100.0%	55.1%	21.9%	5.8%	17.2%
Total, aged 35 to 54	100.0	70.5	23.1	3.7	2.7
Aged 35 to 39	100.0	69.2	26.7	2.2	2.0
Aged 40 to 44	100.0	73.8	21.1	3.1	2.1
Aged 45 to 49	100.0	72.0	20.9	4.1	3.0
Aged 50 to 54	100.0	66.5	23.3	6.0	4.3

Source: Bureau of the Census, Household and Family Characteristics: March 1994, *Current Population Reports, P20-483, 1995*

Workers Aged 35 to 54 Dominate the Labor Force

Nearly half of the nation's workers are aged 35 to 54.

Among the 125 million employed Americans in 1995, 59 million were between the ages of 35 and 54—or 47 percent of the total. The percentage of employed who are aged 35 to 54 exceeds 50 percent in some occupations. Middle-aged workers account for 57 percent of managers, for example, and for 55 percent of professional specialty workers (such as doctors, nurses, and teachers). Behind this dominance is the fact that people aged 35 to 54 are at the peak of their careers. While just 28 percent of all employed Americans are managers and professionals, the proportion reaches 34 percent among people aged 35 to 54.

Middle-aged workers are least represented in the lowest-paid occupations. They account for just 37 percent of service workers, for example, and for only 31 percent of handlers, equipment cleaners, helpers, and laborers. These occupations tend to attract young adults who are just starting out in the labor force. Only 11 percent of 35-to-54-year-olds are employed in service occupations, versus 14 percent of all employed workers.

◆ Because 35-to-54-year-olds are at the peak of their careers, their earnings are also peaking. Baby boomers now hold the nation's top jobs and many are earning high incomes.

Occupations by Age, 1995

(number of total persons and persons aged 35 to 54 employed by occupation, 1994; numbers in thousands)

	total	35 to 54	35 to 44	45 to 54
Total, employed	124,900	58,580	34,202	24,378
Managerial & professional specialty	35,318	19,824	11,211	8,613
Executive, administrative & managerial	17,186	9,839	5,469	4,370
Professional specialty	18,132	9,985	5,742	4,243
Technical, sales, & administrative support	37,417	16,579	9,585	6,994
Technicians & related support	3,909	1,936	1,230	706
Sales	15,119	6,138	3,493	2,645
Administrative support, including clerical	18,389	8,506	4,862	3,644
Service	16,930	6,248	3,733	2,515
Private household	821	305	177	128
Protective service	2,237	979	585	394
Other service	13,872	4,964	2,971	1,993
Precision production, craft, & repair	13,524	6,851	4,200	2,651
Mechanics & repairers	4,423	2,278	1,361	917
Construction trades	5,098	2,418	1,546	872
Extractive occupations	136	87	56	31
Precision production	3,867	2,068	1,237	831
Operators, fabricators, & laborers	18,068	7,686	4,650	3,036
Machine operators, assemblers, & inspectors	7,907	3,661	2,170	1,491
Transport & material moving	5,171	2,487	1,503	984
Handlers, equip. cleaners, helpers, & laborers	4,990	1,539	977	562
Farming, forestry, & fishing	3,642	1,392	823	569
Farm operators & managers	1,446	629	341	288
Other agricultural & related occupations	2,010	683	431	252
Forestry & logging	129	49	34	15
Fishing, hunters, & trappers	58	30	17	13

Source: Bureau of Labor Statistics, unpublished data from the 1995 Current Population Survey

Distribution of Workers by Occupation, 1995

(percent distribution of total persons and persons aged 35 to 54 employed by occupation, 1995)

	total	35 to 54	35 to 44	45 to 54
Total, employed	100.0%	100.0%	100.0%	100.0%
Managerial & professional specialty	28.3	33.8	32.8	35.3
Executive, administrative & managerial	13.8	16.8	16.0	17.9
Professional specialty	14.5	17.0	16.8	17.4
Technical, sales, & administrative support	30.0	28.3	28.0	28.7
Technicians & related support	3.1	3.3	3.6	2.9
Sales	12.1	10.5	10.2	10.8
Administrative support, including clerical	14.7	14.5	14.2	14.9
Service	13.6	10.7	10.9	10.3
Private household	0.7	0.5	0.5	0.5
Protective service	1.8	1.7	1.7	1.6
Other service	11.1	8.5	8.7	8.2
Precision production, craft, & repair	10.8	11.7	12.3	10.9
Mechanics & repairers	3.5	3.9	4.0	3.8
Construction trades	4.1	4.1	4.5	3.6
Extractive occupations	0.1	0.1	0.2	0.1
Precision production	3.1	3.5	3.6	3.4
Operators, fabricators, & laborers	14.5	13.1	13.6	12.5
Machine operators, assemblers, & inspectors	6.3	6.2	6.3	6.1
Transport & material moving	4.1	4.2	4.4	4.0
Handlers, equip. cleaners, helpers, & laborers	4.0	2.6	2.9	2.3
Farming, forestry, & fishing	2.9	2.4	2.4	2.3
Farm operators & managers	1.2	1.1	1.0	1.2
Other agricultural & related occupations	1.6	1.2	1.3	1.0
Forestry & logging	0.1	0.1	0.1	0.1
Fishing, hunters, & trappers	0.0	0.1	0.0	0.1

Source: Bureau of Labor Statistics, unpublished data from the 1995 Current Population Survey

Middle-Aged Share of Occupations, 1995

(persons aged 35 to 54 as a share of total employed by occupation, 1995)

	total	35 to 54	35 to 44	45 to 54
Total, employed	100.0%	46.9%	27.4%	19.5%
Managerial & professional specialty	100.0	56.1	31.7	24.4
Executive, administrative & managerial	100.0	57.3	31.8	25.4
Professional specialty	100.0	55.1	31.7	23.4
Technical, sales, & administrative support	100.0	44.3	25.6	18.7
Technicians & related support	100.0	49.5	31.5	18.1
Sales	100.0	40.6	23.1	17.5
Administrative support, including clerical	100.0	46.3	26.4	19.8
Service	100.0	36.9	22.0	14.9
Private household	100.0	37.1	21.6	15.6
Protective service	100.0	43.8	26.2	17.6
Other service	100.0	35.8	21.4	14.4
Precision production, craft, & repair	100.0	50.7	31.1	19.6
Mechanics & repairers	100.0	51.5	30.8	20.7
Construction trades	100.0	47.4	30.3	17.1
Extractive occupations	100.0	64.0	41.2	22.8
Precision production	100.0	53.5	32.0	21.5
Operators, fabricators, & laborers	100.0	42.5	25.7	16.8
Machine operators, assemblers, & inspectors	100.0	46.3	27.4	18.9
Transport & material moving	100.0	48.1	29.1	19.0
Handlers, equip. cleaners, helpers, & laborers	100.0	30.8	19.6	11.3
Farming, forestry, & fishing	100.0	38.2	22.6	15.6
Farm operators & managers	100.0	43.5	23.6	19.9
Other agricultural & related occupations	100.0	34.0	21.4	12.5
Forestry & logging	100.0	38.0	26.4	11.6
Fishing, hunters, & trappers	100.0	51.7	29.3	22.4

Source: Bureau of Labor Statistics, unpublished data from the 1995 Current Population Survey

Boomers Are
the Elite Workers

Sixty-two percent of all psychologists are aged 35 to 54.

While workers aged 35 to 54 account for 47 percent of all employed Americans, they are a much larger share of some occupations. Examining the age of workers by detailed occupation shows why boomers—and boomer perspectives—seem to be everywhere.

Workers aged 35 to 54 account for fully 63 percent of all registered nurses, 62 percent of all elementary and secondary school teachers, 62 percent of all psychologists, and 69 percent of all actors and directors. They account for a majority of architects, engineers, physicians, college teachers, clergy, and lawyers. Most insurance and real estate salespeople are aged 35 to 54 as well, along with most mail carriers, secretaries, electricians, firefighters, and plumbers.

There are a few occupations in which people aged 35 to 54 are in the minority, such as economists, editors and reporters, advertising salespeople, police, carpenters, truck and taxicab drivers, and farmers, for example. Some of these occupations are dominated by younger adults (ad sales, police, carpentry), while others are dominated by older people (farmers, economists).

♦ The reluctance of so many businesses to target the 35-to-54 age group may be explained by the age profile of people who sell ads. Since so many are under age 35, they may encourage advertisers to chase after people like themselves rather than the more lucrative mid-youth market.

Employed 35-to-54-Year-Olds by Detailed Occupation, 1995

(number of total persons and persons aged 35 to 54 employed by detailed occupation; 35-to-54-year-olds as a percent of total persons employed by occupation, 1995; numbers in thousands)

	total employed	35-to-54-year-olds	
		employed	percent of total
Architects	163	82	50.3%
Engineers	1,934	1,033	53.4
Computer systems analysts and scientists	933	505	54.1
Physicians	693	405	58.4
Dentists	155	93	60.0
Registered nurses	1,977	1,241	62.8
College teachers	846	444	52.5
Teachers, elementary and secondary	2,964	1,834	61.9
Economists	148	66	44.6
Psychologists	260	161	61.9
Clergy	356	180	50.6
Lawyers	894	524	58.6
Authors	118	59	50.0
Actors and directors	114	79	69.3
Editors and reporters	273	126	46.2
Airplane pilots	114	73	64.0
Insurance sales	562	325	57.8
Real estate sales	718	388	54.0
Advertising sales	151	67	44.4
Secretaries	3,361	1,687	50.2
Mail carriers	362	256	70.7
Firefighters	249	135	54.2
Police	519	243	46.8
Automobile mechanics	819	357	43.6
Carpenters	1,255	540	43.0
Electricians	736	368	50.0
Plumbers	502	260	51.8
Truck drivers	2,861	1,364	47.7
Taxicab drivers	213	100	46.9
Construction laborers	780	289	37.1
Farmers	1,223	521	42.6

Source: Bureau of Labor Statistics, unpublished tables from the 1995 Current Population Survey

Most 35-to-54-Year-Olds Work Full-Time

Even women are likely to work full-time.

Most of America's workers work full-time. This is even more the case for 35-to-54-year-olds than it is for the population as a whole. Among middle-aged men, 96 percent work full-time. Among employed women, 77 percent of those aged 35 to 44 and 80 percent of those aged 45 to 54 work full-time.

The typical woman aged 35 to 54 is a full-time worker—a fact of critical importance to marketers. Overall, 57 percent of women aged 35 to 44 work full-time, 17 percent work part-time, and 26 percent do not work. Among those aged 45 to 54, 58 percent work full-time, 14 percent part-time, and 28 percent do not work.

◆ The lives of men and women aged 35 to 54 are full and fast-paced, making them difficult to reach. Research by the Washington, D.C.-based Pew Research Center for The People and The Press shows that boomers are paying less and less attention to the national media because they're so busy. If even major media are having trouble reaching boomers, finding an efficient way to reach these consumers is the greatest challenge facing mid-youth marketers.

Full-Time and Part-Time Workers by Sex, 1995

(number and percent of total persons aged 16 or older and persons aged 35 to 54 employed full-time and part-time, by sex, 1995; numbers in thousands)

| | total employed | | 35-to-54-year-olds employed | | | |
| | | | 35 to 44 | | 45 to 54 | |
	number	*percent*	*number*	*percent*	*number*	*percent*
Total, men	67,377	100.0%	18,374	100.0%	12,958	100.0%
Full-time	59,936	89.0	17,652	96.1	12,423	95.9
Part-time	7,441	11.0	722	3.9	535	4.1
Total, women	57,522	100.0	15,827	100.0	11,421	100.0
Full-time	41,743	72.6	12,240	77.3	9,127	79.9
Part-time	15,779	27.4	3,587	22.7	2,294	20.1

Source: Bureau of Labor Statistics, unpublished tables from the 1995 Current Population Survey

Few Mid-Youth Workers
Are Self-Employed

But people aged 35 to 54 are more likely to be self-employed than workers as a whole.

Though much has been said about the rise of the entrepreneur during the past decade or so, few Americans are self-employed. Only 8 percent of all nonagricultural workers were self-employed in 1995. Among 35-to-54-year-olds, 9 percent are self-employed. This age group accounts for 55 percent of the nation's self-employed.

Men are more likely to be self-employed than women. Among 35-to-54-year-olds in 1995, 11 percent of working men and 8 percent of working women were self-employed. Self-employment increases with age. Among working men, 10 percent of those aged 35 to 44 and 12 percent of those aged 45 to 54 are self-employed. Among working women, 7 percent of those aged 35 to 44 and 8 percent of those aged 45 to 54 are self-employed.

◆ Because these statistics count only those whose primary job is self-employment, they miss many people who have a business of their own on the side. Consequently, these counts of entrepreneurs are conservative.

Self-Employed Workers by Sex, 1995

(number of nonagricultural workers aged 16 or older and aged 35 to 54 whose longest job in 1995 was self-employment, by sex; self-employed as a percent of nonagricultural workers in age/sex group, and age/sex group's share of total self-employed, 1995; numbers in thousands)

	number of self-employed	percent who are self-employed	% of total self-employed
Total self employed	8,902	7.9%	100.0%
Aged 35 to 54	4,906	9.4	55.1
Aged 35 to 44	2,697	8.8	30.3
Aged 45 to 54	2,209	10.2	24.8
Total self-employed men	5,461	9.2	61.3
Aged 35 to 54	3,022	11.0	33.9
Aged 35 to 44	1,658	10.3	18.6
Aged 45 to 54	1,364	12.2	15.3
Total self-employed women	3,440	6.5	38.6
Aged 35 to 54	1,885	7.6	21.2
Aged 35 to 44	1,039	7.2	11.7
Aged 45 to 54	846	8.1	9.5

Source: Bureau of Labor Statistics, Employment and Earnings, *January 1996*

Middle-Aged Labor
Force to Grow

Almost the entire gain will be in the 45-to-54 age group, however.

Between 1994 and 2005, the number of workers aged 45 to 54 will grow rapidly. While the labor force as a whole is projected to grow by just 8.5 percent during those years, the number of working men aged 45 to 54 will expand by 36 percent. The number of working women in that age group will grow by an even greater 50 percent.

The Bureau of Labor Statistics projects that women's labor force participation rates will surpass 80 percent in the 35-to-54 age group. In contrast, men's participation rates are projected to drop slightly. By 2005, the gap in the labor force participation rates of men and women aged 45 to 54 will shrink to just 7 percentage points.

♦ The huge increase in working women in the 45-to-54 age group suggests that women workers will become an even more powerful force in the economy by the early 21st century. Women in this age group are not constrained by childrearing duties as are younger women. Smart marketers will court the rising ambitions of women who are finally free to devote themselves to their careers.

Labor Force Projections, 1994 and 2005

(number and percent of total persons aged 16 or older and persons aged 35 to 54 in the civilian labor force by sex and employment status, 1994 and 2005; numbers in thousands)

	ciivilian labor force		change, 1994-2005		percent of labor force		labor force participation rate	
	1994	*2005*	*number*	*percent*	*1994*	*2005*	*1994*	*2005*
Men, 16 or older	70,817	76,842	6,025	8.5%	54.0%	52.2%	75.1%	72.9%
Aged 35 to 44	18,968	18,787	-179	-0.9	14.5	12.8	92.8	91.4
Aged 45 to 54	12,962	17,616	4,654	35.9	9.9	12.0	89.1	87.7
Women, 16 or older	60,239	70,263	10,024	16.6	46.0	47.8	58.8	61.7
Aged 35 to 44	16,259	17,078	819	5.0	12.4	11.6	77.1	80.0
Aged 45 to 54	11,357	17,070	5,713	50.3	8.7	11.6	74.6	80.7

Source: Bureau of Labor Statistics, Monthly Labor Review, *November 1995*

6

Health and Fitness

♦ Because boomers are involved in exercise and fitness activities, they are more likely to be healthier in old age than is the current generation of elderly.

♦ Overall, the 11 million people aged 35 to 54 who are without health insurance account for more than one in four uninsured Americans.

♦ Women aged 35 or older accounted for only 6 percent of first births in 1994, 10 percent of second births, 15 percent of third births, and 24 percent of fourth or subsequent births.

♦ Despite all the talk about baby boomers being more health conscious than older Americans, people in their 30s and 40s are less likely to have healthy diets than is the average American.

♦ The percentage of people who participate in fitness activities for at least 100 days a year bottoms out at 20 percent among 35-to-44-year-olds.

♦ However, people aged 45 to 54 are much more likely than the population as a whole to participate frequently in a variety of sports and fitness activities.

♦ Fully 31 percent of acute musculoskeletal conditions are experienced by people aged 45 to 64.

♦ The most prevalent chronic condition among 45-to-64-year-olds is arthritis (24 percent), followed by high blood pressure (22 percent).

♦ AIDS ranks second as a cause of death among 35-to-44-year-olds, fourth among 45-to-54-year-olds, and eighth overall.

Most People Feel Good in Middle-Age

A tiny minority say their health is poor.

The percentage of Americans who say their health is excellent changes only slightly as people age. While 39 percent of 18-to-29-year-olds say they are in excellent health—the highest proportion among all age groups—this share declines only slowly as people enter their 30s, 40s, and 50s.

The proportion who report being in good or excellent health begins to decline steadily once people reach their 60s. In this age group, 25 percent report being in excellent health, while 32 percent say they are in fair or poor health. Despite the decline in health that accompanies aging, only 13 percent of people aged 70 or older report being in poor health, while 20 percent say their health is excellent.

◆ Because boomers are more involved in exercise and fitness than were today's older people in middle-age, boomers are more likely to be healthier in old age than is the current generation of elderly.

"Would you say your own health, in general, is excellent, good, fair, or poor?"

(percent responding by age, 1994)

	excellent	good	fair	poor
Total	31%	47%	17%	5%
Aged 18 to 29	39	48	12	1
Aged 30 to 39	35	50	13	2
Aged 40 to 49	32	47	19	3
Aged 50 to 59	28	48	18	6
Aged 60 to 69	25	43	23	9
Aged 70 or older	20	38	27	13

Note: Percents may not add to 100 because no answer is not included.
Source: 1994 General Social Survey, National Opinion Research Center, University of Chicago

Many Middle-Aged Lack Health Insurance

As boomers reach the age of vulnerability, the health care debate will heat up.

Nearly 40 million Americans—15 percent of the population—did not have health insurance in 1994. The fear of losing health insurance is an important reason for middle-aged Americans' high level of anxiety about their economic security.

Fully 16 percent of people aged 35 to 44 were without health insurance in 1994. Among 45-to-54-year-olds, a substantial 13 percent lacked insurance. Overall, the 11 million people aged 35 to 54 who are without health insurance account for more than one in four uninsured Americans.

Middle-aged Americans who are without health insurance are vulnerable to financial catastrophe. Chronic illness becomes much more common as people enter their late 40s and early 50s. With one in eight 45-to-54-year-olds lacking insurance, a financial crisis looms for many.

◆ Baby boomers have never suffered silently. As the generation enters the ages of vulnerability, expect to hear increasingly strident demands for reform in health care financing.

Health Insurance Coverage by Sex, 1994

(number and percent of total persons and persons aged 35 to 54 by health insurance coverage status and sex, 1994; numbers in thousands)

	total persons	covered by private or government health insurance							not covered
		private health insurance			government health insurance				
		total	total	group health	total	Medicaid	Medicare	military	
Total									
persons	262,105	222,387	184,318	159,634	70,163	31,645	33,901	11,165	39,718
35 to 44	42,334	35,555	32,271	29,894	4,628	2,918	711	1,415	6,780
45 to 54	30,693	26,752	24,874	22,897	3,342	1,499	794	1,406	3,942
Total men	128,072	106,762	90,438	79,743	30,894	13,218	14,513	6,032	21,310
35 to 44	20,972	17,174	15,771	14,638	1,991	1,078	393	751	3,798
45 to 54	15,022	13,130	12,212	11,287	1,689	646	484	770	1,892
Total									
women	134,033	115,625	93,880	79,891	39,269	18,428	19,388	5,134	18,408
35 to 44	21,363	18,381	16,500	15,256	2,637	1,840	317	664	2,982
45 to 54	15,672	13,622	12,662	11,609	1,653	853	310	636	2,050
Total									
persons	100.0%	84.8%	70.3%	60.9%	26.8%	12.1%	12.9%	4.3%	15.2%
35 to 44	100.0	84.0	76.2	70.6	10.9	6.9	1.7	3.3	16.0
45 to 54	100.0	87.2	81.0	74.6	10.9	4.9	2.6	4.6	12.8
Total men	100.0	83.4	70.6	62.3	24.1	10.3	11.3	4.7	16.6
35 to 44	100.0	81.9	75.2	69.8	9.5	5.1	1.9	3.6	18.1
45 to 54	100.0	87.4	81.3	75.1	11.2	4.3	3.2	5.1	12.6
Total women	100.0	86.3	70.0	59.6	29.3	13.7	14.5	3.8	13.7
35 to 44	100.0	86.0	77.2	71.4	12.3	8.6	1.5	3.1	14.0
45 to 54	100.0	86.9	80.8	74.1	10.5	5.4	2.0	4.1	13.1

Note: Numbers will not add to total because some people are covered by more than one type of insurance.
Source: Bureau of the Census, unpublished tables from the 1995 Current Population Survey

Boomers Are
Beyond Childbearing

As the youngest boomers enter their mid-30s, they account for few births.

Among the nearly 4 million babies born to American women in 1994, only 11 percent had mothers aged 35 or older. Despite the fact that many baby boomers delayed having children until their 30s, most babies are still born to younger mothers.

Women aged 35 or older accounted for only 6 percent of first births in 1994. This proportion rises to 10 percent for second births and 15 percent for third births. Even among fourth or subsequent births, however, only one in four mothers was aged 35 or older.

◆ As the large and vocal baby-boom generation ages beyond the childbearing years, the abortion issue will fade into the background. Menopause will replace infertility as the hot topic in the reproductive arena.

Births by Age of Mother, 1993

(total number of births, and number and percent to women aged 35 or older, by age of mother and order of birth, 1993)

	number	percent
TOTAL BIRTHS		
Total to all women	4,000,240	100.0%
Total, aged 35 or older	418,453	10.5
Aged 35 to 39	357,053	8.9
Aged 40 to 44	59,071	1.5
Aged 45 or older	2,329	0.1
FIRST CHILD		
Total to all women	1,619,840	100.0
Total, aged 35 or older	88,360	5.5
Aged 35 to 39	76,129	4.7
Aged 40 to 44	11,806	0.7
Aged 45 or older	425	0.0
SECOND CHILD		
Total to all women	1,289,326	100.0
Total, aged 35 or older	127,205	9.9
Aged 35 to 39	111,764	8.7
Aged 40 to 44	15,065	1.2
Aged 45 or older	376	0.0
THIRD CHILD		
Total to all women	645,596	100.0
Total, aged 35 or older	95,146	14.7
Aged 35 to 39	82,795	12.8
Aged 40 to 44	11,939	1.8
Aged 45 or older	412	0.1
FOURTH OR MORE		
Total to all women	445,478	100.0
Total, aged 35 or older	107,742	24.2
Aged 35 to 39	86,365	19.4
Aged 40 to 44	20,261	4.5
Aged 45 or older	1,116	0.3

Source: National Center for Health Statistics, Advance Report of Final Natality Statistics, 1993, *Vol. 44, No. 3 Supplement, 1995*

Most 35-to-44-Year-Olds Have Children

Two is the most popular number for both men and women.

More than 80 percent of women aged 35 to 44 and men aged 40 to 44 have had at least one child. The proportion is slightly smaller among men aged 35 to 39, because many are married to younger women who are likely to have more children in the future.

The largest proportion of men and women in the 35-to-44 age group have two children. More than one-third of women aged 35 to 44 and men aged 40 to 44 have two, as do 29 percent of men aged 35 to 39.

The percentage of men and women in the 35-to-44 age group with three children is slightly greater than the pecentage who have just one. The only exception is among men aged 35 to 39, many of whom are still having children. Only about one in ten men and women aged 35 to 44 has more than three children.

♦ Because few women aged 35 or older have additional children, these childbearing statistics are not likely to change much as boomers age.

Number of Children Ever Born, 1992

(percent distribution of women and men aged 35 to 39 and 40 to 44 by number of children ever born, 1992)

	women		men	
	35-39	*40-44*	*35-39*	*40-44*
Total	100.0%	100.0%	100.0%	100.0%
None	18.9	16.4	28.1	18.9
One	17.0	17.3	17.9	16.2
Two	36.1	37.3	29.4	37.3
Three	17.6	18.6	15.8	16.7
Four	7.1	6.9	5.9	6.8
Five or more	3.2	3.4	2.8	4.1

Source: Bureau of the Census, Fertility of American Men, *Amara Bachu, Population Division Working Paper Series No. 14, 1996*

Eating Habits of Middle-Aged Are Less Healthy

People in their 30s and 40s are too busy to watch their diets.

Despite all the talk about baby boomers being more health conscious than older Americans, people in their 30s and 40s are less likely to have healthy eating habits than is the average American. The busy lifestyles of people aged 30 to 49, many of whom have young children in the home, may prevent them from watching their diets.

On only three measures of healthy eating do people in their 30s and 40s surpass the average. They are slightly more likely than the average American to say they "always or usually" try new food products. Fifty percent of those in their 30s say they balance their eating of healthy foods with less healthy foods they enjoy more. Perhaps in an attempt to do so, people in their 30s are slightly more likely than the average person to read labels on food packages.

♦ Older people are most likely to practice healthy eating—many of them under doctors' orders. As boomers age into their 50s, consumer interest in healthy eating is likely to surge.

Healthy Eating Habits, 1994

(percent of people aged 18 or older and aged 30 to 49 who always or usually follow selected practices when buying food, by age, 1994)

	total persons 18+	30 to 39	40 to 49
Eat healthy foods	79.4%	77.1%	76.3%
Choose foods that are baked or broiled over fried	72.2	69.7	68.9
Choose breakfast cereals that are low in fat	67.7	62.9	66.1
Choose low fat versions of dairy foods	67.5	62.1	65.1
Read labels on food packages	67.0	70.0	62.4
Maintain a low fat diet	54.9	45.8	51.4
Choose whole grain products over those made with white flour	50.6	47.5	47.2
Take vitamin/mineral supplements at least twice/week	48.2	45.4	46.9
Maintain a low cholesterol diet	47.3	34.0	42.3
Balance healthy foods with less healthy foods I enjoy more	44.8	50.3	40.7
Avoid some favorite foods in order to eat healthier	41.2	35.6	32.5
Avoid some favorite foods in order to lose weight	34.5	33.9	31.7
Try new foods products	33.9	34.9	35.1
Maintain a low calorie diet	30.0	21.1	23.1
Avoid foods that contain red meat	27.3	25.7	24.8
Give up convenience for health benefits	27.0	24.8	23.7
Choose foods that do not contain eggs	18.0	11.0	13.8
Choose foods because they contain organic ingredients	16.3	15.6	13.5
Give up good taste for health benefits	14.8	10.1	9.4
Maintain a vegetarian diet	9.7	8.0	6.0

Source: 1994 Healthfocus Trend Report, HealthFocus, Des Moines, Iowa

Fitness Becomes More Important in Middle-Age

But the biggest fitness enthusiasts are people aged 55 or older.

While the percentage of Americans who regularly participate in sports peaks among 12-to-17-year-olds, fitness participation peaks among people aged 55 or older, according to the Fitness Products Council.

The percentage of people who participate in fitness activities for at least 100 days a year bottoms out at 20 percent among 35-to-44-year-olds. Behind this dip are the busy lifestyles of people in this age group. Many have young children at home and cannot find the time to keep fit regularly.

The percentage who frequently participate in fitness activities rises to 27 percent among 45-to-54-year-olds as children grow up and parents can spend more time on themselves. Fitness participation peaks among people aged 55 or older at 28 percent.

♦ With boomers now filling the 45-to-54 age group, the fitness boom has only just begun.

Sports and Fitness Participation, 1995

(percentage of people frequently participating in sports and fitness activities combined, and percent participating frequently in fitness activities, by age, 1995)

	sports and fitness	fitness only
Aged 6 to 11	48.1%	12.8%
Aged 12 to 17	62.5	24.2
Aged 18 to 24	38.5	21.4
Aged 25 to 34	35.9	23.0
Aged 35 to 44	29.0	20.4
Aged 45 to 54	35.4	26.7
Aged 55 or older	32.3	28.2

Note: Frequent participation in sports activities ranges from 15 to 100 days/year depending on the activity, while frequent participation in fitness activities is 100 or more days/year.
Source: Fitness Products Council, North Palm Beach, Florida, 1996

45-to-54-Year-Olds Are Active in Many Sports

People aged 35 to 44 are too busy to play.

There are only a handful of sports and fitness activities in which 35-to-44-year-olds are more likely to participate frequently than is the average American. Behind their lack of participation are busy lifestyles. Many have young children at home and do not have time to participate in sports or fitness activities.

But good times lie ahead. People aged 45 to 54 are much more likely than the population as a whole to participate frequently in a variety of sports and fitness activities. This age group is most enthusiastic—compared to the general population—about fly fishing, rowing machines, cross-country ski machines, resistance machines, swimming, fitness walking, and golf.

Overall, people aged 35 to 54 account for at least one-third of frequent participants in many sports and fitness activities. Their share is greatest among fly fishers (53 percent), target shooters (42 percent), users of resistance machines (46 percent), rowing machines (41 percent), and cross-country ski machines (62 percent).

◆ As boomers age into the 45-to-54 age group, fitness and recreation activities that appeal to older Americans will boom. These include fitness walking, golf, and camping with recreational vehicles.

Participation by Sports & Fitness Activity, 1995

(total number of persons participating frequently in selected sports and percent of total participants who are aged 35 to 54; number of persons aged 35 to 44 and 45 to 54 participating frequently in selected activities and index of frequent participation, 1995; numbers in thousands; frequent participation means 100 or more days/year unless otherwise indicated by an asterisk)

	total participants	participants 35 to 54	aged 35 to 44		aged 45 to 54	
			number	index	number	index
Aerobic dancing (regular)	1,564	25.1%	216	78	177	88
Aerobic dancing (low impact)	2,367	15.9	242	58	135	44
Aerobics (step)	2,176	28.1	326	84	286	102
Bicycling	4,600	19.1	637	78	240	40
Bowling*	9,401	31.7	1,461	87	1,516	125
Camping (tent)**	6,474	28.8	1,131	98	731	87
Camping (recreational vehicle)**	6,609	29.4	686	58	1,257	147
Fishing (fly)*	1,026	53.0	200	109	344	259
Fishing (freshwater, other)*	9,578	35.3	2,037	119	1,345	109
Fishing (saltwater)*	1,578	36.2	425	151	147	72
Fitness walking	17,208	36.6	2,747	90	3,551	160
Golf*	7,562	39.2	1,369	102	1,595	163
Hiking/backpacking**	3,510	33.1	547	87	616	136
Hunting (shotgun, rifle)*	3,794	35.8	700	104	658	134
Free weights	11,355	29.9	1,640	81	1,754	120
Resistance machine	6,235	46.1	1,378	124	1,494	185
Rowing machine	1,708	40.8	190	63	507	230
Stationary bike	9,383	30.5	1,591	95	1,273	105
Multi-purpose home gym	4,406	31.8	704	90	697	122
Treadmill	7,007	34.1	1,386	111	1,006	111
Stair-climbing machine	3,794	34.4	869	129	438	89
Cross-country ski machine	1,066	62.0	300	158	361	262
Racquetball*	1,421	36.2	247	98	268	146
Roller skating (in-line)*	9,435	4.9	182	11	283	23
Running/jogging	9,463	26.5	1,494	89	1,009	82
Shooting (target)*	3,209	41.7	897	157	441	106
Skiing (cross-country)**	378	13.2	32	47	18	36
Skiing (downhill)**	1,799	19.0	249	78	92	39
Softball (slow pitch)*	8,116	16.3	937	65	387	37
Softball (fast pitch)*	1,471	8.1	70	27	49	26

(continued)

(continued from previous page)

	total participants	participants 35 to 54	aged 35 to 44		aged 45 to 54	
			number	index	number	index
Swimming (fitness)***	4,906	27.0%	340	39	984	155
Tennis*	4,950	23.5	365	41	797	125
Volleyball (hard surface)*	6,180	13.4	677	62	152	19
Volleyball (beach)*	1,379	27.3	316	129	61	64

* 25 or more days/year.
** 15 or more days/year.
*** 52 or more days/year.
Note: The index is calculated by dividing the participation rate of the age group by the overall participation rate for that activity and multiplying by 100. A value of 100 indicates participation equal to the average. Example: an index value of 111 indicates that participation by the age group in the activity is 11 percent greater than average. An index of 87 indicates that participation by the age group in the activity 13 percent below average.
Source: Sports Participation Index, 1995, *prepared for the Sporting Goods Manufacturers Association, North Palm Beach, Florida, by American Sports Data, Inc., Hartsdale, New York, 1996*

Acute Conditions Less Likely in Middle-Age

Middle-aged Americans account for a small share of those who suffer from colds and flu each year.

People aged 45 to 64 accounted for only 13 percent of all acute conditions suffered by Americans in 1994, according to the National Center for Health Statistics (NCHS). As boomers move into this older age group, they can expect to catch fewer colds and experience fewer injuries. Because the NCHS uses broad, 20-year age groupings in its analysis of health conditions, it is not possible to see the steady improvement that occurs in the incidence of acute conditions through middle-age. But a look at how frequently conditions strike people aged 45 to 64 compared to people aged 25 to 44 shows that today's mid-youthers can look forward to some improvement in the years ahead.

Just 17 out of every 100 people aged 45 to 64 catch a cold bad enough to send them to bed for at least half a day or to the doctor. This compares with 22 percent of 25-to-44-year-olds. Just 26 percent of 45-to-64-year-olds got the flu in 1994, versus 38 percent of the younger age group. Seventeen percent were injured, versus 25 percent of 25-to-44-year-olds. Only a handful of acute conditions strike 45-to-64-year-olds more than 25-to-44-year-olds, including skin conditions and acute musculoskeletal injuries.

♦ Fully 31 percent of acute musculoskeletal conditions are experienced by people aged 45 to 64. This relatively high share can be explained by the increasing involvement of older people in regular fitness activities. More older Americans are overdoing it, and they take their sprains and strains to the doctor.

Acute Health Conditions, 1994

(total number of acute conditions for all persons, number and rate per 100 people aged 25 to 44 and 45 to 64, and share of total acute conditions accounted for by age group, 1994; numbers in thousands)

		aged 25 to 44			aged 45 to 64		
	total	*total*	*rate*	*share of total*	*total*	*rate*	*share of total*
Total acute conditions	445,169	127,222	153.5	28.6%	56,898	112.9	12.8%
Infective/parasitic diseases	54,201	12,066	14.6	22.3	3,873	7.7	7.1
Common childhood diseases	3,798	380	0.5	10.0	-	-	-
Intestinal virus	11,902	3,124	3.8	26.2	951	1.9	8.0
Viral infections	17,257	3,457	4.2	20.0	1,562	3.1	9.1
Other	21,244	5,106	6.2	24.0	1,360	2.7	6.4
Respiratory conditions	208,930	63,925	77.1	30.6	27,937	55.4	13.4
Common cold	65,968	18,591	22.4	28.2	8,372	16.6	12.7
Other acute upper respiratory infections	30,866	8,333	10.1	27.0	3,351	6.6	10.9
Influenza	90,447	31,351	37.8	34.7	13,058	25.9	14.4
Acute bronchitis	12,149	3,624	4.4	29.8	2,101	4.2	17.3
Pneumonia	4,220	761	0.9	18.0	450	0.9	10.7
Other respiratory conditions	5,280	1,265	1.5	24.0	605	1.2	11.5
Digestive system conditions	15,863	3,918	4.7	24.7	2,084	4.1	13.1
Dental conditions	2,891	771	0.9	26.7	437	0.9	15.1
Indigestion, nausea, vomiting	8,323	2,114	2.6	25.4	687	1.4	8.3
Other digestive conditions	4,649	1,033	1.2	22.2	961	1.9	20.7
Injuries	61,887	20,726	25.0	33.5	8,659	17.2	14.0
Fractures and dislocations	7,893	2,100	2.5	26.6	1,218	2.4	15.4
Sprains and strains	14,195	5,740	6.9	40.4	2,198	4.4	15.5
Open wounds and lacerations	10,874	3,796	4.6	34.9	1,105	2.2	10.2
Contusions/superficial injuries	12,117	3,421	4.1	28.2	1,796	3.6	14.8
Other current injuries	16,807	5,670	6.8	33.7	2,341	4.6	13.9
Selected other acute cond.	71,337	16,900	20.4	23.7	8,703	17.3	12.2
Eye conditions	3,160	774	0.9	24.5	316	0.6	10.0
Acute ear infections	24,123	2,344	2.8	9.7	1,132	2.2	4.7
Other ear conditions	3,781	808	1.0	21.4	421	0.8	11.1
Acute urinary conditions	8,140	2,729	3.3	33.5	1,406	2.8	17.3

(continued)

(continued from previous page)

	total	aged 25 to 44			aged 45 to 64		
		total	rate	share of total	total	rate	share of total
Disorders of menstruation	1,146	436	0.5	38.0%	45	0.1	3.9%
Other disorders of female genital tract	2,652	1,476	1.8	55.7	419	0.8	15.8
Delivery and other conditions of pregnancy	3,707	2,397	2.9	64.7	-	-	-
Skin conditions	6,165	1,161	1.4	18.8	1,186	2.4	19.2
Acute musculoskeletal cond.	9,078	3,083	3.7	34.0	2,827	5.6	31.1
Headache, excluding migraine	3,975	1,363	1.6	34.3	738	1.5	18.6
Fever, unspecified	5,410	329	0.4	6.1	214	0.4	4.0
All other acute conditions	32,952	9,686	11.7	29.4	5,642	11.2	17.1

Note: The acute conditions shown here are those that caused people to restrict their activity for at least half a day, or that caused people to contact a physician about the illness or injury. (-) means not applicable or sample is too small to make a reliable estimate.
Source: National Center for Health Statistics, Current Estimates From the National Health Interview Survey, 1994, Series 10, No. 193, 1995

Chronic Conditions Emerge in Middle-Age

People aged 45 to 64 are much more likely than younger adults to suffer from chronic conditions.

Although the incidence of acute conditions diminishes as people enter their 40s and 50s, chronic illnesses begin to emerge. There are only a few chronic conditions (asthma and hay fever, for example) that are more common among 18-to-44-year-olds than among those aged 45 to 64. Because the National Center for Health Statistics publishes its data on health conditions in broad age groups, it is not possible to see the emergence of chronic conditions as people age from their 40s into their 50s and 60s. But a comparison of the prevalence of conditions in the 45-to-64 age group with those in the 18-to-44 age group reveals which conditions are likely to become much more common as the baby-boom generation ages.

The most prevalent chonic condition among 45-to-64-year-olds is arthritis (24 percent), followed by high blood pressure (22 percent). The proportion of people aged 45 to 64 with these conditions is four times the proportion among 18-to-44-year-olds. Hearing impairments and heart disease also emerge as significant problems in the 45-to-64 age group.

◆ As the large baby-boom generation ages into its 50s and 60s, expect to see an enormous increase in the number of people with arthritis, high blood pressure, heart disease, and hearing problems.

Chronic Health Conditions, 1994

(total number of persons with chronic condition, number and percent with condition among people aged 18 to 44 and 45 to 64, and share of total chronic conditions accounted for by age group, 1994; numbers in thousands)

		aged 18 to 44			aged 45 to 64		
	total	total	percent	share of total	total	percent	share of total
Selected skin and musculoskeletal conditions							
Arthritis	33,446	5,656	5.2%	16.9%	12,045	23.9%	36.0%
Gout	2,485	375	0.4	15.1	963	1.9	38.8
Intervertebral disc disorders	5,994	2,435	2.3	40.6	2,558	5.1	42.7
Bone spur or tendinitis	2,717	890	0.8	32.8	1,207	2.4	44.4
Disorders of bone or cartilage	1,520	438	0.4	28.8	430	0.9	28.3
Trouble with bunions	3,296	1,031	1.0	31.3	1,078	2.1	32.7
Bursitis	5,279	1,700	1.6	32.2	2,119	4.2	40.1
Sebaceous skin cyst	1,239	704	0.7	56.8	238	0.5	19.2
Trouble with acne	5,250	2,856	2.6	54.4	251	0.5	4.8
Psoriasis	2,571	979	0.9	38.1	859	1.7	33.4
Dermatitis	9,192	3,867	3.4	42.1	1,693	3.4	18.4
Trouble with dry (itching) skin	6,166	2,503	2.3	40.6	1,660	3.3	26.9
Trouble with ingrown nails	5,987	2,182	2.0	36.4	1,556	3.1	26.0
Trouble with corns and calluses	4,356	1,645	1.5	37.8	1,462	2.9	33.6
Impairments							
Visual impairment	8,601	3,168	2.9	36.8	2,273	4.5	26.4
Color blindness	3,183	1,367	1.3	42.9	1,009	2.0	31.7
Cataracts	6,473	347	0.3	5.4	872	1.7	13.5
Glaucoma	2,603	315	0.3	12.1	593	1.2	22.8
Hearing impairment	22,400	5,339	4.9	23.8	6,952	13.8	31.0
Tinnitus	7,033	1,756	1.6	25.0	2,334	4.6	33.2
Speech impairment	3,179	988	0.9	31.1	451	0.9	14.2
Absence of extremities	1,404	437	0.4	31.1	392	0.8	27.9
Paralysis of extremities	1,416	339	0.3	23.9	457	0.9	32.3
Deformity or orthopedic impairment	31,068	15,400	14.2	49.6	8,570	17.0	27.6
Selected digestive conditions							
Ulcer	4,447	2,105	2.0	47.3	1,272	2.5	28.6

(continued)

(continued from previous page)

	total	aged 18 to 44			aged 45 to 64		
		total	percent	share of total	total	percent	share of total
Hernia of abdominal cavity	4,778	1,116	1.0%	23.4%	1,574	3.1%	32.9%
Gastritis or duodenitis	3,410	1,451	1.3	42.6	888	1.8	26.0
Frequent indigestion	6,957	3,372	3.1	48.5	2,060	4.1	29.6
Enteritis or colitis	2,014	855	0.8	42.5	659	1.3	32.7
Spastic colon	2,063	923	0.9	44.7	633	1.3	30.7
Diverticula of intestines	2,150	249	0.2	11.6	882	1.8	41.0
Frequent constipation	4,040	1,378	1.3	34.1	619	1.2	15.3

Selected conditions of the genitourinary, nervous,

endocrine, metabolic, or blood systems

	total	total	percent	share of total	total	percent	share of total
Goiter or other disorders of the thyroid	4,509	1,498	1.4	33.2	1,506	3.0	33.4
Diabetes	7,766	1,346	1.2	17.3	3,182	6.3	41.0
Anemias	4,664	2,288	2.1	49.1	889	1.8	19.1
Epilepsy	1,396	652	0.6	46.7	236	0.5	16.9
Migraine	11,256	6,807	6.3	60.5	2,647	5.3	23.5
Neuralgia or neuritis	566	162	0.2	28.6	189	0.4	33.4
Kidney trouble	3,512	1,712	1.6	48.7	867	1.7	24.7
Bladder disorders	3,747	1,353	1.3	36.1	852	1.7	22.7
Diseases of prostate	2,641	316	0.3	12.0	689	1.4	26.1
Diseases of female genital organs	5,052	3,231	3.0	64.0	1,332	2.6	26.4

Selected circulatory conditions

	total	total	percent	share of total	total	percent	share of total
Rheumatic fever	2,006	849	0.8	42.3	623	1.2	31.1
Heart disease	22,279	4,097	3.8	18.4	6,838	12.6	30.7
Ischemic heart disease	8,004	440	0.4	5.5	2,842	5.6	35.5
Heart rhythm disorders	8,934	2,798	2.6	31.3	2,401	4.8	26.9
Other selected diseases of the heart, excl. hypertension	5,342	859	0.8	16.1	1,595	3.2	29.9
High blood pressure (hypertension)	28,236	5,549	5.1	19.7	11,206	22.2	39.7
Cerebrovascular disease	2,978	219	0.2	7.4	919	1.8	30.9
Hardening of the arteries	2,239	39	-	1.7	559	1.1	25.0
Varicose veins of lower extremities	7,260	2,398	2.2	33.0	2,545	5.1	35.1
Hemorrhoids	9,321	4,255	3.9	45.6	3,128	6.2	33.6

(continued)

(continued from previous page)

		aged 18 to 44			aged 45 to 64		
Selected respiratory conditions	total	total	percent	share of total	total	percent	share of total
Chronic bronchitis	14,021	5,047	4.7%	36.0%	3,223	6.4%	23.0%
Asthma	14,562	5,598	5.2	38.4	2,561	5.1	17.6
Hay fever	26,146	13,339	12.3	51.0	6,089	12.1	23.3
Chronic sinusitis	34,902	16,586	15.3	47.5	9,067	18.0	26.0
Deviated nasal septum	2,028	938	0.9	46.3	674	1.3	33.2
Chronic disease of tonsils or adenoids	2,925	1,148	1.1	39.2	150	0.3	5.1
Emphysema	2,028	117	0.1	5.8	497	1.0	24.5

Note: Chronic conditions are those that last at least three months or belong to a group of conditions that are considered to be chronic regardless of when they began.
Source: National Center for Health Statistics, Current Estimates From the National Health Interview Survey, 1994, Series 10, No. 193, 1995

Many Healthy Years Await Mid-Youthers

Most of their remaining years will be healthy ones.

For boomers turning 50 this year, there are 22 good years left, according to an analysis of data from the federal government's National Health Interview Survey. The life expectancy of people aged 50 is 33 years—or a decade longer than the healthy years they have left. In the survey, a nationally representative sample of Americans were asked to describe their own health status (excellent, very good, good, fair, or poor) and the degree to which their activities were limited in any way by health problems.

Overall, 83 percent of noninstitutionalized Americans say they are in excellent health and are not in any way limited by health problems. Only 0.5 percent report being in poor health and unable to care for themselves. In 1990, life expectancy for Americans at birth was 75 years, while healthy life expectancy was 64 years. In other words, people born in 1990 could expect to live well for 85 percent of their lives, assuming death and sickness rates do not change. For Americans aged 35 to 54, from 71 to 65 percent of their remaining years should be healthy ones.

◆ As boomers move into their 50s and beyond, their healthy habits may extend the good years. Boomers exercise more and smoke less than the current generation of elderly did at the same age. They may be rewarded for their efforts not just with a longer life, but a better life.

Years of Healthy and Total Life Remaining

(life expectancy and healthy life expectancy in years, and percent of remaining years that should be healthy, by age at beginning of interval, 1990)

	life expectancy	healthy life expectancy	percent healthy
Aged 0 to 4	75.4	64.0	85%
Aged 5 to 9	75.1	60.1	80
Aged 10 to 14	71.2	55.5	78
Aged 15 to 19	66.3	50.9	77
Aged 20 to 24	61.3	46.5	76
Aged 25 to 29	56.6	42.2	75
Aged 30 to 34	51.9	37.9	73
Aged 35 to 39	47.2	33.7	71
Aged 40 to 44	42.6	29.5	69
Aged 45 to 49	38.0	25.5	67
Aged 50 to 54	33.4	21.6	65
Aged 55 to 59	29.0	18.0	62
Aged 60 to 64	24.8	14.8	60
Aged 65 to 69	20.8	11.9	57
Aged 70 to 74	17.2	9.2	53
Aged 75 to 79	13.9	6.8	49
Aged 80 to 84	10.9	4.7	43
Aged 85	8.3	3.1	37

Source: USDA, Family Economics and Nutrition Review, *Vol. 9, No. 1, 1996*

Causes of Death
Shift in Middle-Age

By the 45-to-54 age group, heart disease begins to take its toll.

Heart disease, cancer, and stroke are the three leading causes of death in the United States. They are not the leading killers of 35-to-44-year-olds, however. For that age group, cancer, AIDS, and accidents are the three leading causes of death. But in the 45-to-54 age group, heart disease becomes a leading killer as chronic conditions become more prevalent.

Death rates nearly double between the 35-to-44 and 45-to-54 age groups, with the death rate per 100,000 people rising from 236 for 35-to-44-year-olds to 460 for 45-to-54-year-olds. This is still far lower than the overall death rate, since most people live well beyond their mid-50s. For the population as a whole, there were 880 deaths per 100,000 people in 1993.

◆ AIDS has hit the baby-boom generation hard, which is why it ranks second as a cause of death among 35-to-44-year-olds. In the 45-to-54 age group, AIDS is in fourth place, while it ranks eighth overall.

Causes of Death, 1993

(total deaths among total persons and persons aged 35 to 44 and 45 to 54, number and percent distribution of deaths by selected cause, and death rate by cause per 100,000 people in age group, 1993)

	number	percent	death rate
Total deaths, all persons	2,268,553	100.0%	880.0
Diseases of heart	743,460	32.8	288.4
Malignant neoplasms	529,904	23.4	205.6
Cerebrovascular diseases	150,108	6.6	58.2
Chronic obstructive pulmonary diseases	101,077	4.5	39.2
Accidents	90,523	4.0	35.1
Pneumonia and influenza	82,820	3.7	32.1
Diabetes mellitus	53,894	2.4	20.9
Human immunodeficiency virus	37,267	1.6	14.5
Suicide	31,102	1.4	12.1
Homicide and legal intervention	26,009	1.1	10.1
All other causes	422,389	18.6	-
Total deaths, persons aged 35 to 44	96,038	100.0	235.5
Malignant neoplasms	16,755	17.4	41.1
Human immunodeficiency virus	15,929	16.6	39.1
Accidents	13,255	13.8	32.5
Diseases of heart	13,121	13.7	32.2
Suicide	6,170	6.4	15.1
Homicide and legal intervention	4,537	4.7	11.1
Chronic liver disease and cirrhosis	3,756	3.9	9.2
Cerebrovascular diseases	2,519	2.6	6.2
Diabetes mellitus	1,697	1.8	4.2
Pneumonia and influenza	1,551	1.6	3.8
All other causes	16,748	17.4	-
Total deaths, persons aged 45 to 54	131,815	100.0	460.0
Malignant neoplasms	42,372	32.1	147.9
Diseases of heart	32,679	24.8	114.0
Accidents	8,029	6.1	28.0
Human immunodeficiency virus	6,487	4.9	22.6

(continued)

(continued from previous page)

	number	percent	death rate
Cerebrovascular diseases	5,057	3.8%	17.6
Chronic liver disease and cirrhosis	4,703	3.6	16.4
Suicide	4,168	3.2	15.1
Diabetes mellitus	3,449	2.6	12.0
Chronic obstructive pulmonary diseases	2,494	1.9	8.7
Homicide and legal intervention	2,052	1.6	7.2
All other causes	20,325	15.4	-

Source: National Center For Health Statistics, Advance Report of Final Mortality Statistics, 1993, *Vol. 44, No. 7 Supplement, 1996*

7

Education

♦ Black and white men aged 35 to 54 are almost equally likely to have graduated from high school.

♦ Among women aged 45 to 54, only 24 percent are college graduates, versus 33 percent of men in that age group.

♦ Among 35-to-54-year-olds, 26 percent of white women, 16 percent of black women, and just 9 percent of Hispanic women are college graduates.

Mid-Youth Men Are Most Highly Educated in History

One in three men aged 45 to 54 has a bachelor's degree.

Men aged 45 to 54 are the most highly educated of Americans. One-third have a college diploma, and 14 percent have an advanced degree. Behind this high level of education is the Vietnam War. In order to avoid being drafted during the 1960s and early 1970s, many young men opted for college deferments. Those men are now in their 40s and early 50s.

When the war ended, so did the pressure to stay in school. Consequently, men aged 35 to 44 are slightly less educated than those aged 45 to 54. Twenty-eight percent have a bachelor's degree, and 10 percent have an advanced degree.

◆ The high educational level of baby-boom men will transform the middle-aged market. Not only does education mean higher earnings, it also changes consumer behavior. Educated consumers are more sophisticated and demanding than those with less education because of their exposure to a broad array of ideas and experiences.

Educational Attainment of Men, 1995

(number and percent distribution of total men aged 25 or older and men aged 35 to 54 by educational attainment, 1995; numbers in thousands)

		aged 35 to 54	
	total men	aged 35 to 44	aged 45 to 54
Total, number	79,463	20,972	15,022
Not a high school graduate	14,520	2,594	2,087
High school graduate or more	64,942	18,377	12,935
High school graduate	25,378	6,872	4,351
Some college, no degree	13,795	3,972	2,564
Associate's degree	5,138	1,659	1,110
Bachelor's degree or more	20,631	5,874	4,910
Bachelor's degree	13,132	3,784	2,766
Master's degree	4,591	1,284	1,324
Professional degree	1,713	517	448
Doctoral degree	1,195	289	372
Total, percent	100.0%	100.0%	100.0%
Not a high school graduate	18.3	12.4	13.9
High school graduate or more	81.7	87.6	86.1
High school graduate	31.9	32.8	29.0
Some college, no degree	17.4	18.9	17.1
Associate's degree	6.5	7.9	7.4
Bachelor's degree or more	26.0	28.0	32.7
Bachelor's degree	16.5	18.0	18.4
Master's degree	5.8	6.1	8.8
Professional degree	2.2	2.5	3.0
Doctoral degree	1.5	1.4	2.5

Source: Bureau of the Census, unpublished tables from the 1995 Current Population Survey

White Men Most Likely to Be College Graduates

Just 57 percent of Hispanic men aged 35 to 54 graduated from high school.

Among men aged 35 to 54, whites are much better educated than blacks or Hispanics. While 31 percent of white men in this age group have a bachelor's degree, only 15 percent of blacks and 11 percent of Hispanics are equally educated.

Black and white men aged 35 to 54 are almost equally likely to have graduated from high school (88 percent of white men and 79 percent of black men are high school graduates). The differences in educational attainment between blacks and whites occur after high school, when family income strongly determines who continues in school and who does not.

Only 57 percent of Hispanic men graduated from high school, far below the rate for whites or blacks. One reason for the low educational level of Hispanics is that many are immigrants who came to the U.S. from countries where schooling beyond the teen years is uncommon.

♦ Because white men are so much better educated than blacks or Hispanics, their incomes are also higher. Until the gap in education closes, the average black or Hispanic man will not earn as much as the average white.

Educational Attainment of Men
by Race and Hispanic Origin, 1995

(number and percent distribution of men aged 35 to 54 by educational attainment, race, and Hispanic origin, 1995; numbers in thousands)

	white	black	Hispanic
Total, men aged 35 to 54	30,538	3,829	2,993
Not a high school graduate	3,551	812	1,282
High school graduate or more	26,988	3,016	1,711
High school graduate	9,393	1,453	792
Some college, no degree	5,545	739	413
Associate's degree	2,452	233	168
Bachelor's degree or more	9,598	591	338
Bachelor's degree	5,806	407	209
Master's degree	2,354	128	64
Professional degree	883	26	44
Doctoral degree	554	30	22
Total, men aged 35 to 54	100.0%	100.0%	100.0%
Not a high school graduate	11.6	21.2	42.8
High school graduate or more	88.4	78.8	57.2
High school graduate	30.8	37.9	26.5
Some college, no degree	18.2	19.3	13.8
Associate's degree	8.0	6.1	5.6
Bachelor's degree or more	31.4	15.4	11.3
Bachelor's degree	19.0	10.6	7.0
Master's degree	7.7	3.3	2.1
Professional degree	2.9	0.7	1.5
Doctoral degree	1.8	0.8	0.7

Source: Bureau of the Census, unpublished tables from the 1995 Current Population Survey

Mid-Youth Women Are also Highly Educated

About one in four is a college graduate.

Unlike their male counterparts, women aged 35 to 54 did not have the threat of being drafted and sent to Vietnam to keep them in college. Older baby-boom women are significantly less educated than their male counterparts. Among women aged 45 to 54, only 24 percent are college graduates, versus 33 percent of men in that age group.

But baby-boom women are much more highly educated than the generations of women that precede them. And unlike men, whose educational attainment peaks in the 45-to-54 age group, younger women are increasingly well-educated. Among women aged 35 to 44, 25 percent are college graduates—not far below the 28 percent of men in this age group who have graduated from college.

♦ Because men and women tend to marry people like themselves, many college-educated men and women are married to one another. With earnings so closely linked to education, college-educated dual-income couples in the 35-to-54 age group are the nation's most affluent households.

Educational Attainment of Women, 1995

(number and percent distribution of total women aged 25 or older and women aged 35 to 54 by educational attainment, 1995; numbers in thousands)

		aged 35 to 54	
	total women	*aged 35 to 44*	*aged 45 to 54*
Total, number	86,975	21,363	15,672
Not a high school graduate	15,992	2,336	2,135
High school graduate or more	70,983	19,027	13,537
High school graduate	31,072	7,230	5,617
Some college, no degree	15,561	4265	2967
Associate's degree	6,756	2,134	1,256
Bachelor's degree or more	17,594	5,398	3,697
Bachelor's degree	12,181	3,604	2,265
Master's degree	4,226	1,360	1,167
Professional degree	715	276	121
Doctoral degree	472	159	144
Total, percent	100.0%	100.0%	100.0%
Not a high school graduate	18.4	10.9	13.6
High school graduate or more	81.6	89.1	86.4
High school graduate	35.7	33.8	35.8
Some college, no degree	17.9	20.0	18.9
Associate's degree	7.8	10.0	8.0
Bachelor's degree or more	20.2	25.3	23.6
Bachelor's degree	14.0	16.9	14.5
Master's degree	4.9	6.4	7.4
Professional degree	0.8	1.3	0.8
Doctoral degree	0.5	0.7	0.9

Source: Bureau of the Census, unpublished tables from the 1995 Current Population Survey

White Women Are Better Educated Than Black or Hispanic Women

Only 58 percent of Hispanic women aged 35 to 54 are high school graduates.

Among women aged 35 to 54, whites and blacks are almost equally likely to have graduated from high school (89 percent of whites and 82 percent of blacks). But while 26 percent of white women in this age group are college graduates, only 16 percent of blacks have a college degree. Black women are as likely as black men to be college graduates, however, while white and Hispanic women are less likely to have graduated from college than their male counterparts.

Only 58 percent of Hispanic women graduated from high school, and just 9 percent have a bachelor's degree. Behind the low educational level of Hispanics is the fact that many are immigrants from countries such as Mexico where educational attainment is generally low.

◆ Until women's educational levels equal those of men, the average woman won't earn as much as the average man. Among blacks, the gap between men's and women's incomes is much smaller than the gap between the incomes of white men and women. Behind the smaller gap is the fact that black men and women are equally educated.

Educational Attainment of Women
by Race and Hispanic Origin, 1995

(number and percent distribution of women aged 35 to 54 by educational attainment, race, and Hispanic origin, 1995; numbers in thousands)

	white	black	Hispanic
Total, women aged 35 to 54	30,815	4,555	3,139
Not a high school graduate	3,291	808	1,314
High school graduate or more	27,523	3,747	1,826
High school graduate	10,713	1,679	901
Some college, no degree	6,053	987	476
Associate's degree	2,886	366	158
Bachelor's degree or more	7,871	715	291
Bachelor's degree	4,995	481	208
Master's degree	2,267	175	62
Professional degree	346	30	11
Doctoral degree	262	27	10
Total, percent	100.0%	100.0%	100.0%
Not a high school graduate	10.7	17.7	41.9
High school graduate or more	89.3	82.3	58.2
High school graduate	34.8	36.9	28.7
Some college, no degree	19.6	21.7	15.2
Associate's degree	9.4	8.0	5.0
Bachelor's degree or more	25.5	15.7	9.3
Bachelor's degree	16.2	10.6	6.6
Master's degree	7.4	3.8	2.0
Professional degree	1.1	0.7	0.4
Doctoral degree	0.9	0.6	0.3

Source: Bureau of the Census, unpublished tables from the 1995 Current Population Survey

8

Attitudes and Behavior

♦ Two out of three boomers believe the lot of the average man is getting worse.

♦ Fully 80 percent of boomers say they have already achieved the number-one component of the American Dream—being true to yourself and not selling out.

♦ Twenty-eight percent of boomers say they are very happy, while 60 percent are pretty happy and 12 percent are "not too happy."

♦ Thirty-five percent of boomers are conservative, versus 28 percent who describe themselves as liberal.

♦ Only 38 percent of boomers—versus 56 percent of the World War II generation—think working mothers are bad for children.

♦ Among workers, boomers are more satisfied with their jobs than are Generation Xers, but they are less satisfied than the Swing generation.

♦ Six out of ten boomers say they believe in God without a doubt, versus only 2 percent who say they don't believe in God.

♦ Fully 39 percent of boomers live in the same place they did at age 16, higher than the proportions for the Swing or World War II generations.

♦ Only 38 percent of boomers watch television three or more hours a day, versus 51 percent of Generation Xers, 46 percent of the Swing generation, and 63 percent of older Americans.

Note: For definitions of Generation X, the baby boom, Swing, and World War II generations, see the glossary.

Many Boomers Are Pessimistic About Modern Life

"Grass is browner" syndrome rules among midlifers.

The old adage that the grass is always greener on the other side of the fence no longer holds true in the United States. Most Americans think others are struggling while they, themselves, are doing fine. The grass on the other side of the fence has browned.

Two out of three baby boomers believe the lot of the average man is getting worse. There is little variation by generation in this attitude, with Generation Xers somewhat more likely than older people to feel this way.

Sharp generational differences emerge when people are asked whether most people try to be helpful. Fully 60 percent of Generation Xers think most people are just looking out for themselves, as do a plurality of baby boomers. In contrast, a majority of the Swing and World War II generations think most people try to be helpful.

When Americans are probed about their own prospects, baby boomers are more optimistic. When asked whether they agree with the statement, "the way things are in America, people like me and my family have a good chance of improving our standard of living," baby boomers are more likely to agree than those younger or older.

♦ Boomers may believe the world is falling apart, but they are upbeat about their own ability to survive. If the lot of the average man is getting worse, then they are anything but average.

Average Man

"In spite of what some people say, the lot of
the average man is getting worse, not better."

(percent responding by generation, 1994)

	total	Generation X	Baby Boom	Swing	World War II
Agree	67.2%	70.0%	66.4%	68.2%	65.6%
Disagree	29.9	27.2	31.9	29.5	28.0

*Note: Asked of those currently working; numbers may not add to 100 percent because "don't know" and no
answer are not shown.*
Source: 1994 General Social Survey, National Opinion Research Center, University of Chicago

Helpful or Selfish?

"Would you say that most of the time people try to be helpful,
or that they are mostly just looking out for themselves?"

(percent responding by generation, 1994)

	total	Generation X	Baby Boom	Swing	World War II
Helpful	46.3%	31.8%	44.8%	53.3%	55.6%
Selfish	46.5	60.9	48.0	41.2	36.2
Depends	6.4	7.1	6.9	4.6	6.1

Note: Numbers may not add to 100 percent because "don't know" and no answer are not shown.
Source: 1994 General Social Survey, National Opinion Research Center, University of Chicago

Improve Standard of Living

"The way things are in America, people like me and my family
have a good chance of improving our standard of living.
Do you agree or disagree?"

(percent responding by generation, 1994)

	total	Generation X	Baby Boom	Swing	World War II
Strongly agree	10.9%	12.1%	12.5%	10.0%	7.1%
Agree	50.5	55.1	51.3	49.3	46.1
Neither	11.7	6.5	13.7	8.9	14.2
Disagree	21.1	21.9	17.7	25.2	24.5
Strongly disagree	3.6	2.8	3.3	5.2	3.5

Note: Numbers may not add to 100 percent because "can't choose" and no answer are not shown.
Source: 1994 General Social Survey, National Opinion Research Center, University of Chicago

What the American Dream Is Made Of

Most boomers believe in the American Dream.

Over half (54 percent) of people born between 1946 and 1964 still believe in the American Dream, although a 68 percent majority think it is harder to achieve today than it was a generation ago, according to a survey conducted in 1996 by Roper Starch Worldwide and sponsored by FirstWave.

Because boomers are highly individualistic, their American Dream is one of self-fulfillment. When asked which components are part of the American Dream for them, the highest percentage of boomers are in consensus about the most personal items. Number one is "being true to yourself and not selling out," cited by fully 97 percent of boomers. Among the top ten components, only one—seeing your children succeed, which ranks 8th—relates to other people. Contributing something useful to society is 14th, and having a happy marriage is 15th. At the bottom of the list (and not shown here) is being wealthy, cited by 42 percent, and having power and influence (36 percent).

◆ Fully 80 percent of boomers say they have already achieved the number-one component of the American Dream—being true to yourself and not selling out. Sixty-one percent have achieved the number-two component—feeling you're in control of your life.

The American Dream

"Everyone has a different definition of the American Dream.
Which of the following items are a part of your personal
American Dream, regardless of whether it
describes your life right now or not?"

(percent of Americans aged 32 to 50 naming item as part of their American Dream, 1996; only top 20 items are shown)

Being true to yourself and not selling out	97%
Feeling you're in control of your life	96
Finding satisfaction within yourself regardless of work or family situations	96
Making enough to insure a comfortable future	96
Maintaining your health and vitality	96
A job that gives you personal satisfaction	96
Having inner peace	96
Seeing your children succeed	95
Owning a home	95
Reasonable work hours	93
Having the money you need to do what you want	93
Being true to your own religious beliefs	93
Being one of the best at the job you do	92
Creating or contributing something useful to society	91
Having a happy marriage	91
Leaving something to your heirs	84
Staying married for a lifetime	83
Having children	81
Staying sexual throughout your life	77
Doing better than your parents did	75

Source: The Balancing Act: Boomers Talk About Life and The American Dream, *sponsored by FirstWave, Inc., and conducted by Roper Starch Worldwide, Inc., 1996*

Most Mid-Youths
Are Pretty Happy

Only 12 percent of boomers are unhappy.

Midlife can be a time of seemingly endless routines—raising children, managing a career, and running a household. Boomers are more likely than the members of Generation X or the Swing generation to say life is pretty routine. Forty-nine percent call their lives routine, while 48 percent say life is exciting. Only the World War II Generation is less likely to find life exciting than boomers.

The proportion of Americans who say they are "very happy" rises slightly with age, from 25 percent among Generation Xers to 32 percent among the World War II generation. Twenty-eight percent of boomers say they are very happy, while 60 percent are pretty happy and 12 percent are "not too happy."

Few boomers have experienced any traumatic events in the past 12 months. In fact, they are least likely among the four generations to have experienced a traumatic event recently—only 32 percent have done so. The Swing generation is most likely to have experienced trauma, with 43 percent saying they have done so in the past 12 months. For many, this trauma was the death of a parent or spouse.

♦ Does happiness increase with age, or are some generations happier than others? High levels of divorce, coupled with economic insecurity, may depress boomers and younger adults. Unless these conditions change, the happiness of younger generations may never match that of older Americans.

Is Life Exciting?

"In general, do you find life exciting, pretty routine, or dull?"

(percent responding by generation, 1994)

	total	Generation X	Baby Boom	Swing	World War II
Exciting	47.0%	53.2%	47.6%	50.0%	37.2%
Routine	48.0	43.1	49.3	44.2	52.9
Dull	4.1	3.6	2.8	4.4	7.1

Note: Numbers may not add to 100 percent because "don't know" and no answer is not shown.
Source: 1994 General Social Survey, National Opinion Research Center, University of Chicago

Are You Happy?

"Taken all together, how would you say things are these days?
Would you say that you are very happy, pretty happy,
or not too happy?"

(percent responding by generation, 1994)

	total	Generation X	Baby Boom	Swing	World War II
Very happy	28.6%	24.8%	27.9%	30.0%	32.4%
Pretty happy	58.7	62.6	59.9	56.7	54.6
Not too happy	12.2	12.3	11.8	12.8	12.4

Note: Numbers may not add to 100 percent because "don't know" and no answer are not shown.
Source: 1994 General Social Survey, National Opinion Research Center, University of Chicago

Trauma in Past Year

Number of traumatic events happening in the past year:

(percent responding by generation, 1994)

	total	Generation X	Baby Boom	Swing	World War II
None	59.7%	61.3%	62.3%	49.4%	60.2%
One or more	35.2	36.6	31.7	42.9	35.6

Note: Numbers may not add to 100 percent because "can't choose" and no answer are not shown.
Source: 1994 General Social Survey, National Opinion Research Center, University of Chicago

Most Boomers Are Cynical About Politics

The youngest Americans are the least cynical.

Three out of four Americans say that most public officials are not really interested in the problems of the average man. This proportion does not vary much by age. Only among Generation Xers is there less agreement, with only 69 percent feeling this way.

Despite the pessimism of boomers and older Americans, voting rates rise with age. In midlife, boomers are just reaching the age at which voting rises substantially. Among 35-to-39-year-olds, 61 percent voted in the 1992 presidential election. This compares with 69 percent of people aged 45 to 49 who voted, electing their peer Bill Clinton—who was 46 in 1992.

While much has been said about the increasing conservatism of boomers, they remain more liberal than either the Swing or World War II generations. Overall, 28 percent of boomers describe themselves as liberal, versus 26 percent of the Swing and 18 percent of the World War II generations. Thirty-five percent of boomers are conservative, versus 36 percent of the Swing and 38 percent of the World War II generations. Generation Xers are more liberal and less conservative than boomers.

◆ While boomers are more conservative today than they were as young adults, they are less conservative than people in their 40s were two decades ago. Society as a whole is tilting more liberal, a trend that continues despite the rise of the religious right.

Cynical About Politicians

"Most public officials are not really interested
in the problems of the average man."

(percent responding by generation, 1994)

	total	Generation X	Baby Boom	Swing	World War II
Agree	73.5%	68.7%	74.3%	73.6%	76.0%
Disagree	23.8	29.5	23.9	24.5	18.0

Note: Numbers may not add to 100 percent because "don't know" and no answer are not shown.
Source: 1994 General Social Survey, National Opinion Research Center, University of Chicago

Voting in the 1992 Presidential Election

(number and percent of people aged 35 to 54 voting in the 1992 presidential election; numbers in thousands)

	voters	percent voting
Total	113,866	61.3%
Total, 35-54	44,561	65.7
Aged 35-39	12,897	61.4
Aged 40-44	12,372	66.1
Aged 45-49	10,814	69.4
Aged 50-54	8,478	67.9

Source: Bureau of the Census, Voting and Registration in the Election of November 1992, *Current Population Reports, P20-466, 1993*

Liberal or Conservative?

"Where would you place yourself on a seven-point scale ranging from extremely liberal to extremely conservative?"

(percent responding by generation, 1994)

	total	Generation X	Baby Boom	Swing	World War II
Extremely liberal	2.4%	3.6%	2.6%	1.9%	1.3%
Liberal	11.0	13.6	11.1	10.9	8.4
Lean liberal	12.6	12.7	14.6	13.0	8.2
Moderate	35.1	34.9	34.3	34.8	37.0
Lean conservative	15.8	14.4	17.4	15.2	14.0
Conservative	16.0	15.0	14.6	14.8	20.8
Extremely conservative	3.4	2.5	3.1	5.6	3.2

Note: Numbers may not add to 100 percent because "don't know" and no answer are not shown.
Source: 1994 General Social Survey, National Opinion Research Center, University of Chicago

Boomer Lifestyles
Are Different

Many boomers broke traditions.

Changes in sexual mores are readily apparent in statistics on cohabitation. Few members of the World War II or Swing generations lived with their spouse before marriage. In contrast, 41 percent of boomers and 46 percent of Generation Xers cohabited before marriage.

A majority of married respondents in all generations say their marriage is very happy. Those most likely to be happily married are Generation Xers—many of whom married recently.

In midlife, most people are beyond their childbearing years. Only 22 percent of boomers say they expect to have more children. Fifty-nine percent of boomers have children at home. Eighty-one percent of boomers have a living mother and 61 percent a living father. These proportions drop to 52 and 20 percent, respectively, for the Swing generation.

Distinct differences in attitudes toward women's roles appear when Americans are questioned about working mothers. When asked whether preschool children suffer if their mother works, only 38 percent of boomers agree. In contrast, 56 percent of the World War II generation think working mothers are bad for children.

♦ Perhaps the greatest differences between boomers and older Americans is in men's and women's roles. Working women—and in particular working mothers—have transformed the lifestyles of boomers and younger adults. In doing so, they have also transformed consumer markets.

Cohabitation Before Marriage

"Did you live with your husband/wife before you got married?"

(percent responding by generation, 1994)

	total	Generation X	Baby Boom	Swing	World War II
Yes	28.7%	45.5%	40.5%	13.1%	7.1%
No	69.7	54.5	57.3	85.5	91.7

Note: Asked only of currently married; numbers may not add to 100 percent because no answer is not shown.
Source: 1994 General Social Survey, National Opinion Research Center, University of Chicago

Do You Have a Happy Marriage?

"Taking things all together, how would you describe
your marriage? Would you say that your marriage is
very happy, pretty happy, or not too happy?"

(percent responding by generation, 1994)

	total	Generation X	Baby Boom	Swing	World War II
Very happy	60.2%	65.7%	59.2%	57.0%	62.7%
Pretty happy	36.0	31.4	36.6	38.9	34.1
Not too happy	3.0	2.9	3.3	3.5	2.1

*Note: Asked only of current married; numbers may not add to 100 percent because "don't know" and no
answer is not shown.*
Source: 1994 General Social Survey, National Opinion Research Center, University of Chicago

More Kids?

"Do you expect to have any (more) children?"

(percent responding by generation, 1994)

	total	Generation X	Baby Boom	Swing	World War II
Yes	20.5	66.7	21.6	-	-
No	74.0	26.4	69.0	98.9	99.1
Uncertain	4.9	6.9	8.9	-	-

Note: Numbers may not add to 100 percent because no answer is not shown.
Source: 1994 General Social Survey, National Opinion Research Center, University of Chicago

Generations in Household

"How many generations are living in your household?"

(percent responding by generation, 1994)

	total	Generation X	Baby Boom	Swing	World War II
One	54.4%	44.1%	37.7%	64.4%	89.4 %
Two: children	41.4	52.6	59.2	27.6	6.8
Two: parents	0.8	0.2	0.8	1.5	0.8
Two: grandchildren	0.6	0.6	0.1	1.5	1.1
Three: children and grandchildren	2.1	1.5	1.9	4.1	1.1
Three: children and parents	0.6	0.8	0.4	0.9	0.8
Four	-	0.2	-	-	-

Source: 1994 General Social Survey, National Opinion Research Center, University of Chicago

Mother Alive?

"Is your mother still living?"

(percent responding by generation, 1994)

	total	Generation X	Baby Boom	Swing	World War II
Yes	62.5%	96.2%	81.2%	51.5%	5.8%
No	36.6	3.8	18.2	46.9	92.6

Note: Numbers may not add to 100 percent because "don't know" and no answer are not shown.
Source: 1994 General Social Survey, National Opinion Research Center, University of Chicago

Father Alive?

"Is your father still living?"

(percent responding by generation, 1994)

	total	Generation X	Baby Boom	Swing	World War II
Yes	45.9%	88.5%	60.7%	19.8%	2.2%
No	51.2	8.4	36.2	76.7	96.0

Note: Numbers may not add to 100 percent because "don't know" and no answer are not shown.
Source: 1994 General Social Survey, National Opinion Research Center, University of Chicago

Working Mother

"A preschool child is likely to suffer if his or her mother works.
Do you agree or disagree?"

(percent responding by generation, 1994)

	total	Generation X	Baby Boom	Swing	World War II
Strongly agree	9.0%	4.4%	9.0%	8.1%	13.4%
Agree	31.7	26.0	28.8	31.9	42.2
Neither	12.1	10.0	13.4	12.1	11.1
Disagree	31.7	37.6	30.9	35.9	25.2
Strongly disagree	13.5	20.8	16.6	10.1	3.6

Note: Numbers may not add to 100 percent because "can't choose" and no answer are not shown.
Source: 1994 General Social Survey, National Opinion Research Center, University of Chicago

Work Begins to Lose Glamour as People Age

Many boomers would stop working if rich.

A third of baby boomers say they would quit their jobs if they had enough money to live comfortably for the rest of their lives. This proportion is greater than among Generation Xers (28 percent), but less than among the Swing generation (45 percent). As people approach retirement age, the chance to do what they want rather than what they must becomes more appealing.

Among workers, boomers are more satisfied with their jobs than are Generation Xers, but they are less satisfied than the Swing generation. Members of the Swing generation are more likely than boomers to be at the peak of their careers, which explains why they are most likely to say they are very satisfied with their jobs.

♦ While most boomers would continue to work if they had the money, this proportion is likely to shrink as boomers age into their 50s. Millions of boomers will look forward to having time on their hands. The only problem is how to pay for it.

Work If Rich?

"If you were to get enough money to live as comfortably as
you would like for the rest of your life, would you
continue to work or would you stop working?"

(percent responding by generation, 1994)

	total	Generation X	Baby Boom	Swing	World War II
Work	64.8%	71.0%	66.0%	53.5%	73.3%
Stop	33.6	28.0	32.7	44.7	20.0

*Note: Asked of those currently working; numbers may not add to 100 percent because "don't know" and no
answer are not shown.*
Source: 1994 General Social Survey, National Opinion Research Center, University of Chicago

Job Satisfaction

"On the whole, how satisfied are you with the work you do?"

(percent responding by generation, 1994)

	total	Generation X	Baby Boom	Swing	World War II
Very satisfied	44.2%	35.3%	44.1%	50.3%	48.9%
Moderately satisfied	38.2	43.8	40.3	37.3	17.4
A little dissatisfied	10.1	14.6	10.6	6.8	5.5
Very dissatisfied	3.3	4.6	3.3	3.1	1.3

Note: Asked of those currently working; numbers may not add to 100 percent because "don't know" and no answer are not shown.
Source: 1994 General Social Survey, National Opinion Research Center, University of Chicago

Most Boomers Believe in God, Without a Doubt

Sixty percent are true believers.

Americans are highly religious, and boomers are no exception. Six out of ten boomers say they believe in God and have no doubts about it. This proportion is slightly smaller than for the Swing (71 percent) and World War II generations (66 percent), but it's larger than among Generation Xers (53 percent). Only 2 percent of boomers say they don't believe in God. Eleven percent—the highest proportion among the four generations—do not believe in a personal God but do believe in a higher power of some kind. These include the followers of New Age religions, popular among many boomers.

Eleven percent of boomers say they have no religious preference, double the proportion among older people but less than the 16 percent of Generation Xers without a religious preference. Most boomers and older Americans are Protestant. In contrast, among Generation Xers, fewer than half are Protestant, while 29 percent—the highest proportion among the four generations—are Catholic.

Perhaps because they are less religious, boomers and younger adults are more likely than older Americans to think people should have the right to end their lives if they have an incurable disease. Two out of three boomers and Generation Xers think this should be a right, versus fewer than half of the oldest Americans.

◆ As boomers enter the oldest age groups, they may change their minds about the right to die, fearing they will be pushed out of the way by younger generations.

Belief in God

"Which statement comes closest to expressing what you believe about God? 1) I don't believe in God; 2) I don't know whether there is a God and I don't believe there is any way to find out; 3) I don't believe in a personal God, but I do believe in a Higher Power of some kind; 4) I find myself believing in God some of the time, but not at others; 5) While I have doubts, I feel that I do believe in God; 6) I know God really exists and I have no doubts about it."

(percent responding by generation, 1994)

	total	Generation X	Baby Boom	Swing	World War II
Don't believe in God	2.4%	4.2%	2.1%	0.8%	2.9%
Don't know if there is a God, no way to find out	2.7	5.5	3.1	1.5	0.4
Higher Power	9.5	8.0	10.7	9.5	7.9
Believe in God sometimes	3.7	3.8	3.8	3.0	4.0
Believe, but have some doubts	15.4	21.4	16.6	11.7	11.2
Believe in God with no doubts	62.0	53.4	60.1	70.5	65.7

Note: Numbers may not add to 100 because "don't know" and no answer are not included.
Source: 1994 General Social Survey, National Opinion Research Center, University of Chicago

Religion

"What is your religious preference?"

(percent responding by generation, 1994)

	total	Generation X	Baby Boom	Swing	World War II
Protestant	59.3%	47.4%	56.6%	65.9%	69.2%
Catholic	25.4	29.2	25.8	23.9	22.5
Jewish	2.0	2.1	1.8	1.3	2.7
None	9.2	15.5	10.8	5.7	3.2
Other	3.8	5.6	4.7	3.0	1.4

Note: Numbers may not add to 100 percent because no answer is not shown.
Source: 1994 General Social Survey, National Opinion Research Center, University of Chicago

Right to Die

"Should people have the right to end their own lives
if they have an incurable disease?"

(percent responding by generation, 1994)

	total	Generation X	Baby Boom	Swing	World War II
Yes	61.3%	67.8%	67.2%	55.0%	49.4%
No	33.5	27.8	28.9	40.1	41.8

Note: Numbers may not add to 100 percent because "don't know" and no answer are not shown.
Source: 1994 General Social Survey, National Opinion Research Center, University of Chicago

Most Boomers Live in Small Cities, Towns, and Country

Only 43 percent live in big cities or their suburbs.

Boomers are less likely to live in big cities than any other generation, since most are raising families. Only 18 percent of boomers live in big cities, while another 25 percent live in the suburbs of big cities. A plurality of boomers—39 percent—live in small cities or towns. Another 16 percent live in the country. Despite the myth that boomers grew up and moved away from home, there are few differences in mobility among the generations. Fully 39 percent of boomers live in the same place they did at age 16, higher than the proportion for the Swing or World War II generations. Only 35 percent of boomers live in a different state than they did at age 16, a smaller proportion than among older Americans.

Sixty-one percent of boomers live in single-family homes. While this proportion is smaller than for older adults, it is much greater than the 38 percent of Generation Xers who live in single-family homes. Few boomers live in apartments, and only 6 percent live in trailers.

♦ It is a myth that family life has been weakened by mobility. Most Americans do not live far from other family members, and boomers are no exception.

Community Type

"How would you describe the place where you live?"

(percent responding by generation, 1994)

	total	Generation X	Baby Boom	Swing	World War II
Big city	19.3%	24.4%	18.0%	19.3%	18.1%
Suburbs or outskirts of big city	23.7	22.7	25.4	26.9	17.7
Small city or town	39.8	43.7	39.0	35.6	42.2
Country village	4.4	2.9	4.9	3.0	5.8
Farm or home in country	10.5	5.0	10.7	13.3	11.9

Note: Numbers may not add to 100 percent because "don't know" and no answer are not shown.
Source: 1994 General Social Survey, National Opinion Research Center, University of Chicago

Mobility

"When you were 16 years old, were you living in this same city or state?"

(percent responding by generation, 1994)

	total	Generation X	Baby Boom	Swing	World War II
Same place	39.4%	49.5%	39.0%	33.0%	37.5%
Different city	25.2	24.4	25.5	25.7	24.8
Different state	35.1	25.7	35.3	41.3	37.4

Note: Numbers may not add to 100 percent because no answer is not shown.
Source: 1994 General Social Survey, National Opinion Research Center, University of Chicago

Type of Dwelling Unit in Which Respondent Lives

(percent responding by generation, 1994)

	total	Generation X	Baby Boom	Swing	World War II
Trailer	6.5%	8.1%	6.4%	7.8%	4.3%
Single-family home	59.8	38.2	60.9	66.9	69.6
Duplex, side-by-side	3.8	6.9	3.6	2.0	3.1
Duplex, vertical	2.9	4.6	2.6	2.4	2.4
3-4 units	1.9	2.9	1.9	1.3	1.4
Row house	5.3	6.9	6.2	4.6	2.7
5+ units, 3 stories	12.1	23.2	11.6	8.3	7.1
5+ units, 4+ stories	5.0	5.8	4.4	3.7	6.9
Commerical building	0.5	0.8	0.5	0.7	0.2
Other	0.6	1.2	0.3	0.4	1.1

Note: Numbers may not add to 100 percent because "don't know" and no answer are not shown.
Source: 1994 General Social Survey, National Opinion Research Center, University of Chicago

Most Boomers Do Not Read a Newspaper Daily

They're too busy to pay much attention to the media.

A minority of boomers read a newspaper daily. Only 43 percent do so, compared with well over half of older Americans. Boomers are not likely to pick up the daily newspaper habit as they age because of the many media competing for their attention.

Mid-youth Americans are too busy to spend much time watching television. Boomers are least likely among all age groups to watch television three or more hours a day. Only 38 percent watch this much TV, versus 51 percent of Generation Xers, 46 percent of the Swing generation, and 63 percent of older Americans.

Seventy-five percent of boomers occasionally drink alcohol. Because the proportion of people who do not drink rises with age, drinking among boomers is likely to diminish as they enter their 50s.

Thirty-two percent of boomers smoke cigarettes, about the same proportion as among Generation Xers or the Swing generation.

♦ Boomers are so distracted by the fast pace of life that many organizations are now struggling to find an audience. Network television is losing viewers and newspapers are losing readers. The greatest challenge to marketers targeting the baby-boom generation is figuring out how to reach these overwhelmed consumers.

Newspaper Readership

"How often do you read the newspaper?"

(percent responding by generation, 1994)

	total	Generation X	Baby Boom	Swing	World War II
Daily	49.6%	31.1%	43.1%	57.5%	71.3%
Few times a week	23.1	31.1	25.8	22.7	11.3
One a week	13.4	19.2	16.2	7.7	7.6
Less than once a week	10.0	16.0	11.0	8.8	4.2
Never	3.9	2.6	3.8	3.3	5.6

Note: Numbers may not add to 100 percent because no answer is not shown.
Source: 1994 General Social Survey, National Opinion Research Center, University of Chicago

Television Viewing

"On the average, about how many hours a day
do you personally watch television?"

(percent responding by generation, 1994)

	total	Generation X	Baby Boom	Swing	World War II
None	3.7%	4.3%	4.6%	3.0%	2.1%
One to two	48.5	44.6	56.6	50.4	34.0
Three or more	47.2	50.5	38.3	46.1	62.9

Note: Numbers may not add to 100 percent because no answer is not shown.
Source: 1994 General Social Survey, National Opinion Research Center, University of Chicago

Do You Drink?

"Do you ever have occasion to use any alcoholic beverages
such as liquor, wine, or beer, or are you a total abstainer?"

(percent responding by generation, 1994)

	total	Generation X	Baby Boom	Swing	World War II
Use alcohol	69.1%	80.6%	74.9%	64.9%	51.7%
Abstain	30.9	19.4	25.1	35.1	48.3

Source: 1994 General Social Survey, National Opinion Research Center, University of Chicago

Do You Smoke?

"Do you smoke?"

(percent responding by generation, 1994)

	total	Generation X	Baby Boom	Swing	World War II
Yes	27.8%	34.4%	31.8%	31.2%	12.7%
No	72.2	65.6	68.2	68.8	87.3

Source: 1994 General Social Survey, National Opinion Research Center, University of Chicago

About the Author

Cheryl Russell is a business demographer and an expert on the baby-boom generation. She is the editor of *The Boomer Report*, a newsletter about the baby boom. She is the author of *100 Predictions for the Baby Boom* and *The Master Trend—How the Baby-Boom Generation Is Remaking America*, both published by Plenum Publishing. She is the editor-in-chief of New Strategist Publications, where the books she has authored include *The Official Guide to the American Marketplace* and *The Official Guide to Racial & Ethnic Diversity*. Ms. Russell has written articles about consumer trends for a variety of publications, including *Barron's, The Wall Street Journal, Family Circle, TV Guide, Redbook, New Woman*, and *American Demographics*. She has spoken to many businesses about trends and has appeared on CBS Evening News, NBC Nightly News, and PBS. She lives in Ithaca, New York, with her husband and two children.

Glossary

adjusted for inflation Income or a change in income that has been adjusted for the rise in the cost of living, or the consumer price index (CPI-U-X1).

baby-boom generation Americans born between 1946 and 1964, aged 32 to 50 in 1996.

consumer unit For convenience, consumer units are sometimes called households in this book, although consumer units are somewhat different from the Census Bureau's households. Consumer units are all related members of a household, or financially independent members of a household. A Census Bureau-defined household may include more than one consumer unit.

dual-earner couples A married couple in which both the householder and the householder's spouse are in the labor force. Also called two-income couples.

earnings One type of income. See also income.

employed All civilians who did any work as a paid employee or farmer/self-employed worker, or who worked 15 hours or more as an unpaid farm worker or in a family-owned business during the reference period. All those who have jobs but who are temporarily absent from their jobs due to illness, bad weather, vacation, labor management disputes, or personal reasons are considered employed.

expenditure The transaction cost includes excise and sales taxes of goods and services acquired during the survey period. The full cost of each purchase is recorded even though full payment may not have been made at the date of purchase. Expenditure estimates include money spent on gifts for others.

family household A household maintained by a householder who lives with one or more people related to him or her by blood, marriage, or adoption.

female/male householder A women or man who maintains a household without a spouse present. May head family or nonfamily households.

full-time, year-round Fifty or more weeks of full-time employment during the previous calendar year.

Generation X Americans born between 1965 and 1976; also known as the baby bust. Generation Xers are aged 20 to 31 in 1996.

geographic regions The four major regions and nine census divisions of the United States are grouped as shown below:

Northeast:
—New England: Connecticut, Maine, Massachusetts, New Hampshire, Rhode Island, and Vermont
—Middle Atlantic: New Jersey, New York, and Pennsylvania

Midwest :
—East North Central: Illinois, Indiana, Michigan, Ohio, and Wisconsin
—West North Central: Iowa, Kansas, Minnesota, Missouri, Nebraska, North Dakota, and South Dakota

South:
—East South Central: Alabama, Kentucky, Mississippi, and Tennessee
—South Atlantic: Delaware, District of Columbia, Florida, Georgia, Maryland, North Carolina, South Carolina, Virginia, and West Virginia

West:

—West South Central: Arkansas, Louisiana, Oklahoma, and Texas

—Mountain: Arizona, Colorado, Idaho, Montana, Nevada, New Mexico, Utah, and Wyoming

—Pacific: Alaska, California, Hawaii, Oregon, and Washington

Hispanic Persons or householders who identify their origin as Mexican, Puerto Rican, Central or South American, or some other Hispanic origin. Unless otherwise noted, persons of Hispanic origin may be of any race. In other words, there are black Hispanics, white Hispanics, and Asian Hispanics

household All the persons who occupy a housing unit. A household includes the related family members and all the unrelated persons, if any, such as lodgers, foster children, wards, or employees who share the housing unit. A person living alone is counted as a household. A group of unrelated people who share a housing unit as roommates or unmarried partners is also counted as a household. Households do not include group quarters such as college dormitories, prisons, or nursing homes.

household, race/ethnicity of Households are categorized according to the race or ethnicity of the householder only.

householder The householder is the person (or one of the persons) in whose name the housing unit is owned or rented or, if there is no such person, any adult member. With married couples, the householder may be either the husband or wife. The householder is the reference person for the household.

householder, age of The age of the householder is used to categorize households into age groups. Married couples, for example, are classified according to the age of either the husband or wife, depending on which one identified him or herself as the householder.

income Money received in the preceding calendar year by each person aged 15 or older from each of the following sources: (1) earnings from longest job (or self-employment); (2) earnings from jobs other than longest job; (3) unemployment compensation; (4) workers' compensation; (5) Social Security; (6) Supplemental Security income; (7) public assistance; (8) veterans' payments; (9) survivor benefits; (10) disability benefits; (11) retirement pensions; (12) interest; (13) dividends; (14) rents and royalties or estates and trusts; (15) educational assistance; (16) alimony; (17) child support; (18) financial assistance from outside the household, and other periodic income. Household income is the combined income of all household members. Income of persons is all income accruing to a person from all sources. Earnings is the amount of money a person received from his or her job.

labor force The labor force tables are based on the civilian labor force, which includes all employed civilians, as well as those who are looking for work (the unemployed).

labor force participation rate The percent of the civilian population in the labor force.

married couples with or without children under age 18 Refers to married couples with or without children under age 18 living in the same household. Couples without children under age 18 may be childless couples or parents of grown children who live elsewhere.

median The amount that divides the population or households into two equal halves; one below and one above the median. Medians can be calculated for income, age, and many other characteristics.

median income The amount that divides the income distribution into two equal groups, half having incomes above the median, half having incomes below the median. The medians for households or families are based on all households or families. The median for persons are based on all persons aged 15 or older with income.

nonfamily household A household maintained by a householder who lives alone or who lives with people to whom he or she is not related.

nonfamily householder A householder who lives alone or with nonrelatives only.

occupation Occupational classification is based on the kind of work a person did at his or her job during the previous calendar year. For persons who changed jobs during the year, the data refer to the occupation of the job held the longest during that year.

part-time or full-time employment Part-time is less than 35 hours of work per week in a majority of the weeks worked during the year. Full-time is 35 or more hours of work per week during a majority of the weeks worked.

percent change The change (either positive or negative) in a measure that is expressed as a proportion of the starting measure. When median income changes from $20,000 to $25,000, for example, it is a 25 percent increase.

percentage point change The change (either positive or negative) in a value which is already expressed as a percentage. When a labor force participation rate changes from 70 percent to 75 percent, for example, it is a 5 percentage point increase.

poverty level The official income threshold below which families and persons are classified as living in poverty. The threshold rises each year with inflation and varies depending on family size and age of householder. In 1994, the poverty threshold for one person under age 65 was $7,710. The threshold for a family of four was $15,141.

proportion or share The value of a part expressed as a percentage of the whole. If there are a total of 4 million people and 3 million are white, then the white proportion is 75 percent.

race Race is self-reported. A household is assigned the race of the householder.

rounding Percentages are rounded to the nearest tenth of a percent; therefore, the percentages in a distribution do not always add exactly to 100.0 percent. The totals, however, are always shown as 100.0. Moreover, individual figures are rounded to the nearest thousand without being adjusted to group totals, which are independently rounded; percentages are based on the unrounded numbers.

self-employment A person is categorized as self-employed in this book if he or she was self-employed in the job held longest during the reference period. Persons who report self-employment from a second job are excluded, but those who report wage-and-salary income from a second job are included. Unpaid workers in family businesses are excluded. Self-employment statistics in this book include only nonagricultural workers and exclude people who work for themselves in an incorporated business.

sex ratio The number of men per women.

Swing generation Americans born between 1933 and 1944, aged 51 to 63 in 1996. Also known as the Silent generation.

unemployed Unemployed persons are those who, during the survey period, had no employment but were available and looking for work. Those who were laid off from their jobs and were waiting to be recalled are also classified as unemployed.

World War II generation Americans born before 1933, which includes everyone aged 64 or older in 1996.

Index

Female-headed families. *See* Families.

Fitness participation, 196-200

Happiness
  of marriage, 238, 240
  of self, 230, 232

Health
  acute conditions, 201-203
  causes of death, 210-212
  chronic conditions, 204-207
  eating habits, 194-195
  fitness activities, 196-200
  insurance, 188-189
  life expectancy, 208-209
  sports activities, 196-200
  status, 186-187

Hispanic. *See also* Race.
  educational attainment of, 216-217, 220-221
  households headed by, 50-51
  income of, 78-79, 88-89
  labor force participation of, 166-167
  marital status of, 60-61
  population, 10-12
  poverty of, 94-95

Homeownership, 98-99, 102-103

Households
  by Hispanic origin, 50-51
  by race, 46-49
  female-headed families
    by Hispanic origin, 50-51
    by number of children, 44-45
    by race, 46-49
    number of, 34-35
    projections of, 37
  generations in, 242
  income
    by Hispanic origin, 72-73
    by race, 72-73
    by type, 68-71
    distribution, 66-67
    median, 64-65
  married couples
    by Hispanic origin, 50-51
    by number of children, 42-43

  by race, 46-49
  number of, 34-35
  projections of, 36-37
  projections, 36-37
  single-person
    by sex, 56-57
    homeownership rates of, 98-99
    income distribution of, 68-71
    number of, 38-39
  size, 38-39
  type
    by Hispanic origin, 50-51
    by race, 46-49
    homeownership rates by, 98-99
    number by, 34-35, 42-45
    projections of, 36-37
  with children
    by age of children, 40-41
    by Hispanic origin of householder, 50-51
    by household type, 42-45
    by race of householder, 46-49

Housing, type of, 253, 256

Income
  household
    by Hispanic origin, 72-73
    by race, 72-73
    by type, 68-71
    distribution, 66-67
    median, 64-65
  of men
    by Hispanic origin, 78-79
    by race, 78-79
    distribution, 76-77
    earnings by education, 80-83
    median, 74-75
  of women
    by Hispanic origin, 88-89
    by race, 88-89
    distribution, 86-87
    earnings by education, 90-93
    median, 84-85

Insurance, health, 188-189

Target American Consumers
with these highly acclaimed books by
demographic and industry experts

) Who We Are

**The Official Guide to the
AMERICAN MARKETPLACE, 2nd ed.**

An in-depth look at the trends that define who we are as consumers—
our education, health, incomes, occupations, living arrangements,
racial and ethnic makeup, spending patterns, and wealth.
(ISBN 0-9628092-4-1; Jan. 1995)   **$79.95**

**The Official Guide to
RACIAL & ETHNIC DIVERSITY**

An in-depth guide to the demographics and spending patterns of
Asians, blacks, Hispanics, Native Americans, and whites, including
ethnic groups among Asians and Hispanics.
(ISBN 1-885070-03-9; April 1996)   **$89.95**

) How We Differ by Age

**The Official Guide to
THE GENERATIONS**

by Susan Mitchell

The demographics and spending patterns of adult consumers—Generation X, born 1965-76; the Baby Boom, born 1946-64; the Swing
Generation, born 1933-45; and the World War II Generation, born
before 1933.
(ISBN 0-9628092-8-4; May 1995)   **$69.95**

**WISE UP TO TEENS
Insights Into Marketing & Advertising to Teenagers**

by Peter Zollo

A ground-breaking book that gives you an in-depth look at teen
lifestyles and values, where teens get their money, how and why they
spend it, and proven, hands-on techniques that you can use to research
and advertise to teens.
(ISBN 0-9628092-9-2;Oct. 1995)   **$34.95**

**THE MID-YOUTH MARKET
Baby Boomers in Their Peak Earning & Spending Years**

by Cheryl Russell

The author, a nationally recognized expert on the baby boom,
examines the demographics and spending patterns of that generation,
which spends more than any other age group.
(ISBN 1-885070-06-3; Nov. 1996)   **$69.95**

) How Much Money We Have

**The Official Guide to
AMERICAN INCOMES, 2nd ed.**

by Thomas Exter

*(the first edition of this book was one of Library Journal's
Best Reference Sources of 1993)*

A storehouse of data on income trends, household and perso
income, discretionary income, household income projections, spe
ing, wealth and poverty.   **$89**
(ISBN 1-885070-00-4; Nov. 1996)

) What We Spend It On

**The Official Guide to
HOUSEHOLD SPENDING, 3rd ed.**

by Hoai Huong Tran

(the first edition of this book was titled Consumer Power)

Who buys? What do they buy? How much do they spend? Here
detailed spending data on almost 1,000 products and services, brok
out by scores of demographic variables.
(ISBN 1-885070-01-2; Oct. 1995)   **$89.**

**Who's Buying
FOOD & DRINK**

by Marcia Mogelonsky

The source of data on who spends how much on food and alco
consumed at home and away from home—the variables include a
income, household type, region, race and Hispanic origin, educati
number of earners in household, and occupation.
(ISBN 1-885070-0407; Oct. 1996)   **$69.**

**Who's Buying
FOR THE HOME**

by Alison Stein Wellner

Who spends how much on products and services for the home—
variables are the same as for *Who's Buying Food & Drink*, and
scores of subjects include maintenance and repairs, utilities, fue
public services, household services and supplies, furniture, and app
ances.
(ISBN 1-885070-05-5; Oct. 1996)   **$89.**